FROMMER'S
1985-86 GUIDE TO
NEW YORK

by Faye Hammel

D1352084

Published by Frommer/Pasmantier Publishers
A Division of Simon & Schuster, Inc.
1230 Avenue of the Americas
New York, NY 10020

ISBN 0–671–52426–7

Manufactured in the United States of America

*Although every effort was made to ensure the accuracy
of price information appearing in this book,
it should be kept in mind that prices
can and do fluctuate in the course of time.*

CONTENTS

MAPS

Inflation Alert

It is hardly a secret that inflation continues to batter the United States as it has everywhere else. The author of this book has spent laborious hours attempting to ensure the accuracy of prices appearing in this guide. As we go to press, we believe we have obtained the most reliable data possible. Nonetheless, in the lifetime of this edition—particularly its second year (1986)—the wise traveler might add 15% to 20% to the prices quoted throughout these pages.

Chapter I

WHYS AND WHEREFORES

IT ALWAYS HAPPENS. People from out of town who've become New Yorkers (like us) are invariably held up as Ultimate Authorities by the folks back home. When our friends come into the city, they are *sure* we can advise them on the best hotels, the newest "in" restaurants, and which plays on Broadway are really worth seeing. And even more important, they expect us to know where they can get the best values for their money, whether they're planning to spend $50 a day or $500. For in a city as complex, as varied—and as expensive—as New York, it's much too easy to waste time and money if you don't have inside information.

And that's what we intend to give you in the pages ahead: the inside dope, the special tips that can make all the difference between your feeling like a native or a newcomer. We'll tell you which hotels, in our opinion, offer the best value for your dollar, from the Waldorf to the "Y"; which restaurants are worth going into bankruptcy for, which will feed you well for a pittance; how to get tickets for a top Broadway musical without paying scalper's rates or even having an uncle who works for the producer; how to enjoy the big and little sights of the city in the most efficient, relaxed manner possible; how to discover the shopping secrets of New York's smartest women in out-of-the-way bargain meccas where the Kaspers and Calvin Kleins go for peanuts; how to find the coziest pub, the latest disco, or the most total "total environment"; how to catch the most interesting entertainments, lectures, concerts with free or nominal admissions; and how to venture into New York's exotic world of swamis, astrologers, and Zen masters. As an added fillip, we'll tell you where to wander, when fancy strikes, off the well-trod road of the major sights and experiences and head off the beaten path for a world of surprises. We hope this catalogue of what we consider the best New York has to offer will be useful to you, whether it's your first trip to the city or your 110th. First, though, let us issue a warning to newcomers.

THE FIRST TIME IN NEW YORK: You should be advised that there is one dangerous aspect of coming to New York for the first time: not of getting lost, mobbed, or caught in a blackout, but of falling so desperately in love with the city that you may not want to go home again. Or, if you do, it may be just to pack your bags. With most visitors to New York, it's usually love or hate at first sight. Either you are so enthralled by the dazzle, the tempo, the sense of adventure that only a great city can give, that you immediately make it your own. Or you may find the noise, the smog, the traffic, the seeming callousness of the natives just too much. But be warned: New York is still the magic town, the beckoning metropolis, the mighty citadel of power. And the younger you are, the more potent is its spell. *Caveat emptor.*

WHAT MAKES NEW YORK TICK: To describe New York fully would take volumes—and besides, it's indescribable. You might study New York history for a year, cram your head with statistics about population and industry and geography, become an expert on urban problems—and still not have the slightest feeling of what New York is about. New York simply must be experienced, in all its incredible variety, to be comprehended. It is really unlike any other city in America, and more like a small (or not-so-small) country of its own. New York is a lot more like London than it is like Chicago or Los Angeles, but it is really an entity only to itself. It is noted for its size (with a population close to eight million, it is the nation's largest city); its diversity (more different kinds of people do their thing here than just about anywhere else); and perhaps most important of all, the magnetism that attracts to it the brightest, most creative, most ambitious, most determined people from everywhere. For this is the central city, the megalopolis, the nerve center of the world's finance and trade, of advertising and publishing and fashion, of theater and ballet and music, and now, with the United Nations here, of world diplomacy as well. It is the vortex that pulls into its center a lot of the best (and worst) people and projects and theories and schemes from everywhere. New York is in the eye of the hurricane. This is what gives the city its special feeling of intensity, the high-powered vibration that is felt immediately by even the most casual visitor. It is what makes New York one of the most exciting places on the planet.

THE WEATHER AND WHEN TO COME TO NEW YORK: Expect hot summers and cold winters in New York, plus sometimes idyllic, 70-degree-ish springs and falls. The city is great to visit anytime you can. Both central heating and air conditioning are practically universal, so the weather is never a problem. The winter is the height of the theater and entertainment season, but if you come in the summer you're ahead of the game, since most residents will be out at the beach, and you have the city practically to yourself. It's much easier then to get into the charming little restaurants, to pick up tickets for Broadway plays at the last minute, and you don't have to fight off the mobs in the big stores.

NEW YORK: AVERAGE MONTHLY TEMPERATURES

Month	Temp	Month	Temp
January	32.3	July	76.8
February	33.4	August	75.1
March	40.5	September	68.5
April	51.4	October	58.3
May	62.4	November	47.0
June	71.4	December	35.9

Chapter II

BIG CITY LOGISTICS

IF YOU COME TO NEW YORK by train or bus, you will arrive at either Pennsylvania Station (34th Street and Seventh Avenue), Grand Central Terminal (42nd Street and Park Avenue), or the Port of New York Authority Bus Terminal (41st Street and Eighth Avenue). All three are located in midtown, minutes from your hotel. If you come by plane, you will arrive at Kennedy, LaGuardia, or Newark International Airports. Carey Transportation buses can take you to Park Avenue and 42nd Street for $6 from Kennedy, $4.50 from LaGuardia. (An express bus-and-subway service—"The Train to the Plane"—also runs from Kennedy to 57th Street and Avenue of the Americas, at a cost of $6. For information, phone 858-7272.) Both Kennedy and LaGuardia have money-saving share-the-taxi programs.

Taxi fare averages $25.50 from Kennedy, $13 from LaGuardia to the midtown area. From Newark Airport, a bus will take you to the Port of New York Authority Terminal for $4.

GEOGRAPHY: Before you arrive at your hotel, though, you should know a little about the geography of the city and the best means of getting around town. You probably already know that New York City is divided into five boroughs: Manhattan, the most important; the Bronx, to the north; Brooklyn, to the south; Queens (where the airports are and the World's Fair was), to the east; and Richmond, or Staten Island, south and east of New York harbor. Since you'll probably be spending most of your time in Manhattan, there's no need to concern yourself with the details of getting around the other boroughs. If you visit them, be sure to get specific directions and pick up some good maps in advance.

Manhattan is, of course, an island, and a rather small one at that (12 miles long, 2½ miles across at its widest point), and its

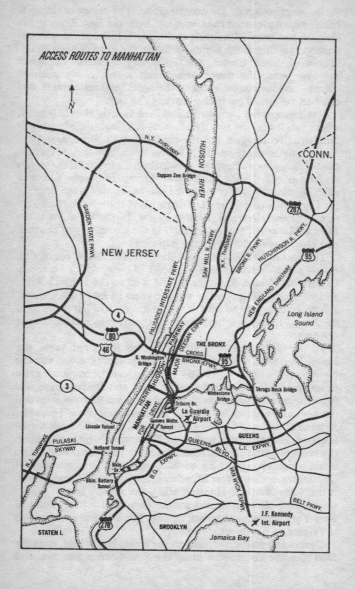

ACCESS ROUTES TO MANHATTAN

varied neighborhoods are easy to get to. The center of things is **Midtown,** an area that runs, roughly, from the East River to the Hudson and from 34th Street to 59th Street. Within this neighborhood you'll find the United Nations, the Empire State Building, Rockefeller Center, the Broadway theaters, the great shipping piers, the major department stores, many business offices—and, of course, most of the hotels and restaurants that cater to visitors. This is the heart of the city.

The area around 34th Street and Broadway is **Herald Square,** where you'll find the two department-store colossi, Macy's and Gimbel's. To the east are the shops of 34th Street and Fifth Avenue; to the west and south, the New Madison Square Garden Center rising above Pennsylvania Station. Below that, the streets become crowded with trucks and throngs of people and men pushing minks on racks along the sidewalks: this is the home of the **Garment Center,** the **Fur District,** and the legendary characters of Seventh Avenue. Farther below, in the West 20s is the **Flower Market** (if you get up early in the morning, you can pick and choose with the city's retail florists).

The next most important area starts at 14th Street, goes south, roughly to Houston, and is the heart of New York's Bohemia: **Greenwich Village.** It begins on the west at the Hudson River and, although Fifth Avenue was for years its eastern boundary, it now extends all the way across town, on to First Avenue to the **East Village,** one-time home of the hippies and the flower children.

To the south, the East Village reverts to its old name, the **Lower East Side,** where thousands of immigrants settled into the New World in the early 1900s—to struggle, to be engulfed, some to conquer. Most of the Jews and Irish and Italians have fled from the ghettos uptown or to the suburbs, but little colonies still remain, although most of the population is now Hispanic. Around Grand and Orchard Streets there is still a Jewish neighborhood, known mostly for incredible Sunday bargain shopping; the heart of **Little Italy** is Mulberry Street, and, of course, there is a **Chinatown,** centering on Mott and Pell Streets. West of Chinatown, around West Broadway, Spring, and Greene Streets, is the **Soho** (south of Houston area), the world's largest collection of cast-iron commercial architecture and the lively home of New York's most vital artists' colony. The area just south of this is **Tribeca,** a newer artists' colony.

Continuing south, we come to the **Brooklyn Bridge,** the **City Hall** and the courthouse area, the South Street Seaport, and finally to the financial district, the site of **Wall Street,** the stock exchange, the giant insurance companies. From here on, Manhattan narrows sharply, winds it way past ancient streets and alleys and old buildings that are being bulldozed to make way for giant office complexes, and slips into the sea.

Picking up again from the Midtown area, we find **Central Park** beginning at 59th Street, and this magnificent sweep of greensward is now the great divide between East and West. To the east is the **Upper East Side,** home of the Beautiful People, the would-be BPs, the fashionable schools and shops, the prestigious **Metropolitan Museum of Art.** On the West, at 65th Street and Broadway, is **Lincoln Center for the Performing Arts,** a veritable fortress of culture (the Metropolitan Opera House, Avery Fisher Hall, the New York State Theater, the Vivian Beaumont Theater, etc.), which leads up Broadway, the heart of the **Upper West Side.** This is mostly a residential district, with the lovely buildings of Central Park West on one boundary, and Riverside Drive on the other. At 112th Street and Broadway is the campus of Columbia University, and as you go up Riverside Drive, you will see the massive structure of Grant's Tomb and the great Gothic spires of Riverside Church. **Harlem** begins at 125th Street on the West Side, and around 110th Street on the East centers the sprawling Puerto Rican neighborhood of New York: **El Barrio.** Farther north on the West Side is **Washington Heights,** a middle-class residential neighborhood and, near the tip of the island, **Fort Tryon Park** and the beautiful Cloisters of the Metropolitan Museum of Art, a serene vantage point from which to contemplate the incredible diversity of incredible New York.

NAVIGATING: If you can count and you know your east from your west, you can find your way around Manhattan. Navigating is, in fact, so simple that the average 12-year-old can do it with aplomb (in fact, we often see 12-year-olds directing their parents around town). All you have to remember is that the streets run east and west and are numbered consecutively; that the avenues run north and south and most have numbers, although a few have names; and that streets and avenues usually bisect each other at right angles. (Unfortunately, this does not apply to Lower Manhattan—Wall Street, Chinatown, Soho, Greenwich Village—since these neighborhoods just sort of grew, before the engineers came up with this brilliant scheme; you'd best have a map for exploring here.)

As for the East and West, the key to the mystery is **Fifth Avenue,** the big dividing line between the East and West Sides of town (below Washington Square, Broadway is the dividing line). So, for example, to get to 20 East 57th Street, you would walk about one block *east* of Fifth; to get to 20 West 57th Street, about one block *west.* To get *uptown* of a certain point, simply walk north of, or to a higher-numbered street than, where you are; *downtown* is south of (or a lower-numbered street than) your current location. Got that? All that is left to learn are the names of the major avenues. Starting at Fifth Avenue and going east (toward the East River), they are: Madison, Park (Park Avenue South below 34th Street), Lexington, Third, Second, First, York (from East 60th Street to East 92nd Street), and East End (from East 79th Street to East 90th Street). On the Lower East Side, First Avenue gives way to Avenues A, B, C, and D. Starting again at Fifth Avenue and working west, we have Avenue of the Americas (everybody calls it Sixth Avenue), Seventh Avenue, Broadway, Eighth Avenue (which becomes Central Park West at 59th Street), Ninth Avenue (becomes Columbus Avenue at 59th Street), Tenth Avenue (Amsterdam Avenue after 59th Street), Eleventh Avenue (becomes West End Avenue from 59th to 107th Streets), and Riverside Drive, beginning at 72nd Street.

TRANSPORTATION: Now that you've got your navigation signals straight (or have a 12-year-old in tow), choose your means of transportation. New York is one of the few cities left in this country where walking is not only encouraged, but altogether feasible, since everything is packed so close together. Walking, in fact, is often the quickest way to get somewhere, especially during the midday lunch crush and the evening rush hour (5 to 6 p.m.), when surface traffic seems to move at the rate of two miles an hour. If you *must* have a car (recommended for trips outside the city, but not for getting around Manhattan), there are many reputable car-rental agencies listed in the phone book.

Taxis

The most convenient way to get around town, of course, is by cab. Since the recent fare hikes, they have become expensive. As soon as you step into the cab, the meter clicks to $1; the charge is then 10¢ for each additional one-ninth of a mile. You are, of course, expected to tip: about 20% to 25%. Incidentally, don't be surprised if the New York taxi drivers do not regale you with a discourse on the city's labor problems or a critique of the current administration; so much has been written on the cab driver's querulous opinions that the most talkative of them have either become shy or graduated to TV talk shows. Your ride is likely to be remarkably silent. Cabs can be hailed on almost any street: a light on top indicates that they are available.

Subways

Everyone should ride the New York subway at least once—just for the experience. If you manage to survive a rush-hour crush (8 to 9:30 in the morning, 5 to 6 in the evening on weekdays), you'll have something to tell the folks about back home. The rest of the time, the subway is relatively uncrowded, and will take you where you want to go quickly (no traffic!), fairly efficiently and at a cost of 90¢ per token, *at this writing*. The two lines that run through Manhattan are the IRT and the IND; the BMT runs mostly from lower Manhattan to Brooklyn and Queens. You can sometimes get a good map of the subway system at any token booth, but in general, keep in mind that the IRT runs trains north and south on both the East and West Sides of town. East Side trains run along Lexington Avenue; the line is popularly known as the "Lexington Avenue Subway." On the West Side, the trains go along Broadway and Seventh Avenue (the Broadway line goes north to Columbia University and Washington Heights; the Seventh Avenue line branches eastward north to 96th Street to Seventh Avenue and Harlem). The east and west branches of the IRT are connected by the Grand Central/Times Square Shuttle, and the 14th Street Canarsie Line. The Queensboro Line runs beneath the shuttle from Times Square to Grand Central and then east into Queens. IND trains run along Sixth and Eighth Avenues, with major stops in Greenwich Village at West 4th Street and Sixth Avenue, at the Port of New York Authority Bus Terminal at 41st Street, and at Columbus Circle (59th Street).

Buses

Slower than subways but cheaper than the taxis, the buses solve a lot of transportation problems. Almost every major avenue has its own bus (they run either north or south: downtown on Fifth, uptown on Madison, downtown on Lexington, uptown

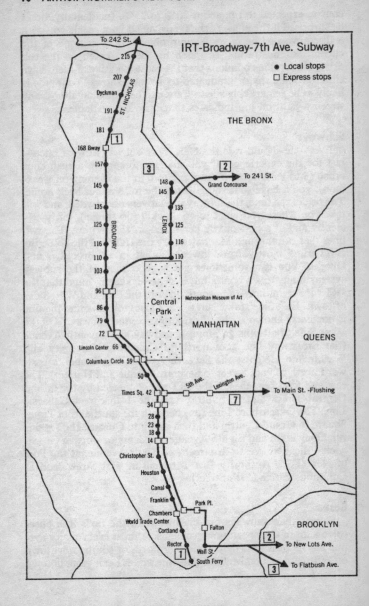

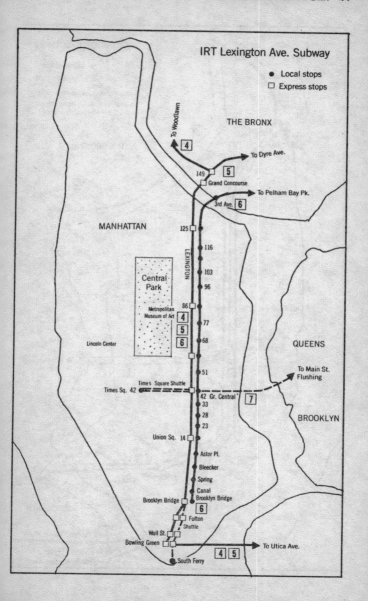

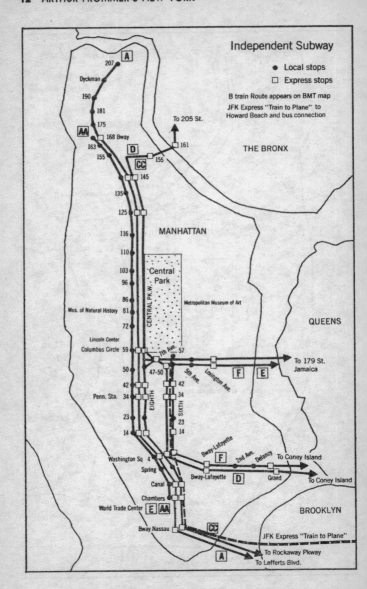

Independent Subway

● Local stops
□ Express stops

B train Route appears on BMT map

JFK Express "Train to Plane" to Howard Beach and bus connection

THE BRONX

To 205 St.

207 Ⓐ

Dyckman

190

181

175

ⒶⒶ 168 Bway Ⓓ

163

155 ⒸⒸ 155 161

145

135

125 MANHATTAN

116

110

103 Central

96 Park

86 CENTRAL PK. W.

Mus. of Natural History 81 Metropolitan Museum of Art

72

QUEENS

Lincoln Center

Columbus Circle 59 7th Ave. 57

50 Lexington Ave. Ⓕ Ⓔ To 179 St. Jamaica

47-50 5th Ave.

42 EIGHTH 42

Penn. Sta. 34 SIXTH 34

23 23

14 14

Washington Sq 4 Bway-Lafayette Ⓕ 2nd Ave. Delancy To Coney Island

Spring Bway-Lafayette Ⓓ Grand To Coney Island

Canal

Chambers

World Trade Center Ⓔ ⒶⒶ

Bway Nassau ⒸⒸ

JFK Express "Train to Plane"

Ⓐ To Rockaway Pkway

To Lefferts Blvd.

BROOKLYN

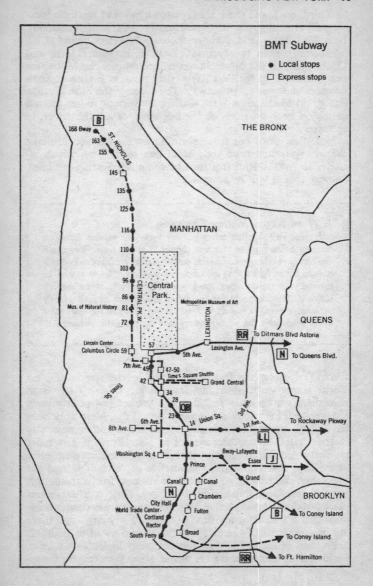

BMT Subway
- Local stops
□ Express stops

THE BRONX

168 Bway
163
155
ST. NICHOLAS
145
135
125
116
MANHATTAN
110
103
96
CENTRAL PK. W.
86
81
Mus. of Natural History
72

Central Park

Metropolitan Museum of Art

LEXINGTON

QUEENS

Lincoln Center
Columbus Circle 59
57
5th Ave.
Lexington Ave.
RR To Ditmars Blvd Astoria
N To Queens Blvd.

7th Ave.
49
47-50
Time's Square Shuttle
42
Grand Central
34
28
QB
23
14 Union Sq.
3rd Ave.
To Rockaway Pkwy
8th Ave.
6th Ave.
1st Ave.
LL

Washington Sq 4.
8
Bway-Lafayette
Essex
J
Prince
Grand

Canal
Canal
BROOKLYN
N
Chambers
City Hall
Fulton
B To Coney Island
World Trade Center
Cortland
Rector
Broad
To Coney Island
South Ferry
RR To Ft. Hamilton

TIMES SQ.

on Third, etc.), and there are crosstown buses at strategic locations all around town: 8th Street (eastbound), 9th (westbound), 14th, 23rd, 34th, 42nd, 50th (eastbound), 51st (westbound), 65th (eastbound), 66th (westbound), 79th, 86th, 96th, 116th, and 125th. Some of the buses, however, are erratic: the M104, for example, starts at the East River, then turns at Eighth or Sixth Avenues and goes up Broadway. The buses of the Fifth Avenue line go up Madison or Sixth and follow various routes around the city. Check the maps on the bus signs, or ask the driver, to be sure.

Note that since bus drivers are no longer allowed to make change, you must have your exact fare ready: 90¢, which includes an Add-A-Ride (for transfer to an intersecting bus line). Subway tokens will be accepted.

A Word About Money Changing

Foreign visitors often arrive in New York City without American currency believing that they can change it at any time. They can't! The foreign exchange companies maintain **only** Monday to Friday 9 a.m. to 5 p.m. hours: they are closed on weekends. Be sure, then, to change your money when you arrive in New York, at the airport. Canadian visitors should also be advised that their money is not freely negotiable here, as is ours in their country. They're the ones most often stuck with the wrong money and no place to exchange it.

SAFETY: Despite the fact that "crime in the streets of New York" seems to be about the favorite gag of every television comedian, we honestly feel that the subject has been grossly exaggerated. Let's look at the facts, first. True, New York does have a high incidence of crime, but so does every other major city in the United States; because it's in New York, it gets more publicity. Second, considering that some eight million people live in the city, that hundreds of thousands more come in and out every day, and that all go about their business freely, the out-of-towner's frequent impression that New York is a dangerous place just doesn't make sense. However, there are certain precautions that it's wise for a visitor to take—in any city—and there are certain areas of the city that we would avoid at night. It helps, first of all, if one does not obviously look like a tourist, flashing a big camera and a big wallet. Keep your camera inconspicuous, put your money in travelers checks, and leave your valuables in the hotel safe or at home. Third, there are certain areas much worse than others at night: one is the East Village, and the second is the area around Times Square, particularly between Seventh and Eighth Avenues, now lined with lurid pornographic theaters and bookstores. Although it may appeal to some, its appeal is most certainly limited, and nobody says you have to go there. Since there have been so many complaints, the city is now promising to clean up the area—and we're keeping our fingers crossed. The parks are taboo after sundown, unless you're going to a festival or theatrical performance in Central Park, in which case the access routes will be well lighted. And it's safer to take a cab home late at night than a subway. (Stay well back from open subway platforms.) One final tip: On the cab ride from the airports to the city, foreign visitors should be wary of cab drivers demanding huge sums (several foreigners have recently been victimized badly); only take a metered cab, and only pay *exactly* what the meter reads, plus a tip and toll charges. Follow the rules, and a trip to New York should be no more dangerous than one to, say, your own hometown.

Chapter III

NEW YORK'S BEST HOTEL VALUES

NEW YORK CITY has more hotel rooms than some small countries have people. In a city where at least a handful of establishments can accommodate 2000 guests, where a "small hotel" is considered one with fewer than 1000 rooms, you won't spend your nights sleeping in Central Park. But—and it's a rather big but—getting exactly the kind of hotel room you want, in the location you want, at the price you want to pay is another cup of tea. If you haven't done your homework, you might not be too happy with where you stay. Sometimes it seems that choice hotel rooms in New York are as scarce as hot tickets to the top show on Broadway. But it needn't be that way, not if you understand some of the guidelines of the New York hotel scene.

First, of course, is the question of what you'll want to pay. So varied are the accommodations you can find in New York that you might easily spend $1000 a night in a sumptuous suite overlooking Central Park—or settle for a room with bath at $70 for a double. But you will, in general, be paying more for hotel accommodations in New York than in almost any other American city. Inflation is rampant at the moment and, what with real estate taxes and labor costs plus everything else constantly zooming up, the hotels are raising and raising and raising their rates. (In most cases, it's been necessary; in some, we suspect, it's taking advantage of what the traffic will bear.) In general, the price picture breaks down like this. To stay in one of the top, elegant hotels of the city, those geared to international business travelers and other members of the expense-account set, you can expect to pay between $125 and $200 and up for a double room. To stay where most people stay, in one of the city's first-class, efficiently run, and comfortable hotels, expect to spend $90 and up for a double; and to stay in a still-comfortable but more modest establishment, prepare to part with around $70. You can also, particularly if you're a student or a single person traveling alone, still find some respectable establishments where you can get a room for around $35 a night. We have, therefore, divided our hotels into four categories and, allowing for some inevitable overlapping, they break down like this: (1) Elegant and Expensive; (2) First Class; (3) Good Buys; and (4) For Budgeteers.

If, however, you're coming to New York just for the weekend, you're in luck. That's when business travelers clear out and expensive hotel rooms go empty. Rather than let this happen, some of the loveliest hotels in town woo the vacationer with attractive weekend package rates, which often include some meals, sightseeing, theater tickets, and many extras. Because these packages vary greatly and change frequently, your best deal is to call the hotel you're interested in, and/or write the **New York Convention and Visitors Bureau,** 2 Columbus Circle, New York, NY 10019, requesting their brochure, "New York City Packages Directory."

You will note that we have described here some 50 hotels—which, admittedly, is only a segment of the huge number in the city. And we do not necessarily claim that they are the best in the city. They offer, however, in our opinion, excellent values in each price category, and they are representative of what you will find everywhere in New York.

Now, a few more preliminary remarks. All of the rates listed, unless otherwise stated, are for European Plan only, which means that no food is served, not even breakfast. The rates given are "transient rates": for those who stay in some hotels on a weekly or monthly basis, lower rates are usually available. Reservations in advance are *always* a good idea, especially during the busy summer months: from Easter to October is high season in New York. If you haven't planned in advance, you will almost always be able to get some sort of room, but perhaps not just the one you would like. And please note that although we have made every effort to be absolutely accurate about prices, the hotel business presents a highly competitive, changing situation, and prices may go up or down (usually up) a bit, depending on the season and the demand for rooms. Since new labor contracts are usually settled around the middle of the year, some of the hotels may raise their prices in June. But give or take a few dollars (and inflation notwithstanding), these rates will still represent excellent value for the dollar spent.

Finally, all rates are subject to an 8¼% New York City Room Tax, plus a $2-a-day occupancy tax.

FOR MOTORISTS ONLY: Here's a tip for those of you who are driving to New York. When you park your car in a New York hotel garage, it is assumed that you will keep it in more-or-less dead storage. There is really not much point in driving a car in Manhattan; everything is within easy bus or subway or cab distance, and besides, the parking situation is terrible. It could cost you more to pay for a garage than it would to take a cab. But if you will need your car, if you're driving out of the city or whatever, advise the hotel of this when you check in. That way, the car will be stored in an easy-to-reach part of the garage, and for an extra $1 or so tip per use to the bellhop, you will have it handy. Also note that even when parking is free, as in most motor hotels, there is usually an in-and-out service charge of several dollars each time the car is used.

One more word to the wise motorist: When checking out of a motor hotel, call for your car *two hours* before check-out time. It *is* conceivable that it will arrive earlier, but the worst that can happen is that you ask the bellhop to watch it while you're having your breakfast—and it's much better to have the car wait for you than the other way around.

And now, the details of finding the city's best hotel values. We'll begin in the pastures of plenty where the beautiful people play, where a room for the night goes, roughly, for $125 . . . and way up.

Elegant and Expensive: $125 and Way Up

THE NEW BEAUTIES: New York has seen an explosion of new hotel construction in the last several years—at least half a dozen major establishments and some 6000 new rooms, with more coming up in the next year or two. Of these, perhaps the grandest is the $100-million **Helmsley Palace Hotel**, 455 Madison Ave., NY 10022 (50th St.; tel. 212/888-7000), surely one of the foremost luxury hotels of the world. Above the landmark turn-of-the-century Villard houses, a neo-Renaissance Italian palazzo built in American brownstone for railroad tycoon and journalist Henry Villard, rises a 51-story bronzed glass tower, making this the tallest hotel in New York. While the painstakingly and magnificently restored public rooms have won nothing but praise from the critics, the new tower has been dubbed, in contrast, a "mediocrity." Never mind. The rooms inside are lovely, and the public rooms are perhaps the finest in New York. Guests may enter through the Villard cobblestone courtyard, proceed up the grand marble staircase to view the red Verona marble fireplace of August St. Gaudens, and are surrounded everywhere by works by such noted artists of the day as Louis Comfort Tiffany, John La Farge, and George Breck.

Amid all this splendor are all the conveniences of modern hotel living: a multilingual staff, concierge service and room service 24 hours a day, a parking garage underneath the building, air conditioning and soundproofing throughout. All of the 775 standard guest rooms, which rent from $175 to $225 single and $165 to $245 double, look exactly alike, except that some have king-size beds with gilded headboards and others have two doubles. Interior colors are soft pastels, with peach velvet chairs and carpeting. Rooms are air-conditioned and soundproofed, have remote-control color TV and in-house movies, digital clock radios, direct-dial (national and international) phones, and mini-refrigerators, a welcome extra. Electric blankets are available. Bathrooms are sumptuous. There are 100 suites, beginning at $500 for one-bedroom apartments and going up to $1500 for fairytale triplexes with their own room gardens and solariums. Weekend packages are available. Note that rates are subject to change.

For reservations, phone, toll free, 800/221-4982.

Not quite as grandiose as the Helmsley Palace, but handsome in its own right, is the second Helmsley Hotel to open in New York in the past few years, the **Harley of New York,** 212 East 42nd St., NY 10017 (tel. 212/490-8900). The 41-story, 800-room, brick-and-bronze glass tower is a model of grace both in its luxurious appointments and efficiency, the kind that top-level business executives demand: concierge, fast check-in and check-out service, foreign currency exchange, multilingual secretarial and business services, and even a special continental breakfast elevator whizzing early-morning wake-up platters to the rooms. You might also have your breakfast at Harry's New York Bar down in the lobby, which is also known for decently priced lunches and fantastic free hors d'oeuvres during the busy cocktail hour. Breakfast is also served at Mindy's, the hotel's full-service restaurant, where you could take lunch and dinner as well—the finest French cuisine—in a glorious multilevel setting with many trees and plantings, and an entire glass wall overlooking an open-air landscaped plaza.

As for the sleeping rooms, they are beautifully decorated, especially those with king-size beds and blue Oriental-motif spreads; rooms with two double beds have pale beige or apricot-and-green color schemes. All are outside rooms, and all have 25-inch color TVs with cable and remote controls, digital alarm clock radios, and such amenities as oversize down pillows and skirt hangers in the closet (Leona Helmsley, president of Harley Hotels, has taken special care to cater to the needs of women travelers). The bathrooms are luxurious, with both phone and scale, plus sheet-size bath towels and the usual package of toiletries found in luxury hotels. Rates for these rooms run from $125 to $185 single, from $125 to $200 double, depending on floor and location. Suites, all situated on corners on the top five floors, are $280 a night. There is a full garage on the premises, and parking is free on weekends, when attractive packages are available. Note that rates are subject to change.

For reservations, phone, toll free, 800/221-4982.

The striking new hotel that heralded the renaissance of 42nd Street, the **Grand Hyatt New York,** Park Ave. at Grand Central Terminal, NY 10017 (tel. 212/883-1234), is perhaps the most dramatically modern of New York hotels. Created on the structural skeleton of the old Commodore Hotel, the $100-million reconstruction produced a 1407-room, 34-story building that has been hailed as a high-water mark of modern architectural design. From the silver-mirrored facade that reflects such neighborhood landmarks as the Chrysler Building and Grand Central Terminal to the four-story plant-filled atrium with cascading waterfall and 100-foot bronze abstract sculpture, the effect is one of dazzle and glitter. Fresh flowers everywhere become part of the decor. Dining rooms and lounges continue the glamor theme, especially the Sun Garden Lounge, a sidewalk café and cocktail spot cantilevered spectacularly right over busy 42nd Street. The Crystal Fountain, the hotel's full-service restaurant, is handsome, with a reflecting pool in the center of the room and a mirrored ceiling that reflects the busy goings-on of the street. Sunday brunch is a lavish treat here. The decor at Trumpets, an elegant haven of nouvelle cuisine, is more traditional and subdued.

Also quiet and subdued, in contrast to the fantasy world on the first floor, are the guest rooms, done in deep earth colors of brown, green, and burgundy, and decorated with handsome prints. All rooms have color TV with in-room movies, clock-radios, plush carpeting, skirt hangers in the closets, luxurious bathrooms with an amenity basket of toiletries. Rooms rent from $125 to $155 single, from $145 to $180 double; the deluxe king room, with its separate seating area, desk, and chair, is at the top of the scale. (Rates are subject to change.) Even more luxurious, at $175 single and $195 double, are the 110 rooms in the Regency Club, which occupies the entire 31st and 32nd floors, and with the services of a special concierge and a hospitality lounge, is like a small and private hotel within the larger hotel itself.

The Grand Hyatt abounds with services: there's an electronic-card key system, valet parking is available one block away, a concierge is at the ready, free morning newspapers come with your order from room service or are available in the public dining rooms, and HBO and sports programs are free on guest room TV sets. There is easy access to nearby tennis courts and health club facilities. And a number of well-priced weekend packages are especially attractive.

For reservations, phone, toll free, 800/228-9000.

If you love Paris in the springtime, then you're surely going to love the new **Hotel Parker Meridien,** 118 West 57th St., NY 10019 (tel. 212/245-5000), since that's exactly the feeling one gets any time of the year at New York's first French hotel. This $75-million, 41-story newcomer is the North American flagship of Meridien hotels, a division of Air France, and from its splendid entrance promenade with 65-foot-high gold-leaf ceiling and marble arch, to the lobby and balconied atrium alive with trees and plantings, to the elegant restaurants, guest rooms, and roof-top swimming pool, there's a special ambience here of the good life, à la française. Dining facilities reflect art as well as the art of dining: there's a splendid Oriental carpet in the hotel's premier restaurant, Maurice, where superb nouvelle cuisine is served— even at breakfast (see Chapter IV's restaurant recommendations); 16th- and 17th-century French tapestries and modern sculptures lead the way to Le Patio, a smartly casual rendezvous for breakfast, buffet lunch, Sunday brunch, and cocktails; and works by the French Impressionists are reproduced in lighted, chiseled glass in Montparnasse, a convivial *boîte* for everything from croissants to nightcaps and lunch in between.

Guests who need to work off some of the calories can make use of the hotel's Club La Raquette, below the lobby level, complete with regulation racquetball, squash and handball courts, and fitness equipment. On the roof is a splendid glass-enclosed pool, with a beautiful view of both a Bernard LaMotte mural and Central Park far below. There are indoor and outdoor sundecks and a jogging path, as well.

As for the 600 guest rooms and suites, they are beautifully done, with blonde built-in oak furniture, blonde marble tops, accents of brass, and art imported from Paris. Beds are usually king-size or double-doubles. Bathrooms are floor to ceiling marble and include a telephone. Room rates go from $125 to $185 single, $145 to $205 double. Junior suites are $225; one-bedroom suites, $350; two-bedroom suites, $450. Family plans are available, and there is an especially well-priced "Le Weekend Français" package, which includes many amenities at rates of $110 per person, double occupancy, for two nights and three days, but all rates are subject to change.

For reservations at the Parker Meridien, phone, toll free, 800/223-9918.

Vista International, 3 World Trade Center, NY 10048 (tel. 212/938-9100), is the first major hotel to be built in the downtown area since 1836. From all indications, it's been worth waiting for. The $70-million, 23-story flagship of Hilton International in the continental United States, it's quickly gaining a reputation as a superbly efficient homebase for business travelers (the lobby rings with international accents) during the week and as a resort destination in the heart of New York's most historic neighborhood on the weekends. Throughout the hotel—from the dramatic gold mylar sculpture of "sails" that sweeps upward between the first two levels to the rooftop swimming pool—an aura of quiet, understated elegance makes its presence known. It's visible, of course, in the hotel's splendid quartet of dining and wining facilities: in the American Harvest Restaurant, serving traditional American recipes from a menu that changes with the seasons and the harvests; in its popular-priced Greenhouse Restaurant, glass enclosed and brilliant with trees and flowers, with free-standing buffets and a wine bar; in the graceful Vista Lounge, the place for continental breakfast, light lunch, and a sunset spectacular at cocktail time; and in the Tall Ships Bar, a handsome nautical setting with etched-glass murals of American clipper ships, serving seafood and meat pies for lunch, plus clams, oysters, and chowder.

The quiet elegance extends to the hotel's 829 guest rooms, which have some of the most striking vistas in the city. Done in soft earth tones of dusty peach, beige, and muted greens, with blonde oak and rattan furniture, they all feature color TV and in-house movies; Uniquey, an electronic keyless lock system;

handsome bathrooms; and little extras like toiletries, turn-down service, and chocolates on the pillow at night. These rooms go from $98 to $160 single, $128 to $190 double. For rates of $175 single, $205 double, guests can stay at Vista Executive Floor rooms on the 20th and 21st floors, where they have their own special check-in facilities and their own concierge, and can take complimentary continental breakfast in the morning and cocktails in the evening in their own Club Lounge. Again, rates are subject to change.

Business travelers, who make up most of the hotel's population during the week, can avail themselves of the services of the Executive Business Center, which can arrange for secretarial, translation, and reference services. Vacation travelers can use the hotel's shuttle bus to make excursions to the shopping and historic areas of Lower Manhattan or to Broadway theaters. Weekend packages, which include free parking, bicycles, and sometimes walking tours, are especially attractive, and start as low as $50 per person, double occupancy. And all visitors have use of the Executive Fitness Center with racquetball courts, a jogging track, and a glorious rooftop pool.

For reservations, phone the number above, or any office of the Hilton Reservation System.

THE CLASSIC STANDBYS: Synonymous with New York elegance, the **Plaza,** Fifth Ave. at 59th St., NY 10022 (tel. 212/PL 9-3000), has been attracting the cognoscenti since early in the century. Built in 1907, it has officially been designated as a "landmark of New York." Frank Lloyd Wright called it his home-away-from-home; Eloise grew up there, and it is a favorite choice of visiting royalty. Looking incongruously like a European château on the New York skyline, the French Renaissance structure is full of splendid touches, inside and out. Rooms have 14-foot ceilings, copper window frames, ornamental plaster moldings, and thick mahogany doors, while parlors also have carved marble fireplaces and crystal chandeliers. Many of the rooms afford spectacular views of Central Park and Fifth Avenue. All rooms have private bath, air conditioning, and color television, and 24-hour room service is available. The Plaza's dining rooms include the romantic, garden-like Palm Court (perfect for hand-holding), especially popular for Sunday brunch and afternoon tea; the classic Edwardian and Oak Rooms (the Oak Bar is the place to celebrity-watch and be seen); the casual Oyster

Bar, a cross between an English pub and a fish house; and Trader Vic's, for South Seas feasting. Single rooms go from $100 to $290, doubles from $160 to $290, suites from $350 to $600, prices subject to change. Inquire about reduced weekend rates that may be offered from time to time, as well as special weekend packages. The Plaza is owned by Westin Hotels.

The toll-free reservations number is 800/228-3000.

Ranking right up there with the Plaza, the **St. Regis-Sheraton,** Fifth Ave. and 55th St., NY 10022 (tel. 212/PL 3-4500), is another longtime favorite with the social, diplomatic, and international set. Also built early in the century, it still has its European charm and grandeur (its magnificent marble-floored, 20-foot-high lobby has recently had its ceiling restored), its large and graceful rooms with, of course, all the modern benefits of air conditioning, color television, and private baths. Sheraton Hotels took over the St. Regis a few years ago, and the result has been an unusually happy synthesis of old and new. Rates here go from $130 to $190 for a single; from $160 to $220 double and twin; and one- and two-bedroom suites begin at $260 and run up to $545. Down in the lobby, you can find just about the nicest shops: Bijan of Beverly Hills, Godiva, Fred Joalliers of Paris, all the names dear to the beautiful people. Elsewhere in the hotel, you can join the crowd for dinner and entertainment in the King Cole Room, for a drink at the St. Regis Grill, or perhaps for dancing to a band at Astor's, in a relaxed and elegant atmosphere.

The toll-free reservations number is 800/325-3535.

Another beauty on this fashionable strip facing the greensward of the park is **St. Moritz-on-the-Park,** 50 Central Park South, NY 10019 (tel. 212/PL 5-5800), a hostelry with a delightfully European air about it. The lobby suggests a place both elegant and exciting and, for further proof, take a look at the famed Rumpelmayer's, which is a combination old-world restaurant, soda fountain, candy-and-toy shop, and probably the most sophisticated place in New York to take your moppets for an ice-cream soda. You can also enjoy the leisurely life at Harry's New York Bar or the Café de la Paix, one of New York's few sidewalk cafés. Upstairs, the guest rooms are spacious, very well appointed, and all have air conditioning, color TV, and private baths. Rates (subject to change) run from $95 to $155 single, from $115 to $175 double or twin. One-bedroom junior suites go from $185 to $285; two-bedroom suites range in price from $275 to $575. Ask about special July and August rates, and weekend packages all year round.

The toll-free reservations number is 800/221-4774.

Another of New York's newer hotels, the **United Nations Plaza Hotel** at One United Nations Plaza, NY 10017 (East 44th St. just west of First Ave.; tel 212/355-3400), is a masterpiece of understated elegance, perfectly befitting the ambassadors, diplomats, and heads of state who choose it for the kind of serenity and security that few other New York hotels possess. Just across the street from the United Nations, and owned by it (although its rates are too steep for most U.N. personnel), the hotel was designed by Kevin Roche of Kevin Roche–John Dinkeloo and Associates, and his fine hand is seen everywhere, especially in the stunning Ambassador Grill and Lounge, whose ceiling of mirrored glass, reflecting and refracting light in a series of prisms within prisms within prisms, makes the 14-foot ceiling seem cathedral-high. Sleeping rooms begin on the 28th floor, so there's scarcely a whisper of traffic noise, and all have beautiful views, subtly modern decor, TVs and radios, air conditioning, and all the amenities. Rooms and halls are decorated with beautiful ethnic art from U.N. member countries. Guests may swim in the glorious glass-enclosed swimming pool in the sky, use the facilities of the Turtle Bay Health Club, and play tennis at a reduced fee. The Ambassador Grill serves breakfast, lunch, and dinner; there's music in the adjoining Ambassador Lounge. Room service is available around the clock. The United Nations Plaza Hotel is a small place, with only 289 rooms, so its staff (among them they speak 27 languages) is able to give its guests all sorts of personal services—it can even provide heating pads, rollers, plug adapters, voltage transformers, and a butler! And in the European manner, shoes can be polished overnight.

As for the rates, single rooms run from $125 to $165; $20 additional should be added for double occupancy. Fabulous suites begin at $400 per night. Rates are subject to change.

More reasonable rates are reserved for weekenders, and the package—inquire at the hotel for current prices—includes weekend membership in the health club, plus a credit toward the incredibly popular Sunday brunch in the Ambassador Grill. (Some of New York's most glittering celebrities can often be seen standing in line for the noon or 2 p.m. sittings.)

The United Nations Plaza Hotel is a Hyatt International Hotel, and reservations can be made by phoning 800/228-9000, toll free.

Could there be anyone who has heard of New York who has not heard of the **Waldorf-Astoria**? As much a part of the New York scene as the Empire State Building (the site of the original Waldorf-Astoria), this grande dame of New York's luxury hotels holds forth at Park Ave. and 50th St., NY 10022 (tel. 212/355-3000). We often think that its lushly carpeted and beautifully furnished lobby, with its meandering arcades and quiet little corners, is one of the few true hotel lobbies left in the city. Waldorf guests have always included the world famous: you might run into anyone here from Frank Sinatra to Mrs. Douglas MacArthur. Not content to rest on its laurels, however, the Waldorf, under the Hilton banner, has refurnished and redecorated all of its rooms, and equipped them, of course, with all the necessities: individual air conditioning, color TV (with first-run cinema service), private baths (many with boudoir), direct-dial telephones, and old-world amenities like nightly turn-down service. Special arrangements have been made for families (children occupying the same room as their parents are free) and for honeymooners (champagne and room service breakfasts at no extra charge). Rates for all this largesse (subject to change) run from $105 to $165 for a single, from $140 to $200 for a double, from $300 to $435 for a one-bedroom suite, and $440 to $595 for a two-bedroom. A third person in the same room is charged $35 a night. Oscar's, the famous coffeeshop at the Waldorf, is decorated as an indoor garden; the Bull & Bear has a giant Maltese-cross bar of African mahogany with a footrail, and serves both English and American food; Sir Harry's Bar has an African safari setting; and Inagiku serves Japan's finest food. And, of course, there's still Peacock Alley which has always been, to our minds, one of the nicest *intime* spots in town. Now featuring Cole Porter's own piano, it is the scene, every Sunday, of mind-boggling brunches that are just about the most lavish in town (see Chapter IV, "Restaurants").

For reservations, phone your local Hilton Reservation Service.

One of New York's landmark hotels has undergone a $15-million renovation, and the results are visible everywhere in the beautiful **Drake Swissotel**, at Park Ave. and 56th St., NY 10022 (tel. 212/421-0900). The premier North American hotel for Swissotels, the prestigious Swiss chain, it combines the best features of American hospitality and Swiss innkeeping. The jewel-like lobby is the setting for both the Champagne and Wine Bar, and La Piazetta, a gourmet continental restaurant. The 640 rooms are nicer and bigger than many we've seen elsewhere: sprightly floral color schemes, lacquered white or fruitwood furniture, desks, full-length mirrors, plants in every room, colored sheets, and sunny lemon-yellow halls give the feeling of guest bedrooms in a country home. Special extras include fool-proof locks, peepholes and buzzers, extra telephones and radio speakers in the bathrooms, ice buckets, digital alarm clocks in addition to the color TVs, in-house movies, satin hangers, special soaps and toiletries in every room—even refrigerators. And all rooms have double-double beds. There are independent heating and air conditioning controls. Rates (subject to change) run from $145 to $205 single, from $165 to $225 double, and from $350 to $500 for suites.

Inquire of the hotel about its "Critic's Choice," "Drake Weekender," and "Classic Celebration" packages, which offer good value for a weekend on the town.

When it opened in the 1920s as a "residence for men accustomed to the finer things of life," the Shelton Towers Hotel was considered one of the city's finest hotel architectural achievements. The beautiful old details are still there, but the old hotel has undergone a bright new metamorphosis as **Halloran House,** 525 Lexington Ave. at 49th St., NY 10017 (tel. 212/PL 5-4000 or toll free 800/223-0939). The lobby, with its dark wood, marble floors, chandeliers, and a busy but graciously subdued feeling, recalls the past. The bedrooms are big-city contemporary, with such details as extra phones in the bathroom, safe-deposit boxes in the closet, bedside remote controls for the color TV, radio alarm clocks, and wide-angle peepholes. Rooms are nicely furnished, with either king-size or two double beds, and the suites, some with mini-refrigerators, modern and Oriental decor, and wrap-around terraces, can be spectacular. Services include the ministrations of a concierge and room service. Guests can dine at Norman's of New York, an elegant room offering American-continental cuisine; Biff's Place, fun for lunch and live entertainment every night; and the Green Thumb, a pleasant coffeehouse adjoining Norman's.

Rates (subject to change) run from $105 to $120 single, $120 to $135 double, $210 to $500 for suites. Children under 18 stay free in their parents' room. An excellent weekend package is available.

It's been called "the only gallery on Fifth Avenue that will give you a bed for the night." And that, indeed, is the feeling one gets from **American Stanhope Hotel,** Fifth Ave. at 81st St., NY

10028 (tel. 212/288-5800), a landmark hotel across the street from the Metropolitan Museum of Art and at the foot of New York's "Museum Mile." Thanks to the passionate interest in Americana of the hotel's owner, Mimi Russell (an American granddaughter of Winston Churchill), this small and intimate hotel houses the country's largest single private collection of 19th-century American art and antiques. They spill over from the gracious public areas downstairs (each representative of a different period of American history) up to the 296 guest rooms above. Each room is furnished with original Empire period antiques, plus wallpaper, draperies, and quilted comforters in matching country prints. Of course there are all the modern amenities of color TV, AM-FM radio, direct-dial telephone, and full bathroom with tub and shower. Guest services include babysitting, room service, concierge, same-day valet and laundry service, valet parking, and weekday limousine service to midtown. Some of the rooms overlook Central Park. This kind of elegant simplicity does not come cheap: prices range from $125 to $165 single, $148 to $185 double or twin, $185 to $200 for a junior suite studio, and $300 to $620 for one-, two-, and three-bedroom suites. A third person in the room is $20.

American regional cuisine and decor are featured in all of the dining areas. At the Saratoga, a gracious 19th-century American Empire-style dining room, you may find Jackie O. having breakfast or a group of society women planning a ball over lunch. Dick Cavett, Paul McCartney, and Bianca Jagger are frequent patrons. Local families can often be found celebrating children's birthday parties in the Furnished Room, which looks like a turn-of-the-century Victorian-style front parlor; everything is washable, and kids rave about the foot-long hot dogs. New York's oldest sidewalk café, the Terrace, is still one of the best spots in town for sophisticated people-watching.

The American Stanhope has an especially good weekend package: for $115 per couple, you stay at the hotel for two nights, have breakfast at the Saratoga, and get free admission to all the museums on "Museum Mile." Corporate rates and special services are also available.

Over on the West Side of town, the **New York Hilton at Rockefeller Center,** Avenue of the Americas between 53rd and 54th Sts., NY 10019 (tel. 212/586-7000), is one of the major hotels of New York. The soaring, glass-sided column is one of the pioneers of the modernistic architecture of the city and especially of the Rockefeller Center area. The largest hotel in town

(2131 rooms), the Hilton boasts convention halls big enough for small armies to parade in (meeting and banquet rooms can service anywhere from 15 to 3000), and guest rooms whose wall-to-wall blue-tinted windows provide dramatic vistas of New York's skyline. The rooms are nicely decorated with a modern touch, all have individually controlled heating and air conditioning, direct-dial phones, color TV with in-house movies at a nominal charge, and an electronic message and wake-up system. Special rooms are available for the handicapped. There are ice machines on most floors. The tab here runs from $95 to $140 in a single, from $120 to $165 in a double or twin, from $290 to $325 for parlor and one-bedroom suites, from $400 to $435 for parlor and two-bedroom suites. Executive Tower, a hotel within a hotel on the 39th through 44th floors, features its own registration desk, a private lounge and Boardroom for guests, concierge service, and its own manager and staff. Room amenities here include refrigerators, bathroom scales, radio alarm clocks, and other extras; rates are $175, single or double. There is no charge for children sharing their parents' room, and rates are subject to change. There's plenty of wining and dining excitement at the Hilton. Hurlingham's, an elegant restaurant with a polo theme, has the ambience of a British club; a pianist performs nightly. Sybils has a disc jockey and dancing until 4 a.m., and is popular with a chic crowd. The Café New York coffeehouse is open 24 hours every day. Mirage, the lobby cocktail lounge, is highlighted by two huge, antique marble sphinxes; a pianist entertains every evening, and there are complimentary hors d'oeuvres from 5 to 7 p.m. And the International Promenade is great fun for cocktails and people-watching through floor-to-ceiling windows. The Hilton's staff, by the way, is multilingual (some 35 different languages are spoken), there is an International Visitors Information Service, and guest information, signs, and menus are in several languages. The cashiers can exchange foreign currency 24 hours a day.

Hilton's Rainbow Weekend package is an attractive deal. For reservations, phone the number above or your local Hilton Reservation Service.

On its way to becoming the premier facility in the worldwide network of Sheraton hotels, the **Sheraton Centre New York,** Seventh Ave. at 52nd St., NY 10019 (tel. 212/581-1000), is a 50-story, 1847-room hostelry alive with excitement and a wealth of comforts for the huge number of conventioneers who gather here. A multi-million-dollar conversion project has created a futuristic lobby; Café Fontana, a continental café in the European sidewalk tradition, complete with trees and fountains; Ranier, a prestigious Italian restaurant; and La Ronde, a nightclub with live entertainment and dancing. The Sheraton Towers is a luxury "hotel within a hotel"; a private club entrance leads the way to five floors of exquisitely appointed guest rooms and suites that feature such niceties as refrigerators, electric blankets, terry shower robes, fine china, and silverware. Free continental breakfast, afternoon tea and pastries, cocktails, and other meals are served in the private Towers Club. Rates for singles here run $175 to $190; for doubles and twins, $195 to $210. Suites go from $350 to $495. In the main body of the hotel, rooms are comfortably furnished in sunny color schemes, boast two armchairs, clock radios, cable TVs, and, on request at certain times, small refrigerators. These rooms go from $95 to $155 single, from $105 to $175 double; suites range from $350 to $795. (Rates are subject to change.) Sheraton Centre also offers a host of vacation package plans at good prices. Guests may use the swimming pool at the Sheraton City Squire, directly across the street, free of charge.

The toll-free reservations number is 800/325-3535.

First Class: From $75, Double

MIDTOWN WEST SIDE: If you've come to New York to go to the theater, to see the sights, to conduct business, or just to be in the heart of everything, you can't pick a more convenient location that the midtown West Side area. Choose a hotel in this area, bounded on the north by Rockefeller Center in the 50s, passing through the Broadway theater district in the 40s, and bordered on the south by Madison Square Garden Center, and, chances are, you'll be within walking distance of just about everywhere you want to be.

Finding a New York hotel with a swimming pool is not an easy matter; they are few and far between. If you'd like to take a swim before (or even after) a hard day's sightseeing, then the **Sheraton City Squire Hotel**, on Seventh Ave. at 52nd St., NY 10019 (tel. 212/581-3300), is an excellent choice. A $15-million renovation has recently been completed. The lobby is pleasant, with its shops and bar, and all rooms, smartly furnished, have picture windows. Some have private terraces and striking views as well. But best of all is the view from the glass-enclosed swimming pool, open year round. It's great fun to swim or lie back

in a comfortable chair and gaze at the crazy, mixed-up beach—
the skyscrapers of New York surrounding you. Air conditioning,
TV, private bath, of course, and the prices are as follows: singles
go from $90 to $150; doubles or twins, from $98 to $170; suites,
from $250 and up. An extra person is charged $20 per night.
Children may stay in their parents' room free. Parking is $12 per
night. Right at the hotel is the Movenpick Restaurant, which
serves Swiss and continental cuisine and includes both a lounge
and a "croissanterie" which serves fresh, baked-on-the-premises
items.

For reservations, toll free, phone 800/325-3535.

The **Windsor Harley,** 100 West 58th St., NY 10019 (tel. 212/
265-2100), is the kind of gracious, small hotel that people tell
their friends about. A favorite for almost half a century, the
Windsor is close to Central Park and has a beautiful old-world
lobby with mirrored ceiling, fireplace, and chandeliers. The old-
world theme is carried out in the generously sized rooms (even
the singles have king-size beds!) with their French Provincial
furniture, wall-to-wall carpeting, and good closets (most rooms
have two). Computerized no-key locks assure absolute protec-
tion. You'll find performing artists (the hotel is near the major
music and theater centers), corporate types, and international
visitors enjoying the peacefulness of a stay here. Singles run from
$95 to $105; doubles or twins, from $105 to $115; one-bedroom
suites, $155 to $175; two-bedroom suites, from $250 (rates sub-
ject to change).

The toll-free reservations number is 800/321-2323.

One of New York's best hotel swimming pools opens to the
sun on the roof of the **Holiday Inn–57th Street,** 440 West 57th
St., NY 10019 (between Ninth and Tenth Aves.; tel 212/581-
8100), and that's just the beginning of the creature comforts that
abound at this super-size city version of the popular chain. The
location is way west, near the Hudson and the passenger ship
piers, not far from the Coliseum and Lincoln Center. A rather
unimpressive outside that resembles an apartment building gives
way, on the inside, to a complex beehive of 606 rooms and
extensive facilities for pampering travelers, including free underground car parking (refreshing!), room service, and that lovely
rooftop pool. The sleeping rooms, some of which are marvelously spacious, are bright and airy. Attractively appointed, they
have modern paintings on the walls, good closet space, color TVs
with radio, direct-dial phones, and most also have a work/eating
area. Prices range from $80 to $103 for singles, $90 to $113 for

The Literary Life—An Off-the-Beaten-Path Choice

We know of no hotel lobby in New York that is so full of fascinating ghosts as that of the **Hotel Algonquin,** 59 West 44th St. (tel. 212/840-6800). Every time we sit down at one of the plush little sofas in the oak-paneled lobby-lounge and ring the bell for a glass of scotch—or a spot of tea—we are reminded of the generations of actors and writers and celebrated wits who have held forth here since 1902. But although Robert Benchley and James Thurber and H. L. Mencken and Laurette Taylor are part of the Algonquin's storied past, the current crop of celebrities is equally as bright: you might find Jean-Luc Godard or Sir Laurence Olivier or Truman Capote or Simone Signoret engaged in heated conversation or being interviewed by the *Times,* for the Algonquin is as much a literary and artistic club as it is a hotel. But it is a hotel, very much in the European manner of an inn, where the management tries to know each guest and make each one feel at home. And you really needn't be a celebrity to stay here. The 200 rooms and suites, comfortably furnished and with all the modern amenities of private baths, TV, direct-dial phones, guest-controlled air conditioning, plus the extraordinary security of "Cardgard" room entry in place of keys, are open to all comers. They range in price from $84 to $100 for a single, from $87 to $103 for a double, from $90 to $106 for a twin-bedded room. Most one-bedroom suites are $160 to $182. There is free parking on weekends for those staying at least two nights. Once you get to the Algonquin, do have a meal at the celebrated Rose or Oak Rooms or, at least, a drink in the lobby. Could that be Peter Ustinov over there to your right?

---

twins; the family plan (two double-double beds) is $98 with no charge for children under 12. Extra adults in the same room are $10; rollaway beds, another $10. Spacious "King Leisure" rooms with a king-size bed are $102 single, $112 double. Suites are available, as are group rates.

There's no shortage of places to dine right at home. The Greenery is the place for breakfast, or a buffet or regular lunch. Derby's, handsome in the 18th-century English manner, has an extensive menu of international specialties. And finally, there's the Study, a cocktail lounge of subdued atmosphere and a wine rack with ivy-filled planters on top and hundreds of wine glasses hanging below. There's entertainment nightly.

For reservations from outside New York state, phone, toll free, 800/231-0405.

Heading south a bit, in the heart of the busy area in the low 30s that encompasses the Madison Square Garden Center, Pennsylvania Station, the Garment District, and Macy's and Gimbels, there are two distinctive hostelries, one big and exciting, the other small and peaceful. The first is the **New York Penta**, 401 Seventh Ave., at 33rd St., NY 10001 (tel. 212/736-5000), just across the street from Madison Square Garden and Pennsylvania Station, and the closest hotel to the gigantic New York Convention Center on 35th St. and Eleventh Ave. With some 1737 guest rooms, the 21-story Penta is one of the largest in the city, and one of its prime convention and exhibit hotels. The Penta, which began life as the New York Statler back in 1919, was designed by McKim, Meade and White; its new owners, a European hotel group, are completing a loving, lavish, $20-million renovation on this landmark property, and the excitement will be evident everywhere: in the newly restored white exterior, in the stunning new lobby designed by Ellen McClusky, the new Globetrotter and Bierstube restaurants (the first a full-service restaurant, the other a German-type pub for beer, wine, and European snacks), and in the guest rooms, whose prize-winning design was chosen after a competition by four noted interior designers.

Depending on what floor you stay on, you'll be either in a pale gray-green room with camel accents, or a dusty teal-blue one with shades of vanilla and beige. The wooden furniture is lacquered in pale colors, and although the rooms are not large, they are designed to give a feeling of comfort, with a desk, lounge chairs, a cylinder drum table, and art prints and engravings (many with an Oriental feeling) on the wall. Bathrooms are all newly redone too, with superb makeup lighting, courtesy of an incandescent vanity strip light. Conveniences include color TV and individually controlled air conditioning, room service until 10:30 p.m., same-day valet and laundry service, valet parking, an electronic guest security system, and the attentions of a multilingual staff. The hotel aims to provide first-class service at reasonable prices. For New York, this translates to singles from $69 to $125, twins from $89 to $145. One-, two-, and three-bedroom suites, many of them on special "executive floors," will be available; rates on request.

Weekend visitors can realize substantial savings with two plans: "New York Penta Plain and Simple" at $29.95 per person per night (Thursday, Friday, and Saturday), and "New York Penta Pampered Weekend" at $54.95 per person per night.

For toll-free reservations, phone 800/223-5588 in New York state; elsewhere, 800/223-8585.

A door or so away from the excitement going on at the Penta is a hotel with all the feeling of a quiet, gracious home. That's **Southgate Tower,** at 31st St. and Seventh Ave., NY 10001 (tel. 212/563-1800). The Southgate is one of the few hotels in New York where every room—even a studio—has a fully equipped, modern kitchen, so you can happily settle in here for a few days, a week or two, or even longer; many corporations keep rooms here for their executives. The 1000 rooms of the original Governor Clinton (later Penn Garden Hotel) were remodeled a few years ago and turned into 500 apartments. Spacious rooms, some with terraces, are beautifully furnished, and the housekeeping is tops; if you don't want to cook in, there's a restaurant in the lobby and room service available as well. Southgate Mall, the main lobby, is like a European street with fountains and plantings, and shops and services lining each side of the plaza. There is a parking garage right on the premises. Considering all you get here, and the not inconsiderable savings of eating in, this has to be one of the best values in town. Single rooms go from $79 to $89; twin rooms, from $89 to $99. One-bedrooms go from $95 to $125.

THE EAST SIDE: New York's East Side is traditionally known for being a bit more peaceful, a bit less frenzied than the West Side. Some—especially women—feel it's safer at night. Some of the most elegant hotels—like the Waldorf-Astoria, the Pierre, and the Carlyle are East Side addresses. But there are also less expensive hostelries here, and the location couldn't be better. You're near Grand Central Terminal, the United Nations, and the Fifth Avenue department stores. The posh specialty shops of Madison Avenue and the swinging boutiques of Lexington and Third Avenues are all nearby.

A big favorite on the East Side is the comfortable **Loews Summit,** at Lexington Ave. and 51st St., NY 10022 (tel. 212/752-7000). This one features an in-hotel garage, a lobby beauty and barber shop, a gift shop, a health club, Maude's Restaurant for good dinners, the Lobby Bar for drinks; in short, it's the kind of hotel that has enough so that one could just stay in on a rainy day and be well provided for. The Summit offers a luxurious lobby and rooms in attractive modern decor, all with color TV, radio, in-room movies, direct-dial phones, bar-refrigerators, and that extra phone in the bathroom, too. Central air conditioning, of course. Now for the rates: from $90 to $120 for a single, $110 to $140 for a double or a twin. Suites, some with balconies, begin at $168 for Tower (junior) suites, and go from $240 for one-bedroom arrangements, $330 for two bedrooms. A third person in the room is $15 additional, and there is no charge for children under 14 sharing their parents' room. (Rates are subject to change.)

A recent $3-million renovation has made the gracious, European-style **Hotel Beverly,** Lexington Ave. and 50th St., NY 10022 (tel. 212/PL 3-2700), lovelier than ever. There's a quiet, calm feeling about this 300-room, family-owned hotel, refreshingly unusual in the hubbub of the city. Also unusual is the fact that this is largely a suite hotel. Which means that for scarcely more than the cost of a bedroom in other hotels, you can have all the comforts of a private apartment—and that includes living room, bedroom, bath, and full kitchenette, complete with refrigerator, cooking unit, dinnerware, and utensils—enough for any meal. And even regular rooms, without kitchenettes, all have refrigerators. Rooms are individually decorated in fine taste, and although the decor varies from traditional to contemporary, all are spacious and lovely with the kind of roominess one can find in the older New York hotels. Some of the studios have a sofa and desk area. Rooms are air-conditioned and have cable color TV. The hotel is especially proud of its new security walk-in closets (you are given a separate key for closet, and nobody can open it but you). It's like a giant safe deposit box, but big enough to hold luggage, attaché cases, and precious possessions. Many corporations keep permanent hold on rooms here for their executives; it seems they find the location and ambience congenial. So, too, do tourists from all over the world, U.N. people, and visiting families, and for the same reasons. In addition, children can stay in the same room with their parents free. (All parties of four are placed in suites.)

The Beverly's lobby has been newly redone too, with warm fruitwood-paneled walls, an Oriental-pattern carpet, and traditional furnishings that create the feeling of an 18th-century English living room. A concierge is at the ready, there's valet parking, room service, and Kenny's Steak Pub, one of the most popular steakhouses in town, is on one side of the lobby. On the other side of the lobby is a 24-hour pharmacy.

To make things even nicer, readers of this book who reserve directly with the hotel will be granted a $10 discount per night off the regular rates, which are $89 to $98 single, $99 to $109 double, $99 to $119 for junior suites, $150 to $175 for one-bedroom suites, and $250 to $300 for two-bedroom suites. In addition, the Beverly has some terrific weekend packages that start as low as $64 per person, double occupancy, for three days and two nights (no discounts on these).

For reservations from outside New York state, phone, toll free, 800/223-0945.

The same people who run the lovely Doral Hotels in Miami Beach are in charge at the **Doral Inn,** Lexington Ave. at 49th St., NY 10022 (tel. 212/PL 5-1200), long one of our favorite hotels on the East Side. The location couldn't be more convenient, since it's smack in the midtown shopping area, across the street, in fact, from the Waldorf-Astoria. It's a busy, with-it hotel, the original one in New York to have indoor squash courts on its premises, available to guests at a nominal fee. When you're not chasing the ball around the court, you can enjoy the feeling of quiet comfort in the well-appointed rooms, decorated in green-and-white or blue-and-white color schemes, with a Floridian air, all with their own private bath, air conditioning, and color TV with AM-FM radio. Small refrigerators are available on request. Rates for single rooms, depending on size and location, run from $82 to $100; doubles and twin-bedded rooms go from $94 to $112. An extra person is $12 more. Two-room suites, perfect for family living, run from $175; three-room suites, from $275. Some of the newer suites contain their own sauna baths, and the penthouse floor has executive rooms and suites, subdivided by terraces. A laundry room and ice machines are available.

Downstairs, the Pantry coffeeshop serves 24 hours a day, and the lovely Mormando Restaurant offers lunch, dinner, and supper until 1 a.m. The same management is also in charge at the Doral Park Avenue Hotel, the Tuscany and Tuscany Towers hotels in New York as well as at the Miami and Miami Beach Dorals. Contact Trudy Cohen, sales manager, for reservations, and you'll be well taken care of.

East and West have met at the pleasant **Hotel Kitano,** 66 Park Ave. at 38th St., NY 10016 (tel. 212/685-0022), the only Japanese-owned and -operated hotel in New York, and the results are pleasing to both Japanese and American clientele (guests usually number about 50% of each), who find this small hotel in the quiet Murray Hill neighborhood an oasis in New York. (Not far from the Garment District, the hotel attracts many women buyers.) While the small lobby and most of the 112 guest rooms are strictly American style, there are still charming Oriental touches; in an authentic tea ceremony room, in the Hakubai Restaurant which serves up delectable Japanese specialties, and in just a few tatami suites, authentic down to their bedrolls and furos (hot tubs). The attractively decorated rooms all have color TV, central heating, and air conditioning, and are of decent size; some have small refrigerators and electric ranges available at no extra charge. Rates (subject to change) run from $85 to $100 for singles, $105 to $115 for doubles and twins, $116 to $270 for suites, and $170 for the Japanese tatami suites. Inquire about the "Japanese Fantasy in New York" package, which includes a meal at Hakubai along with a room or suite.

The toll-free reservations number is 800/223-5823.

The **Middletowne Harley Hotel,** 148 East 48th St., NY 10017 (tel. 212/PL 5-3000), is one of the real finds in the New York hotel scene. Since it was converted just a few years ago from an apartment building, its 191 rooms still have apartment amenities; these are gracious-sized rooms, each with two large closets and, best of all, fully equipped walk-in kitchens, wonderfully handy for corporate executives and diplomats who must entertain, as well as for visitors who wish to save on the high cost of always eating out. Rooms are prettily furnished with bright color schemes, boast full carpets, wallpaper in the bathrooms, floral spreads, in addition to the usual features (12th-floor rooms have tiny terraces). The lobby is small and strictly functional. Rates (subject to change) go from $95 to $105 single, $105 to $115 double or twin, $155 for junior suites, $175 for larger suites. Monthly rates are available on stays of two months or longer.

For reservations, telephone, toll free, 800/221-4982.

One of the more relaxed and quiet hotels on the East Side (all the windows are soundproofed) is the 200-room **Roger Smith,** 401 Lexington Ave. at 47th St., NY 10019 (tel. 212/775-1400). If you can't bear to leave the family pet back home, this is one of the few hotels that won't complain or refuse to accommodate you: they understand the attachment you feel for your pet. The rooms are spacious and well furnished, all with automatic coffee-makers, bath, air conditioning, and color TV (sometimes radios), some with ice-cube machines, small refrigerators are available on request. Rates (subject to change) are $67 to $84 for singles, $79 to $96 for doubles. The suites all have serving pantries with cooking units, and some, since this is an older hotel, boast the presence of terraces or even fireplaces. These one-bedroom, huge living room suites, which range in price from $120 to $160, could be perfect for families, since children are free and the pantry allows for eat-in meals. The Nibbles restaurant serves all three meals at popular prices; free continental breakfast is available to guests on weekends and holidays. Those with cars can use the adjoining garage at an extra charge, or join the New Yorkers who scramble for curbside spaces on 47th Street, free from 7 p.m. until 8 a.m. the next morning. Many Europeans and United Nations personnel frequent the Roger Smith. And, oh yes, there's a travel agent—as well as a dentist—right on the premises.

Few New Yorkers ever gain access to lively Gramercy Park, the only private park in the city, and even fewer visitors—unless they're smart enough to stay at the **Gramercy Park Hotel,** a charming older hotel at 2 Lexington Ave. at 21st St., NY 10010 (tel. 212/GR 5-4320). Nestled amid historic landmarks and beautiful old houses, the Gramercy Park offers a combination rare for New York—elegance and grace at surprisingly little cost. It's a joyful throwback to the heyday of the 1920s, when architect Stanford White (of *Ragtime* renown) lived in the corner brownstone, one of the six houses that occupied the site where the hotel now stands.

People in the arts have long had a special affinity for this hotel: Humphrey Bogart's first wedding took place here, S. J. Perelman called it home, and theater luminaries like Siobhan McKenna and James Cagney have all been guests. And you'll know why as you walk along the airy, tree-lined block into the traditional lobby with its waterfall-of-crystal chandelier and green-and-orange rug.

Although you could get a perfectly fine single room for $75 to $85, or a standard double room (with double or king-size bed) for $80 to $90, it's more fun to stay in one of the suites, which make up 40% of the hotel's accommodations. And at prices of $100 to $125 for standard inside suites, $150 to $175 for deluxe, they are veritable bargains compared to prices at other hotels. All of the eight deluxe suites are spacious, and individual in decor and furnishings. Some have marble fireplaces that were designed by Stanford White and used in his home: one has such details as a French writing desk, leather chairs, and ginger-jar lamps. All suites have two closets and one bathroom; some have serving pantries with a two-burner stove, hotplate, sink, and refrigerator. In the South Building, the second section of the hotel, there's another lobby geared toward relaxed sitting. Living quarters here are primarily for long stays, and all suites have pantries and large closets, and face the park.

The hotel's elegant dining room serves fine continental food, and the Gramercy Café, a cocktail lounge, is the place for piano or guitar music. (Incidentally, if you're planning a large party, the Roof Garden, enclosed in a canvas awning and filled with fresh flowers, provides a terrace for city-gazing and an inside dance floor and bar for up to 250 people.) The Gramercy Park Hotel is near bus and subway routes, and just a few minutes away from the heart of midtown.

For reservations, phone, toll free, either 800/221-4083 or 800/221-4098.

The Good Buys: Doubles Around $60

THE WEST FIFTIES—MUSIC, ART, AND EXPOSITIONS: Still very close to the center of things, but a bit removed from the hustle and bustle of Times Square, the West 50s are an ideal place to stay. The big attractions here are Rockefeller Center; Carnegie Hall; the Coliseum, home to many expositions; Lincoln Center, not far north; the art galleries and elegant shops of 57th Street and Fifth Avenue.

One of the nicest hotels here is the **Hotel Gorham,** 136 West 55th St., NY 10019 (tel. 212/CI 5-1800), built in 1938, when hotel builders could afford to be generous with space. Walk into the lobby with its cathedral ceiling and European ambience and you'll immediately get a feeling of quiet, unhurried comfort. It's a small hotel with just 116 rooms and suites, each styled for easy living, with serving pantries (kitchenettes with refrigerators, hotplate, or range, and sink) in all. There are lockable closets in all rooms (security is tight here) and charming murals of European scenes. All double rooms are large and are priced from $63 to $80, with the higher rates for rooms so large they often accommodate two queen-size beds. All have private bath, air conditioning, color TV, separate clock radio, direct-dial telephone, and a blessed feeling of space. Singles go from $53 to $70. Very attractive single suites are available from $75 to $90. Each extra person is charged $10. But you need pay no more than $85 for a family suite which can sleep up to six persons! (Rates are subject to change.) On the premises is Castellano's, a gourmet European restaurant awarded two stars by the *New York Times*. Theatrical people, tourists, buyers, and many Europeans all seem to feel comfortable at the Gorham.

On the same street, a bit closer to Fifth Avenue, the **Shoreham Hotel,** 33 West 55th St., NY 10019 (tel. 212/247-6700), is a gracious small (120-room) hotel that caters to a largely repeat clientele, many from South America and Europe. Some 90% of its clients, management claims, make return visits, and these travelers are attracted neither by flamboyant surroundings nor prices. What they are attracted by is a fine location, comfortable rooms at good prices, and a staff that still knows about old-fashioned courtesy. The recently renovated traditional lobby has lounge chairs of the comfy, plunk-yourself-down variety for resting after a hard day's sightseeing or shopping. Security is excellent, as elevators are operated manually, and operators and desk people keep an eye on who's coming and going. Rooms are done either in earth-color motifs or cool-color blends of greens and aquas; all have color TV, writing desk, table, and chair for dining, a serving pantry (with some dishes and an electric coffee pot), a newly done bathroom, and air conditioning. Single rooms go for $62 to $72; doubles, from $76 to $86. Suites, which can sleep four in living room and bedroom, and moderately priced for New York: $95 to $130. The Shoreham has a glamorous tenant, the superb La Caravelle restaurant, which you can enter through the lobby; but be advised that a dinner here might well cost you more than your night's lodging.

We're accustomed to seeing **Howard Johnson's Motor Lodges** on highways, but here in New York you'll find a member of this famous family right in the midtown area. It's located on Eighth Ave., between 51st and 52nd Sts., NY 10019 (tel. 212/581-4100), within walking distance of Broadway theaters and all the cultural attractions of the West 50s. The 300 rooms here are all very attractive, with modern decor, wall-to-wall carpets, air conditioning, large bathrooms, color TVs that also show first-run, in-house movies (for a few extra dollars). Right on the premises, naturally, is a Howard Johnson's Restaurant (the kids can indulge in a different flavor of ice cream every day) and a cocktail lounge. You can choose a studio room (with two studio couches) or a more traditional room. Singles run $65, $75, and $85; doubles or twins, $77, $87, and $97; suites, $130 and up. A third person staying in the room is charged $15. There is no charge for children not requiring an extra rollaway bed. Parking is included in the above rates, plus a moderate in-and-out service charge each time the car is used. Rates are subject to change.

For reservations, phone, toll free, 800/654-2000.

MIDTOWN WEST SIDE: If the lure of the theater has brought you to New York, you can't pick a more convenient headquarters than the new **Milford Plaza Hotel,** which sits smack in the heart of the theater district at 270 West 45th St., NY 10036 (tel. 212/869-3600), and exudes "star quality." There's electricity in the atmosphere here, since the hotel is very much dedicated to show business: celebrities like Elizabeth Taylor and Gilda Radner are among the many who have chosen to have their opening-night parties here. The three-story marble lobby is a stunner with its large cone-shaped chandeliers, red-and-black carpeting, and black-and-gray chairs—a fine spot for cocktails or espresso as you survey the passing crowd.

There are 1300 rooms on the 28 floors in this hotel, and every door has a star on it. There are stars on the bedspreads too. Rooms are not large, but they are distinctively designed in contemporary fashion, and all have color TV-radio combinations, washable wallpaper, direct-dial phone, and individually controlled air conditioning. Single accommodations are from $66 to $76, twins or doubles from $80 to $99, one-bedroom suites from $175 to $250, and two-bedroom suites from $225 to $360. Security is a priority here; all guests must present a key before going up to their rooms.

A Best Western hotel, the Milford Plaza has done a nice job on its dining facilities. Its breakfast buffet, served every morning between 6:45 and 11 a.m. for $6.95, including tax and tip, is very popular. The Stage Door Canteen, a revival of the original one and lined with photographs from the 1940s, serves three meals a day and light after-theater snacks; so does the Celebrity Deli, a typical New York deli; both are popular hangouts. Kippy's Pier 44 is known for delicious seafood, and bedecked as it is in the manner of a 19th-century sailing ship with portholes and brass fittings, it's a show in itself.

As you check out the lobby on your way to the travel- and theater-ticket desk or the sundries shop or the beauty salon, you might want to note two unusual windows on the ground floor, overlooking the 44th Street side: one reveals the freezer room with first-class meat hanging in full view; the other displays fresh seafood. And on the Eighth Avenue side, check out the bank of theater posters on parade.

For reservations, phone, toll free, 800/221-2690; in New York state the toll-free number is 800/522-6449.

A longtime haven for theatrical folk, the **Hotel Royalton,** 44 West 44th St., NY 10036 (tel. 212/730-1344), has been home not only for theater-goers, but for those who make theater happen: Julie Harris and Tennessee Williams, George Jean Nathan and William Inge are just a few of the luminaries who have enjoyed the quiet comfort of this turn-of-the-century hotel, built by Stanford White in the early 1900s, and long an exclusive men's club. From the graceful entrance with its pillars-in-the-round, the lobby with its light-orange marble walls and arches, to the unusually spacious rooms, the Royalton is almost an anacronism in cramped, contemporary hotel-land.

Each of the 142 rooms at the Royalton is different in size and decor—no standard hotel issue here. They're all immaculate, however, and have air conditioning, large closets, roomy bathrooms, carpets, color TV (some with radios as well), and writing desks (wouldn't it be fun to know which plays and essays were written at which desks?). Although there are small but sufficient rooms here at $45 single, $55 double, fine if you're on a tight budget, we'd definitely opt for one of the higher priced rooms, which are spacious, charming, smartly decorated, and furnished with such accoutrements as easy chairs, bookcases, and possibly a fireplace with andirons. The one-bedroom suites, some traditional, some modern, are also handsomely done. Refrigerators are available on request, the coffeeshop will provide room service, and the valet will locate babysitters. At the time of this writing, a major renovation of the Royalton was being planned; alas, it should considerably raise rates over the $63 doubles and under-$100 suites available at this time. The Royalton is very popular with TV production people (especially from France and England), fashion industry executives, and the literary and theatrical set, so reserve early.

A good place to stay with children is the **Ramada Inn,** at 790 Eighth Ave., NY 10019 (between 48th and 49th Sts.; tel. 212/ 581-7000), one of the few family-oriented hotels in the area. There's no fancy hotel formality here, kids are welcome to stay in their parents' room free (under 18), and they'll love the open-air pool up on the roof with its cozy cabana deck and snackbar for poolside lounging. The 366 rooms are nicely furnished, with picture windows, air conditioning, color TV with in-room first-run movies, oversize bed, direct-dial phones, and good-size closets. Wolfie's Restaurant provides three meals a day. Single rooms are $65 to $95; doubles and twins are $77 to $108; parlor and one-bedroom suites are $130 to $155; and parlor and two-bedroom suites are $175 to $225 (rates subject to change). Parking is free, but there is a small in-and-out charge for each use. For reservations, call, toll free, 800/228-2828.

The **Century-Paramount,** 235 West 46th St., NY 10036 (tel. 212/246-5500), continues to hold its own as one of the best mini-priced hotels in town. The 700 rooms in this older but refurbished building are nicely done with fairly modern furniture; all are air-conditioned and have TV and private bath. Prices are easy to take: double-bedded and twin rooms go from $50 to $60; singles run from $40 to $50; and there's an extra charge of $6 for a rollaway bed. A family of four might choose a large room with two double beds from $65 to $75. Rates are subject to change. Housekeeping is good. The clientele is fascinating: you might run into an airlines captain in the elevator, or a South American diplomat's family in the lobby or coffeeshop. Especially nice is the courteous and helpful attitude of the management. Advance reservations are always advised, especially if you plan to be in New York between Easter and October, high season for the Century-Paramount.

You'd hardly know you were in the heart of New York once you step inside the **Travel Inn** at 515 West 42nd St., NY 10036 (tel. 212/695-7171), it's so much the typical American motor hotel, what with an outdoor swimming pool and recreation areas, lots of family groups, and free self-parking which allows you to use your car as often as you like with no extra charge. Travel Inn, formerly part of a national chain, is situated in the new off-off-Broadway theater area of New York, just a few blocks (and a short bus ride) west of Times Square. There are 155 rooms in the main building, which have all been redone in cheerfully coordinated color schemes, with nice furnishings and all the comforts; the 100 more rooms in the new building across the street are even prettier, with green carpets and floral spreads, off-white furniture, and a nice dressing room area off the bathroom. Many of the rooms in the main building face a courtyard overlooking a lovely outdoor pool and sunning area; there's garden furniture outdoors in the new building. Rates are reasonable for this feeling of being far away from the hustle-bustle: $50 to $65 single, $65 to $80 double (subject to change), and group rates are available. The Stage Restaurant is on the premises, and there are many others within a one-block radius.

Call 800/223-1900, toll free, for reservations.

EAST SIDE: Clean, cheerful, well priced, and located in a charming, safe, and convenient neighborhood—what more could the price-conscious traveler ask for in a hotel? That's what you'll find at the **Madison Towers Hotel,** Madison Ave. at 38th St., NY 10016 (tel. 212/685-2800), the happy result of a $5-million renovation of a 60-year-old neighborhood hotel. The new hotel sparkles from bottom to top, from its small but pretty lobby with its leather sofas, marble floors, and mirrored ceilings, to the 17 stories of guest rooms above. Rooms are irregularly shaped, which makes them interesting; most are twin-bedded and pleasantly decorated in matching tones of green, blue and peach, fully carpeted, have color TV, and are furnished with reproductions of American antiques. Bathrooms have marble-like sinks, full tubs and showers—and even extra phones. Air conditioning and heat are individually controlled. Rates are modest for New York: $75 single, $85 double, $10 per extra person.

Many of the guests of the Madison Towers are buyers and others involved with the fashion industry (the Garment Center is just across town). You can often find them having a drink or entertaining clients in front of the baronial, wood-burning fireplace at the Whaler Bar, a stunning re-creation of a popular New York cocktail lounge of the 1940s and 1950s. Should you get carried away by the whaling theme, you can sign up for a weekend travel package to Mystic Seaport, Connecticut, for $130 per person, including taxes. The Madison Towers' regular weekend package is a bargain at $37.50 per person per day, double occupancy, Friday or Saturday arrival, which includes full American breakfast, taxes, and a welcome cocktail in the Whaler Bar.

For reservations, call, toll free, 800/225-4340.

If you'd like a bit of turn-of-the-century ambience to go with your room for the night, then the **Prince George Hotel,** 14 East 28th St., NY 10016 (tel. 212/532-7800), might be just the place. One of the better hotels in this neighborhood that attracts many gift buyers and participants in merchandise and trade shows, this handsome old hotel, newly refurnished and brought up to date with all the modern conveniences of air conditioning, private bath, and color TV in every room, still retains its early 1900s charm in the restored lobby (note the intricate woodwork, the carved ceiling, fireplace, chandeliers, and a 15-foot-tall English clock that has been ticking since 1691!). Rooms are pleasant, if on the small side, well furnished with individual decorative touches, and well priced at $60 to $70 single, $70 to $80 double. Some 20 suites are available, from $150 for one or two bedrooms.

(Rates are subject to change.) There's a congenial lounge and cocktail bar in the lobby, and dining facilities include the elegant Regency Room, with its Georgian architecture and gourmet food; the informal Tap Room for lunch and cocktails; and a coffeeshop serving all three meals.

For reservations, phone, toll free, 800/221-4972.

There's an old-world feeling about the lobby of the **Hotel Seville,** Madison Ave. and 29th St., NY 10016 (tel. 212/532-4100; toll free tel. 800/431-5022), complete with Spanish architectural details and live trees in front of each large window overlooking the street. In another part of the lobby there are ficus trees under an atrium and, to be completed as part of an ongoing renovation, a lovely restaurant with antique fireplace and a grand piano offering largely American-style food with Chinese specialties.

As part of this major renovation, this older hotel is updating its rooms and getting better all the time. It now has about 250 rooms for transients, pleasantly decorated with yellow-and-white bamboo-trimmed furniture, chocolate-covered velvet drapes and matching bedspreads, writing desk and chair, ginger jar lamps, and other nice touches. All rooms have color TV, air conditioning, and marble bathrooms. Some even have bay windows that look out on Fifth Avenue. The rates are old-fashioned, indeed: from $43 to $49 single, from $49 to $61 double with a queen-size bed or very large double-doubles. Suites cost $80. Children under 12 are free; an extra adult is $6. Continental breakfast is delivered to your room free of charge, and a nearby coffeeshop provides room service most of the day and evening. The hotel is handy to the Madison Avenue bus which takes you to midtown in just about ten minutes.

The **Hotel George Washington,** Lexington Ave. at 23rd St., NY 10010 (tel. 212/GR 5-1920), is, to be sure, a bit off the usual tourist circuit, but what you lose in a slightly out-of-the-way location you make up for in savings. This 600-room Carter Hotel has many long-term guests, but there are at least 250 rooms for transients, all recently redone, and all with pleasant furniture including a writing desk and lounge chairs in every room, attractively coordinated drapes and bedspreads, color TV in most rooms, and air conditioning in all. The hotel's twin-bedded rooms (reconverted from two small ones) have two closets and two bathrooms, a real feeling of spaciousness, and are a good buy from $48 to $70; smaller doubles go for the same price. Singles run from $38 to $60. No charge for children under 14. Suites for two to four persons are available for $90, and a family room with two large double beds goes for $70. Weekly room rates, from $140 single and $190 and up for a small mini-twin, can be arranged by writing to Mr. Sergio Solorzano, general manager. (Rates are subject to change.) There are special rates for students, faculty, theatrical people, airline employees, government personnel, and "Visit USA" guests from overseas. Some of the rooms at the George Washington have a view of nearby Gramercy Park, one of the loveliest spots in the city. A coffeeshop (open until 1 a.m.), and a bar and lounge, are at the ready, and within a block are bus and subway lines to take you, in about ten minutes, to 42nd Street and the heart of the city.

Although we don't suggest you skip a visit to the United Nations, it sometimes seems to us that the sightseeing in the lobby of the **Hotel Tudor,** 304 East 42nd St., NY 10017 (tel. 212/YU 6-8800), is almost as good, especially during the sessions of the General Assembly, as African chiefs in tribal costumes and Indian ladies in silk saris parade through. But besides being very close to the United Nations and the home of many delegates, the Tudor is also a nicely run tourist hotel and a good value, considering its midtown location (the crosstown 42nd Street bus takes you in minutes to the department stores and the Broadway theater area). Rooms with all the comforts go from $65 single, $70 double, $85 for twins, $110 for triples, $130 for quads, and from $130 for suites. (Rates are subject to change.) Their showpiece King Suite, actually a lovely two-bedroom, three-bathroom apartment, complete with Jacuzzi whirlpool, is well priced at $300. The hotel is constantly redecorating and upgrading itself, but we have had an occasional housekeeping complaint. The lobby is an attractive one, bright and mirrored in front, and divided in the rear, in European style, into comfortable conversational nooks with brass highlighting rich red and black furnishings. Next to the sparkling modern bar, the hotel's reasonably priced restaurant, Jeanne's, a formal room handsomely styled in silver gray, specializes in original continental dishes with a touch of nouvelle cuisine.

The toll-free reservations numbers are 800/221-1253 and 221-1254.

LINCOLN CENTER—AND POINTS NORTH: You can't get much closer to all the excitement of Lincoln Center than the **Hotel**

Empire, just across the street from the main plaza, 44 West 63rd St. on Broadway, NY 10023 (tel. 212/265-7400). The Empire is, in fact, the "official" Lincoln Center hotel. It is an older, 600-room hotel, refurbished and brought back to its former standards by the savvy Carter Hotel chain (which also owns the George Washington, mentioned above). All rooms are attractively decorated (coordinated drapes and bedspreads, and nice furniture), and all have color TV, direct-dial phones, and air conditioning. Rates (subject to change) are $60 to $75 single, $70 to $85 double or twin, $10 for an extra person (children under 14 free in their parents' room). Families will also do well in the small two-bedroom suites (no living rooms) which can comfortably house four or five at $80 to $95; rooms with two double beds, suitable for four, are the same price (the latter are all outside rooms). Special guaranteed rates for students, faculty, overseas guests, clergy, theatrical, and government visitors. And if you're a view nut, request one of the suites that commands a view of the Metropolitan Opera House, Avery Fisher Hall, and the Hudson dropping off into the distance.

There are scads of good restaurants within walking distance of the Empire, but the hotel has its own Theatre Coffee Shop and Cocktail Lounge, a special hangout, it seems, for ballet buffs, and the trendy O'Neal's Baloon, right on the premises.

One of the best choices in the Lincoln Center area is a hotel that few visitors have ever heard of. That's the **Hotel Olcott,** 27 West 72nd St., NY 10023 (right off Central Park West; tel. 212/TR 7-4200), and the reason most out-of-towners don't know this place is because it's largely a residential hotel—most of its guests are either longtime residents or entertainers, diplomats, U.N. people, and the like, in New York for a few months. But at any one time, there will be at least 25 suites available to transients, and as anyone who's discovered the Olcott will tell you, they are among the top buys in the city for the money. These are full, one-bedroom apartments, comfortable enough to live in for a long time (which most of the guests do), and their size ranges from large to enormous. Each has a living room, a twin-bedded bedroom, a private tile bath and shower, and that great money-saver, a kitchenette, complete with dishes and cooking utensils. They rent for $75 a night, $450 per week— you'd pay almost as much as the latter figure *per night* for suites in some of the midtown hotels. There's a $7 daily charge ($35 per week) for each additional rollaway bed needed (up to four people can be comfortably accommodated). Single and double bedrooms are also available at rates of $55 per night, $320 per week single, and $60 per night, $350 per week double. All rooms have air conditioning and direct-dial phones; color TV is available for $3 per day, $15 per week. The furniture is comfortable. Your fellow guests may well be Metropolitan Opera singers, Broadway actors, South American and European business and government people, as well as an occasional resident of the two-doors-away Dakota (New York's most famous and celebrity-studded apartment building), here while their apartment is being redecorated. There's a fantastic budget restaurant off the lobby, a softly lit, modernistically decorated room with live country music (see Chapter IV, "Restaurants"). Plus 72nd Street abounds with coffeeshops, restaurants, and gift boutiques, and is one of the most interesting thoroughfares on the West Side. It's a short bus or subway ride to midtown and the theater district, a short walk to Lincoln Center.

The management states that weekly rentals, reserved in advance, are given preference; however, with luck, you may get a room or suite for a night or two on short notice.

For Budgeteers: Rooms for Around $35

THREE COED Y's: Many business and professional people—as well as tourists and students—choose to stay at the **Vanderbilt YMCA**, 224 East 47th St., NY 10017 (tel. 212/755-2410), which boasts an excellent East Side location not far from the United Nations, a very cordial staff, and small but scrupulously clean rooms. All rooms have TV, some have air conditioning, but none has a private bath. Singles rent for $22 to $34 per day and doubles are $16 to $19 per person—and this includes Y membership. Weekly arrangements are sometimes available after a personal interview. The physical facilities here match those of any health club, and are frequented by many of the big names of New York; you might find yourself sharing the swimming pool, sauna, and gymnasium with U.N. personnel, entertainers, and other VIPs. As for women, the Y is not chauvinistic; facilities are now fully coed. Advance reservations are requested.

Anyone who's been to the **Sloane House Y**, 356 West 34th St., NY 10018 (tel. 212/760-5860), in the last few years is in for a big surprise. The venerable old building (the largest residential Y in the world, and the first to go coed) has undergone a major facelift, and it's more than just cosmetics. Changes include a bright lobby, a computerized registration system, and nine completely renovated floors reserved exclusively for travelers. It's especially popular with students from all over: some 3500 British students have stayed here in the last few years, and there is now a resident student population of 600 plus. The Y's "Hospitality and N.Y. Information Center" provides helpful hints on the "young" way to see New York and helps arrange ongoing travel and YMCA accommodations. Single rooms go from $23 to $27 with air conditioning, TV, and private baths available at rates up to $35. A limited number of twin-bedded rooms is available at $30, $41 with private bath. Group rates are even cheaper: $17 per night for 15 or more. And student rates (semester only, ID card required) are lowest of all: $67.90 per week. There's no pool at Sloane House, but the convenient midtown location, spacious lounges, game rooms, a gym, and a beautiful new cafeteria (with an excellent lunchtime salad bar) and carpeted dining rooms are all pluses. All transients are now accommodated on the new floors.

For those who would like a Y facility uptown near the Lincoln Center area, the **West Side Y**, 5 West 63rd St., NY 10023 (tel. 212/787-4400), is a first-rate choice. This very attractive building, right off Central Park (and around the corner from New York's famed Ethical Culture Society and School), has single and double rooms, some with private bath and TV, some without. These start at $25 minimum for singles and $34 for doubles, on a daily basis. The place is perfect heaven for sports enthusiasts: it has no fewer than two swimming pools, four handball courts, two squash courts, three gyms, three weight rooms, and a running track (so the joggers can run either indoors here or outdoors in Central Park). Residents can use them all. Off the tiled Spanish lobby is a good cafeteria. There are usually some rooms for women, but most are for men. Both men and women students, however, may be accepted on a semester basis at special rates, upon application. An advance of one night's rent is required for all reservations.

MOSTLY FOR WOMEN: The all-women's hotel is a vanishing breed in New York, as it is elsewhere in this country. The famed Barbizon Hotel for Women, home to generations of young hopefuls, has now become the Barbizon, a first-class luxury hotel (thanks to a $15-million renovation) with singles in the $60 to $115 range. But women traveling alone looking for suitable inexpensive accommodations can still do well at the **Martha Wash-**

ington Hotel, 30 East 30th St., NY 10001 (tel. 212/MU 9-1900), where the atmosphere is much like that of a college dorm. Although many students and young career women do live here permanently, many transient rooms are also available. The pleasant, but rather worn-looking lobby contains huge tableaux of Martha Washington and Mount Vernon on the walls. The rooms are small but cozy, some of them have kitchenettes and air conditioning, and TV sets can be rented. Singles with bath are $38; twins with bath, $55; and if you're willing to share a bath with a few other girls, prices go down to $28 for a single, $40 for a double. Conveniences dear to the hearts of traveling women: a second-floor laundry with turquoise washers and dryers; irons and ironing boards brought to your room on request.

The Great Exchange

If you live in Los Angeles or San Francisco, or Tampa, St. Petersburg, or Orlando, Florida, or in greater London, you can now stay in New York City for practically nothing. That's the good news from a new travel company called the Great Exchange. In cooperation with Pan American World Airways, it offers a carefully computed and ensured match with people who have comparable homes and lifestyles in all of these cities. Unlike other vacation exchanges, this company does it all: working from a detailed questionnaire that specifies travel plans and home or apartment details, it makes a congenial match (you agree based on photos and written details), and inspect both properties. Especially for families on lengthy visits, this could be a lifesaver. There is a $25 application fee and a $40 one-time home visit and lifetime membership fee. Flying arrangements must be via Pan American. For information, you can contact Pan American ticket offices, your travel agent, or the Great Exchange, P.O. Box 12028, Glendale, CA 91214. For the toll-free number in your area, phone 800/555-1212.

Chapter IV

THE BEST BUYS IN NEW YORK RESTAURANTS

SOME YEARS AGO, a friend of ours determined that he was going to eat his way through every restaurant in New York City. To approach the task systematically, he opened the pages of the classified phone directory, turned to the restaurant listings, and began proceeding from the Acropolis Restaurant to the Zoevetta Luncheonette. About five years and more than a thousand meals later, he gave us a triumphant progress report: he was all the way down to "H." All of which is by way of saying that there is no shortage of restaurants in New York. But unless you have time on your hands, money to burn, and a nonstop compulsion like our friend's, you will obviously have to be a great deal more selective. Restaurants surround the visitor on every side. Which are the best? Which offer the most value for the dollar spent? Where are the unusual, the off-the-beaten-path "finds" that the natives adore and that tourists seldom find? Here's where we come in.

To help you make your way through the perplexing maze of the New York restaurant world, we have set forth some very simple guidelines. We have chosen those restaurants which, in our opinion, offer the best buys in dining in New York, regardless of how much you spend. (Some other New Yorker might come up with a very different selection; but no matter—getting two New Yorkers to agree on their list of favorite restaurants is like getting Yankees fans and Mets fans to agree on their favorite ballplayers—and that's part of the fun.) And because the price range in New York restaurants is enormous, we have grouped these selections into various price categories. You should first know, however, that thanks to inflation, the cost of dining in New York is at an all-time high. New Yorkers expect to pay around $20 for what they consider a good dinner, and that's even before considering cocktails, wines, taxes, and tips; if they get by with less, they consider themselves lucky. And there seems to be no limit to how much restaurants will charge or people will spend; at a very posh restaurant the $100+ meal is not uncommon, especially with a good bottle of wine. Our price categories, then, are set forth as follows: (1) "In" and Expensive: Dinner for $50 and Up; (2) Expensive: Dinner for $35 and Up; (3) Well Priced: Dinner for $25 and Up; (4) Modest: Dinner Around $18; and (5) Fast Foods, Friendly Prices: Meals from $3 to $7.

LUNCH: You will note that we have, for ease, broken these categories down in terms of dinner prices. A good way to stretch your food budget is occasionally to eat your main meals at lunch, when the values are always best. Even some of the most expensive restaurants, where dinner is all à la carte, offer prix-fixe lunches for reasonable fees. In most places, lunch runs 15% to 20% less than dinner.

BEVERAGES: If you want cocktails before your meal, plan on spending about $3 to $4 per drink. Be careful when you buy wine: a prize year vintage in a luxury restaurant could skyrocket your bill to the tune of $35 to $45 or more. The cost of a bottle of wine will vary in each restaurant, depending on vintage and cachet. If you are not familiar with the subtleties of wines, put yourself in the hands of the waiter or wine steward and ask him to suggest the proper wine to accompany your dinner. In most cases, he'll stay away from the expensive vintages and select a good, moderately priced wine. For four people, order a full bottle; for two or three, a half bottle will do nicely. To save on the tab, order the "vin de maison" or house wine, good and less expensive than bottled wines; it can be bought by the glass or in a carafe.

DRESS: Yes, women can now wear pants, even at the poshest preserves (but dressy pants, not sporty slacks), and casual dress for men is permitted in most places. However, if you're going someplace really elegant, double-check on the dress requirements when you phone for your reservation.

RESERVATIONS: The more expensive the place, the more imperative the need for a reservation. A few places do not accept reservations and, if so, they will tell you when you phone. But it never hurts to phone in advance and reserve, especially at dinnertime.

TIPPING: Leave your slide rule at home and relax. At most places, the rule is to give the waiter 15% of your check (an easy way to approximate this is to, roughly, double New York's 8¼ tax added to all meal tabs). At a very *luxe* establishment, consider 18% to 20%. If a captain is involved, he should receive 5% more.

WHERE AND WHEN: Most of the restaurants are in the prime tourist areas of either midtown (East and West Sides), Greenwich Village, or Soho, but a few are slightly uptown or downtown; none of them, however, will be more than a 15-minute ride from midtown by bus, subway, or cab. Hours of operation are listed for each restaurant, and you can safely assume that lunch is served from noon to 2:30 or 3 p.m. weekdays almost everywhere; and dinner from 5:30 or 6 to 10 or 10:30 p.m. Many restaurants also serve after-theater suppers on Saturday night. Many are closed on Sunday and, during summer, some take rather long vacations. So it's best always to check before you go.

PLEASE NOTE: Although we have made every attempt to be accurate, menu prices are always subject to change, and in times of inflation, there is no telling where prices will go. In any case, the restaurants mentioned will still, we feel sure, be offering the best values for the money.

Now, then, let's begin.

"In" and Expensive: Dinner for $50 and Up

CUISINE—HAUTE AND NOUVELLE: One of the ultimate French restaurants in New York must surely be **Lutèce,** 249 East 50th St. (tel. PL 2-2225), where a genius named Andre Soltner serves what many consider the finest haute cuisine in the city. We like to sit in the greenhouse-like setting where the city landscape is reflected hazily under the mylar dome or, in colder weather, upstairs in the elegant dining room typical of many of the formal dining rooms in New York's private town houses. The food can be as unreal as this gracious setting. Lunch is prix-fixe at around

$27, and this may well be the meal to choose, since dinner can be expected to go upward of $50 per person, plus wines. Among the appetizers, the fish pâté, or any of the pâtés en croûte, are superbly flavored. For your main course, ask what the chef has dreamed up for the day; it is sure to be outstanding. Or go with menu choices like boeuf à la mode (beef in wine), délice de veau (veal with cheese and ham), or the beautifully delicate filet of sole amandine. Everything is prepared in the grand manner and served with flair. For dessert, what better than soufflé glacé framboise (frozen raspberry soufflé) or success à l'orange (frozen orange mousse with almonds)? If you do come for dinner, you may want to try the house specialty, the mignon de bouef en croûte Lutèce (a variation of beef Wellington), or the poussin Basquaise (baby chicken). And for dessert, the classics: crêpes flambées or white peaches flamed with Kirsch. Open for lunch from noon to 2 p.m. Tuesday to Friday, for dinner from 6 to 10 p.m. Monday through Saturday. Be sure to reserve well in advance.

La Caravelle, 33 West 55th St. (tel. 586-4252), has long been considered one of the great French restaurants of New York, although food and service are no longer as consistently grand as they once were. We, personally, have never been less than enchanted with the experience of dining here: the pretty, springlike room, the celebrated crowd, the appropriate Parisian *hauteur* of the waiters, and the food, the food, the glorious food. Dinner is à la carte, from $24.75 to $34 for entrees, and the specialties change every day. You might have a very fine maigret à la fricassée de champignons, or perhaps the côte de veau Caravelle, a veal chop with a cream sauce of cognac and foie gras. The fish dishes are always incredible: imagine the likes of quenelles de brochet, a feathery-light mousse of pike in the most delicate of sauces; cold salmon in summer; the broth of mussels (Billi-Bi); seafood au gratin and the crabmeat. All are memorable. And although the regular desserts are beautiful enough, we think it would be a shame not to partake of the soufflé glacé, $6.75 extra at dinner. Lunch is prix-fixe at $24.75, and, again, the specialties change every day. Coffee is extra. La Caravelle serves lunch from 12:15 to 2:30 p.m., dinner from 6 to 10:15 p.m. Monday through Saturday. It is closed Sunday, holidays, and for the month of August.

La Côte Basque, at 5 East 55th St. (tel. 688-6525), has long been one of the great dining places for the Beautiful People, and beautiful it is. The Bernard Lamotte murals make you feel you're dining by the seaside in a French café; the service is gracious and courtly, and the company is heady. Again, it's far from inexpensive, but the menu is prix-fixe: $25 at lunch, $42 at dinner. Salad and coffee are not included. The food is classic and superbly prepared; you might try the quiche de jour or garlic saucisson or asperges vinaigrette among the appetizers, or choose from the likes of noisettes de veau, steak au poivre, ragoût de homard, or bay scallops de Long Island (fish is always special here). Game dishes are also well done here. For desserts, there are heady temptations of sorbets and pâtisseries, sinful delights like soufflés tous parfums or Grand Marnier. Fruit tarts are memorable. Lunch is served from noon to 2 p.m, dinner from 6 to 10 p.m., Monday through Saturday. Closed in July. Now that La Côte Basque has come under the direction of Jean-Jacques Rachou, noted for his brilliant triumphs at Café Lavandou (see below), it is better than ever.

While some of New York's bastions of haute cuisine make the newcomer feel, if not exactly welcome, only politely tolerated, **Café Lavandou,** 134 East 61st St. (tel. 838-7987) is a happy exception: all comers are treated with gracious hospitality and made to feel right at home. Home, in this case, is a long, lavishly decorated room with comfortable banquettes and chairs that afford spacious seating. The friendliness extends to the generosity of the portions, the relatively moderate tariff for classic cuisine of this order (lunch prix-fixe at around $18, dinner prix-fixe at around $28, excluding coffee). The food is beautifully presented, with each vegetable a flower and garnishes small triumphs of art. We like to start our meal here with one of the fish appetizers: perhaps the mousse of red snapper in feuilletage or the quenelles of pike, mildly flavored with a Pernod sauce. The plat de jour is always excellent, and so are such menu choices as the cassoulet Toulousain (a hearty peasant dish of beans and meats), la belle poularde poêlée aux morilles (chicken in cream sauce with wild morels), sweetbreads in madeira sauce, or fish mousse. And save room for a splendid soufflé or Grand Marnier mousse for dessert. Café Lavandou serves lunch from noon to 2:30 p.m., dinner from 6 through 10 p.m., Monday through Saturday. Reservations several days in advance are advised.

Although the menu is continental rather than strictly French haute cuisine, the **Four Seasons,** 99 East 52nd St. (tel. 754-9494), ranks right up there with the best restaurants in town. One of the great showplace restaurants of New York, it is seasonal in mood and menu, with changing floral displays and artwork (the

Picasso, however, is there year round). You can dine in either the more formal **Pool Dining Room** with its bubbling marble pool in the center of the room; or in the more casual (and slightly less expensive) **Bar Room**, an informal hangout greatly favored by people in publishing and the wine trade. There are several menus at the Four Seasons. In the Pool Dining Room, an à la carte lunch is served from noon to 2:30 p.m., with entrees going from $27 to $32.50. At dinner, 5 to 11:30 p.m., entrees are in the $28 to $35 bracket. There is a special pre-theater dinner from 5 to 6:30 p.m., and an after-theater dinner from 10 to 11:30 p.m., prix-fixe at $30. We'd call this your best bet here: you can have entrees such as shrimp and scallops in lobster sauce, stuffed cabbage with pheasant, or roast duck with red cabbage. And you can also choose from the newly developed Spa Cuisine menu for the health conscious: appetizers like whole-wheat linguine with sliced breast of quail and main courses like escalope of striped bass with eggplant. Wonderful desserts on this menu include tangerine soufflé and white chocolate mousse. In the Bar Room, lunch is served Monday to Saturday from noon to 2 p.m., and entrees run $15.50 to $23.50; dinner is on Monday to Friday from 7:30 to 11:30 p.m., with à la carte entrees from $21 to $24.50. Closed Sunday. Reservations are a must.

Candlelit and quiet, a sheltered oasis away from the busy world outside—it's hardly what one expects but exactly what one finds at **Trumpets,** in the midst of the glamorous, glittering lobby of the new Grand Hyatt Hotel, 42nd St. at Grand Central Terminal (tel. 850-5999). A traditional setting done in tones of beige, brown, and rust, with burled elm and beveled mirror panels, plus graceful flower arrangements, acts as backdrop for a continental menu with many touches of nouvelle cuisine. The appetizers, gorgeously displayed on a round "Buffetière," present a surfeit of choices; you'll do well with the poached salmon in dill sauce, the mushroom terrine, or the ahi-tuna sashimi (prices range from $6 to $8 for most). Don't miss the bracing cream of mussel soup with saffron. As for the main courses, which run à la carte from about $16 to $20, we can recommend the fresh Dover sole on leaf spinach, the salmon paupiette in duxelles sauce, and an excellent marinated rack of lamb, with the lightness of rosemary and the pungency of Dijon mustard. The dessert selection, again, is an embarrassment of riches: you might settle for the very rich chocolate cake and flavor it with Grand Marnier—scented whipped cream, or have a delicious kiwi tart. Wines are expensive, along with the rest of the offerings. An après-theater dinner, served from 5:30 to 7 p.m., with a choice of four entrees, plus salad, appetizer, sorbet, and dessert, is priced at $29. Service is cordial, and little gracious touches like your name printed on the matchbooks add to the overall feeling of well-being.

Trumpets serves lunch Monday through Friday from noon to 2:30 p.m. and dinner daily between 6 and 11 p.m. An elegant cocktail lounge, with piano music at night, adjoins Trumpets.

A bastion of "American nouvelle cuisine" exists in exotic Brooklyn (yes, Brooklyn), at the **River Café**, 1 Water St. (tel. 522-5200). One of city's see-and-be-seen restaurants, River Café is built on a barge underneath the Brooklyn Bridge and commands a truly spectacular view of lower Manhattan and New York Harbor. Perfect for a romantic rendezvous at night, it has a special daytime appeal too, as you watch the river busy with waterborne traffic. Beautifully appointed in pale tones, with each table sporting a tiny shaded lamp evocative of a 1930s supper-club, the River Café is movie-star glamorous. But the food—using only American products (even to the caviar and olive oil)—is not to be ignored. Appetizers like fresh wild American mushrooms in a puff pastry and smoked gulf salmon with a Great Lakes golden caviar sauce are quite special. Such dinner entrees as poached salmon, trout, roast saddle of veal in a creamy shallot sauce, and rack of prime western lamb with spinach and Michigan morel in puff pastry are priced from $16.50 to $40. All are served à la carte, with vegetables, potato, and salad extra. At lunch, lighter fare like omelets and salads, as well as prime aged sirloin steak and fish of the day, is available, from $13 to $17.50. And Sunday brunch, 11.30 a.m. to 2 p.m. is a felicitous time to enjoy a wide range of choices, from buttermilk pancakes with pure maple syrup at $9 to black Angus beef with corncob-cured bacon at $15. Service, alas, can be quite poor, and the dining room can get noisy.

Lunch is served daily from 11:30 a.m. to 2:30 p.m., and dinner from 6:30 to 11:30 p.m. Sunday to Thursday, from 7 p.m. to midnight on Friday and Saturday. You can also just drop by for a drink at the Café Room or at the bar of the dining room, to enjoy the same view and piano music as the diners do.

Is the **Sign of the Dove** New York's most beautiful restaurant? Many would agree that there is nothing quite like the Dove, at 1100 Third Ave. at 65th St. (tel. 861- 8080), anywhere else in the city, perhaps in the world. Sitting in the most beautiful of its four dining rooms, the Greenhouse, with its skylight and natural brick walls, flagstone floors, and lush plantings, surrounded by baroque statuary and European objets d'art, enjoying the sunlight streaming in from the skylight by day or the glow from crystal lanterns shaped like grape clusters by night, one has the uncanny feeling that the outside world of noise and bustle and crowds has simply fallen away. Here, indeed, is the most romantic, the most exquisite of settings. But such rarified elegance does not come cheap; Sign of the Dove, in fact, is one of those places where if you have to ask the price you really shouldn't be here. Most meals for two will easily go over the three-figure mark, when you start adding up items like escargots at $9, mixed green salad at $6 (roquefort dressing is $1.50 extra), broiled veal chop at $26, desserts at $6, coffee at $2.75. Now that we've taken care of *that,* what shall you treat yourself to? At a recent Sunday brunch (brunch is a lovely meal here since it borrows from both the lunch and dinner menus and adds some specific brunch specialties), our party started with broiled honeyed grapefruit with figs ($5.50), then went on to a refreshing heart of radicchio and endive salad in a tangy lime and peanut oil dressing. We could have had a main course of pasta, but we chose it as an appetizer; the house does these particularly well, and our angel-hair pasta with wild mushroom sauce ($22) was memorable. Steamed fish of the day with cucumber and tarragon sauce was moist and tender, and the warm lobster salad with artichoke hearts, mushrooms, French-cut string beans, and avocadoes ($24.50) was unusual. Other good main dishes might include tiny grilled baby lamb chops ($22) or calf liver sauteed with sage and onions ($19.50). Desserts are splendid, stylishly presented from the cart: we sampled a rich bitter-chocolate mousse, a delicious although very sweet white chocolate mousse, and a refreshing pineapple Bavarian cream. For accompaniment, a cup of espresso was just about perfect.

The Sign of the Dove serves dinner from 6 p.m. to midnight (until 1 a.m. weekends), lunch from noon to 3 p.m., Tuesday through Saturday; Sunday brunch from 11:45 a.m. to 4 p.m. There is music at lunch and dinner, and entertainment at the piano bar Tuesday through Saturday from 5:30 p.m. on. Reservations are essential.

Expensive: Dinner for $35 and Up

Now we move from the temples of gastromony to the places where we ordinary mortals feel a bit more at home. Described below are 12 restaurants that are among our favorites in the city. All of them are special—in atmosphere, in food, in value. None is inexpensive, but for the value received they are good buys. Dinner will probably cost you $35 or more per person, before wines, tips, taxes, etc. The restaurants are listed according to nationality group or special interest.

DINING IN THE SKY: The quintessential New York restaurant experience? We'd say it's at **Windows on the World**, that dazzling showplace in the sky, 107 floors up, up, up above the city at the top of the World Trade Center, the almost-tallest building in the world. Windows on the World is one of those magic, mind-blowing places that leaves even jaded city sophisticates gasping, a place that reaffirms the greatness and glamor of New York. Encompassing a veritable acre of glass, the various dining rooms, cocktail lounges, and private rooms afford 360-degree views of the city, the bridges lacing the rivers, the busy traffic of sea and sky; on a clear day, one can see 50 miles. Within, the decor is almost as stunning as the ever-changing floor show outside. Using muted tones of gold and beige and pale rose, lavish touches of mirror and brass and wood, exquisite plants and fresh flowers everywhere, architect Warren Platner has created an ambience that is futuristic yet warm, a brilliant tour-de-force of almost science-fiction-like splendor. Walking along a mirrored reception chamber lined by huge, semiprecious rocks, being greeted by waiters in white uniforms with flashing gold epaulets, seated in a multitiered dining room where ingenious use of mirrors affords full views to every diner, one gets the feeling of floating in a gigantic luxury liner, suspended in a sea of sky.

With so much going for it, it really wouldn't matter what the food at Windows on the World was like, but it happens to be good—very good, in fact, which is more than one can say for most skyscraper restaurants. Actually, there are two distinct dining areas which must be considered separately. The first is the Restaurant, which serves a prix-fixe dinner at $25.95 Monday through Saturday; there are also à la carte selections from $14.95 to $21. The veal steak is excellent, as is the rack of spring lamb James Beard. Poached sea scallops in sweet red pepper sauce make a succulent beginning to the meal, and the desserts are impeccable, worth every last calorie. Choosing between the golden lemon tart, with slices of lemon baked right into it, the white-chocolate mousse, and the blueberry parfait is simply too painful; best to come with a group of friends and sample a little bit of everybody's dessert! Those same desserts make a smashing finale to the Grand Buffet, which takes place on Saturday from noon to 3 p.m., on Sunday from noon to 7:30 p.m., Prix-fixe at $17.95, it's a taste trip around the world: bulghur wheat salad with cumin, marinated shrimp with huge peppercorns, Japanese noodle salad with mushrooms, smoked chicken, hot curries, etc., suggest the lavish fare. Reservations are essential.

Another part of the restaurant that's both charming and popular is the Hors D'Oeuvrerie, which requires reservations only for Sunday brunch; other times, you'll wait in line a bit, but it moves quickly. The Hors D'Oeuvrerie is an internationally minded cocktail lounge and grill, most romantic, where you can nibble on hors d'oeuvres like chicken yakitori, a sushi and sashimi platter, or taramosalata with hot pita bread as appetizers, or order enough of them, or of the grilled entrees, plus dessert, to make a full meal, at about $14. Sunday brunch is special fun, since then you can choose from Mexican, Chinese, and Scandinavian meals, plus omelets, brioches, and the like à la carte, from $6.95. There's afternoon tea from 3 to 6 p.m. And at night, when the sun goes down and the lights wink on over the city and the music begins at the grand piano, the Hors d'Oeuvrerie (with the adjoining City Lights Bar), is one of the most idyllic spots in town for dreaming and dancing.

Parking is free for Windows on the World patrons in the basement of the World Trade Center. By subway, take the IRT Seventh Avenue local to Cortlandt Street, or the IND AA or E train to Chambers Street. Reservations: Write Windows on the World, No. 1 World Trade Center, New York, NY 10048 (tel. 938-1111).

AND ON THE GROUND: Down on the concourse on the ground level of the World Trade Center, there's also excellent dining available at the **Market Dining Room and Bar** (tel. 938-1155), a restaurant that recaptures the spirit of the old Washington Market that once occupied the site. It is now dedicated to serving market-fresh products in hearty American portions, with the emphasis on the little extras, like free dishes of carpaccio (thin slices of raw beef) or lentil salad before your meal, or fresh fruit juices in the drinks, and fresh eggs given to departing dinner guests. A turn-of-the-century club-like atmosphere prevails, with globe lamps, large wooden booths, enormous napkins with a buttonhole to secure it to your shirt, and baskets of fresh produce standing about. Steaks (20-ounce sirloin for $22.50), charcoal-grilled butterflied leg of lamb, and broiled swordfish with lemon butter are typical of the hefty all-American fare. Most entrees run $10 to $17. At lunch you might try a platter of seasonal vegetables for $7.50, or a frittata of the day for $7.25.

Market Dining Room and Bar serves lunch weekdays from 11:30 a.m. to 2:30 p.m. and dinner Monday through Saturday from 5 to 10 p.m.

If you step out of the Bar Room and onto Market Square you'll find the Café, an indoor sidewalk café with waitress service but lighter fare, like half-pound burgers, chili, and stews. Prices begin at $4.25. Open Monday through Saturday from 11:30 a.m. to midnight.

STEAKHOUSES: Those of you who have come to New York in quest of the perfect steak need search no further. Some of the best steak and lobster houses anywhere are right here, and all you need is a well-stuffed wallet (or a generous expense account) and an enormous appetite. For the New York Steak Experience, don't miss **The Palm**, 837 Second Ave., between 44th and 45th Sts. (tel. 687-2953). It's noisy, it's crowded, there's sawdust all over the floors, and the waiters are rushed and can be curt. But the true trencherman overlooks all such indignities, for those thick grilled steaks, those succulent fried onion rings and hash brown potatoes, those monstrous lobsters can be duplicated in few other restaurants. Prices vary, according to the market; at a recent meal, filet mignon was $20; and lobster, out of sight! (We always find one order of four-pounds-plus of lobster perfectly adequate for two—it's almost big enough for three.) There's no menu, but the waiters will tell you about the clams Casino (baked clams with bacon) among the appetizers, and the terrific cheesecake, for dessert. That is, if you have room for anything else after those steaks!

If there's no room at the Palm, you'll be just as happy at **Palm Too**, at 840 Second Ave., just across the street (tel. 697-5198)—same mood, same food, same madness. The Palms are open from noon to 11 p.m. Monday through Friday, on Saturday from 5 to 11 p.m. Closed Sunday, and on Saturday during July and August. You can reserve at lunch only.

Whether the Palm or **Christ Cella** is the city's greatest steakhouse is a question that's been hotly debated by New York's beefeaters for eons now. Suffice it to say that both are memorable. Christ Cella (pronounce it Krisella if you want to sound like a New Yorker), located at 160 East 46th St. (tel. OX 7-2479), is perhaps a trifle more genteel than its counterpart, the noise level a few decibels less, and the service can be more leisurely. Its prices are also rarified, as expensive as the well-heeled crowd that gathers to consume lobsters that go for about $37, steaks for $24.50. Hash browns, baked potatoes, or french fries come with the entree. The menu also offers a wide assortment of fish as well as other meat dishes, and the freshly made soups (cream of asparagus, onion) and the salads—especially the spinach salad with bacon—are excellent. French pastries, cheesecake, and delicious napoleons are among the desserts.

Like the Palms, Christ Cella caters mainly to a business crowd, and is open weekdays from noon to 10:30 p.m., on Saturday from 5 p.m.

ITALIAN EXCELLENCE: Eating at **Barbetta,** 321 West 46th St. (tel. 246-9171), is an experience best compared to dining in a wealthy friend's villa. Barbetta's century-old brownstone on the theater district's Restaurant Row exudes refined elegance. There's a small, gracious cocktail lounge where you might sip an apéritif before dinner in the stately dining room with its tall draped windows and classic table settings. In summer months, tables in the city's prettiest restaurant garden are highly prized.

As for the food, it's definitely northern Italian with hardly a tomato sauce in sight. The seasonal menu features Italian white truffles during their short fall-to-winter season, and in summer, a true culinary delight is available: vitello tonnato, pure white cold veal in a piquant tuna sauce. In spring try the fresh pesto Genovese, the pounded garlic, basil, and pine-nut paste that tops fresh pasta. But year round Barbetta's menu glows with intriguing fare, from succulent whole squab to baby salmon. Risotto can replace pasta here (in true northern Italian fashion), and this rice dish is available in several varieties, including one with wild porcine mushrooms. You might accompany your entrees with the excellent salad of paper-thin sliced mushrooms.

Monday through Saturday, Barbetta is open for lunch from noon to 2 p.m., when a full-course luncheon runs from $18.95 to $24.95 and for dinner, with entrees from $18.95 to $23.95, with the exception of pastas (around $12, evenings only). There is a 75¢ cover charge for à la carte dining in the evening. A pre-theater dinner is $28.

TIFFANY TRIUMPHS: Imagine an art deco palace, gleaming with mirrors and brass and signed Tiffany glass and antique chandeliers, touches of brilliance and beauty wherever you look. Imagine the most affluent and gregarious singles in town—singles of the category of, say, David Frost or Princess Lee Radziwill—congregating at the bar and the tables. And imagine a first-rate kitchen to boot. No need just to imagine it: **Maxwell's Plum** is there, at First Ave. at 64th St. (tel. 628-2100), one of New York's most stunning watering holes.

Restaurateur Warner LeRoy (the son of film director Mervyn LeRoy) scoured the world to furnish Maxwell's with authentic turn-of-the-century artworks, reproductions that fit in beautifully with the originals, and daring innovations like the ceiling of Tiffany glass behind the bar and café in the Back Room. It's here that the food is the most exciting: on the all à la carte menu, you can choose from entrees like veal piccata sauteed with lemon butter, charcoal-grilled swordfish, shrimp and scallop curry, steak tartare, or filet of beef sauté with crisp vegetables and pasta, in a price range from $6.50 to $15. A pre-theater menu is served Monday through Saturday between 5 and 7 p.m., for $12.50. Appetizers like steamed rock shrimp or mussels can indeed be special—as are such desserts as pecan pie with whipped cream and chocolate mousse.

More inexpensively, the café area of Maxwell's offers a wider range of specialties—everything from omelets and very good hamburgers on, and the Back Room lunch menu is also widely priced, starting with fancy burgers for $5.45. Weekend brunch (Saturday from noon to 5 p.m., Sunday from 11 a.m.) is a great time to bring older children, who'll enjoy the ambience as much as any adult. Maxwell's Plum is open every day, from noon to 1:30 a.m.

Ten years after he dazzled New York with Maxwell's Plum, Warner LeRoy encored with the re-creation of **Tavern on the Green,** New York's venerable restaurant right in Central Park, 67th St. and the Park (tel. 873-3200). Again, the decor is fantasyland come to life. Rooms of crystal and frosted mirrors, of glass and sparkling lights reflected from the trees in the park, of dazzling chandeliers and Tiffany-style lamps, of carved wood statues and carved plaster ceilings create a kind of modern rococo setting. When you call for reservations, ask to be seated in the Crystal Room with its three walls of glass and ornate chandeliers; you feel as if you're inside a huge, transparent wedding cake. And the mood is as festive as a wedding too, with masses of flowers everywhere and all kinds of festivities and celebrations going on at neighboring tables. Service is deft and professional, but be prepared for a leisurely meal. Tavern on the Green has four separate menus: for dinner (5:30 p.m. to 1 a.m.), for lunch (noon to 4 p.m.), for pre-theater dinner (5:30 to 6:15 p.m. weekdays only, costing $16.50, including tax, for a three-course meal), and for Saturday and Sunday brunch (10 a.m. to 4 p.m.). The brunch is an especially nice meal here, since you can have anything from traditional breakfast specialties like omelets or eggs Benedict to sophisticated fish preparations, grills, and steaks. Prices are slightly less than on the dinner menu, as they also are at weekday lunches. We started a recent brunch with a superb appetizer of baked goat cheese and a piquantly dressed salad of arugula and radicchio, arranged nouvelle fashion like a flower (appetizers run $3.75 to $10.95). Our soup of the day was a creamy vegetable leek. For main courses, we chose two quiches: one of smoked salmon, the other of brie, both tangy and unusual. And our red snapper on a bed of julienne vegetables with a light cream sauce was tender and juicy. Entrees run from $8.50 for the egg dishes, up to $15.50 for fish and $19.50 for steak. The bread basket is laden with treasures: a soft-as-silk black bread, a whole-grain bread studded with nuts. Do save some room for desserts here, as creations like a chocolate Grand Marnier charlotte with raspberry sauce or a chocolate fudge cake with mocha sauce should not be missed. Even simple strawberries with sour cream come dressed for a party in a delicate basket-like pastry shell. Cappuccino or espresso or caffé with schlag makes a superb ending to the meal.

Tavern on the Green is open every day, and offers outdoor garden seating in warm weather. On summer weekends, there's music: a strolling concertina player on Saturday between 11 a.m. and 3 p.m., a flute, guitar, and cello trio on Sunday. It's extremely popular, so do make reservations well in advance.

THE THIRTIES REVISITED: Stepping into the **Rainbow Room**, 30 Rockefeller Plaza (tel. PL 7-9090), is a bit like going back into the time machine, since it's a classic art deco room—all glass, chrome, and multilevel—where the swing-time ambience of the

1930s still lives. Perched 65 floors above the crowds, the Rainbow Room is *the* place for dinner-dancing in the sky, and the food, while not quite as glorious as the ambience, is always commendable. The dinner menu is à la carte, with entrees like filet of beef Wellington, breast of chicken Kiev, and roast Long Island duckling, priced from $15.25 to $19.50. The seafood crêpe Napoleon is a tasty appetizer, the watercress salad refreshing, and the dessert specialties like Grand Marnier or chocolate soufflés memorable. Remember this place if you're going to the theater. A pre-theater meal, prix-fixe at $21, is served nightly, beginning between 5 and 6:30 p.m., with departure guaranteed by 8 p.m. After-theater supper is served after 11 p.m. every night except Monday. The regular dinner begins at 5 p.m. A band plays for dancing every night except Monday (music charge), and usually it's the justly popular Sy Oliver. The $17.50 Sunday brunch, 11 a.m. to 3 p.m., is lots of fun, with dishes like hot Bloody Mary soup, crêpes, omelets, beef Stroganoff, and fancy desserts.

EGYPTIAN EXCELLENCE: "Andrée's" reads the name on the small blue half-moon canopy over the door of a town house on East 74th Street, between First and Second Avenues. Actually, the restaurant is called **Andrée's Mediterranean Cuisine**, and the exact address is 354 East 74th St. (tel. 249-6619). It looks and feels like someone's home, and it is: Andrée Abramoff, who hails from Egypt, lives here and cooks wonderful Middle Eastern and North African specialties for anyone who wants to come to dinner. You're all invited, Tuesday through Saturday. Since the restaurant opened just a few years back, Andrée has gained a fine reputation among the food elite for imaginative, very fresh food served in a gracious atmosphere: a two-story dining room with Oriental rugs, tapestries, artifacts hung along the brick walls, kaftaned waitresses dispensing the lovely fare. You may order either à la carte (entrees from $17.50 to $21.50), or have either a well-priced pre-theater dinner for $27.50 (on Tuesday, Wednesday, and Thursday from 5:45 to 6:45), or an expanded dinner for $32.50. The pre-theater dinner begins with appetizers like spinach and cheese puffs, tabbouleh, or hummus; and offers a choice of soup or salad, and three entrees—shrimp Alexandria, moussaka (with beef or vegetarian, and very good), and couscous Moroccan-style, studded with nuts and raisins—plus a dessert of chocolate walnut torte, a Middle Eastern fruit salad, or pistachio baklava, and coffee. The more elaborate $32.50 meal has an expanded menu which includes stuffed grape leaves or baba ganoush, soup or salad, entrees such as duck with green peppercorns, rack of lamb, or Cornish hen stuffed with pine nuts, bulghur, and raisins. For dessert, there's a lovely chocolate mousse or a mocha crème caramel, plus espresso and Middle Eastern coffee, very dark, very good.

Andrée's Mediterranean Cuisine is closed on Sunday and Monday, and open Tuesday through Saturday from 6 to 9:30 p.m.

VILLAGE CHARM: The Village Green, 531 Hudson St. (tel. 255-1650), is gorgeous. This quaint, country tavern in an old brownstone is on two levels: flickering candles light rosy brick walls and a stunning array of fresh flowers and lush plants. Wood-burning fireplaces burn upstairs and down in cold weather. Murray Grand at the piano bar draws a convivial crowd of fellow performers and composers who, like the rest of us, dote on the fine French-inspired cooking. Highlights on the all à la carte menu, with entrees from $16 to $24, include loin of lamb with cucumber-mint sauce, fresh fish baked in parchment with fresh pesto, lump Maryland crab imperial, and beautifully prepared boneless duckling with tangerine glaze. Fresh oysters with Beluga caviar, rabbit terrine, and smoked salmon with crème fraiche are satisfying beginnings, mousses of the day and crème brûlée tempting ends. Dinner is served every day, from 5:30 p.m. to 11:30 p.m. Sunday brunch is on from noon to 5:30 p.m.

DOWNTOWN DELICACIES: Everything in Soho seems to have been turned into something other than what it was, and Raoul's, at 180 Prince St. (tel. 966-3518), was an old neighborhood bar and restaurant which has been turned into a popular bistro that serves excellent French food. The decor has not been altered considerably, except for the white tablecloths, but the food certainly has been—and of course, so have the prices and the clientele. Entrees are priced from $13 to $20 à la carte, and people come from all over the city to eat them. Start with an appetizer of the house pâté, oysters in season, soup of the day, smoked trout, or smoked salmon, or . . . The blackboard menu changes every day. There's always a peppersteak, a veal chop, sweetbreads, and at least three fish dishes, but the sauces, the spices, and the specials depend on the chef's mood and what's in the market that day. Desserts, which run from about $3 to $3.50, are all made at the restaurant and are never heavy: fruit tarts (apple, pear, or what's in season), mousses, crème caramel. Raoul's is open seven days a week for dinner only, 6:30 to 11:30 p.m.

As the lofts of Tribeca become as elegant as those of Soho, new restaurants must cater to elegant tastes, and so we have **The Odeon,** 145 West Broadway, corner of Thomas St. (tel. 233-0507). And just as these lofts are in one-time warehouses or factory buildings, so the Odeon, wonderfully art deco, is a one-time cafeteria. Old-fashioned venetian blinds cover the large windows, and the old cafeteria decor remains in a polished, sophisticated way. White linen cloths cover the tables; the waiters wear white shirts and ties. The food is expensive and delicious, but—just as important to know—the Odeon is relaxed and friendly; you'll feel just fine there spending money. But it's also way downtown and one of the "in" places, so don't go without a reservation. Your fellow diners will be assorted and colorful, in a variety of costumes. The chef leans to a nouvelle cuisine menu, and he is an expert, so you can expect superb food, no matter what you order; the menu changes with the season, and with what's fresh in the market. Entrees run from about $9 for pasta de jour up to $23 for a succulent roast rack of lamb with sage and parsley, more (depending on market price) for lobster removed from the shell and poached in a heavenly sauce. Appetizers and desserts, vegetables and salads are all extra on this à la carte menu. If the season permits, try oysters in champagne sauce or snails in garlic and cream for appetizers. For desserts, there are wonderful daily specials, plus standbys like a cold poached pear on a bed of pistachio ice cream, served with chocolate sauce.

Lunch and late-supper menus differ from dinner and are less expensive: an omelet, bay scallops, or a steak are about $4.50, $8.75, and $15, respectively. Sunday brunch, noon to 3 p.m., averages about $10. The Odeon is open for lunch Monday through Friday from noon to 3 p.m., for dinner every evening from 7 p.m. to 12:30 a.m., and for late supper every night from 1 to 2:30 a.m.

Well Priced: Dinner for $25 and Up

WEST SIDE: Richard Lavin, the owner of **Lavin's,** 23 West 39th St. (tel. 921-1288), is a man for whom food is an art form. Everything about his handsome restaurant reflects a serious commitment to serving the finest of American wines and the best of the New American Cuisine. His menu is eclectic, drawing from various cuisines of the world, but always with a distinctly American point of view—and that includes using the freshest of marketplace ingredients, and an emphasis on low-sodium, low-cholesterol ingredients (his sauces are wine-, rather than cream-based, for example). The handsome dining room, high ceilinged and oak paneled, was once the Grill Room of Andrew Carnegie's Engineer's Club; it is one of the treasures of old New York. Lace curtains, bentwood chairs, and fresh flowers on white tablecloths are a pleasant surprise when you walk in off drab 39th Street. Lavin's is perfect for midtown shoppers, but most of the busy lunch and dinner crowd is made up of people from the publishing, architecture, apparel, and food and wine communities—many of the latter from Europe. There are frequent visits by vineyard owners during the week and free wine tastings. The wine list (both domestic and imported vintages) changes weekly, and you can order anything from a two-ounce tasting to a glass from the Cruvinet (a temperature-control machine that enables the house to offer a glass of wine from a "good" bottle and still keep the wine for a period of time) to a bottle.

As for the food, it's superb, as delicious to eat as it is beautiful to look at. Lunch and dinner menus are similar, with entree prices running from $12 to $16 at dinner, slightly less at lunch. Among the appetizers ($5 to $7), the gravlax wrapped around a bundle of julienned vegetables, the corkscrew pasta with aged goat cheese, and the marinated bay scallops are all wonderful. So are main courses like pasta primavera, poached breast of chicken with shiitake mushrooms, grilled calf liver with wine-shallot butter, and the cold poached salmon, which is considered one of the best in New York. In season, you can dine on buffalo steak (quite tasty), venison, and pheasant. The dessert menu is limited but choice: one of the best crème brûlées in captivity, a heavenly chocolate mousse, and a flavorful apple tart for those who aren't counting calories; shaved ice granite and fresh fruit plate for those who are.

Lavin's is open Monday through Saturday, and reservations are a must: lunch seatings are from noon to 2:30 p.m., dinner from 5 to 10 p.m., Monday through Friday. In fall and winter, Saturday dinner as well. Closed Sunday.

Celebrity Stuff

The words "show business" and "Sardi's" are practically synonymous in our town, since **Sardi's**, at 234 West 44th St. (tel. 221-8440), is undoubtedly the most famous theatrical restaurant in the world. No doubt that you'll catch at least a few celebrities —perhaps Dustin Hoffman or Betty Bacall or Barbra—as you look up over your spaghetti or antipasto (the Sardis are Italian, and so is much of the menu). The house special appetizer, hot shrimp à la Sardi, is tasty, and for a main course, you might have suprême of chicken served with broccoli and duchesse potatoes, roast beef, or a pasta of the day. The spinach, bacon, and zucchini salad is crispy; and for dessert, we like the frozen cake with zabaglione sauce. Dinner entrees go from $13.95 to $22.95. Complete dinners are priced at $29.95 Monday through Saturday, $18.95 on Sunday. Lunch is less expensive, and the Sunday buffet brunch is a good value at $11.95. You'll have fun here anytime, but if you can, try to come after the opening night of a Broadway play. Then it's traditional for the star of the show to make a grand entrance—to cheers if the show is a hit, to polite applause if it's a bomb. Broadway openings or not, Sardi's keeps serving from 11:30 a.m. to 2 a.m. (the bar stays open later), every day. A special late-dinner menu goes into effect at 9 p.m.

There a gracious, old-world feeling about dining at the **Hotel Algonquin**, 59 West 44th St. (tel. 840-6800). Located just a few steps away from the Broadway theaters, the Algonquin has long been host to the great names of the English and European theater who couldn't imagine staying anywhere else when they have an engagement in New York; dining with them here, you have the feeling of being in a very special English club, where the food is always excellent, the service impeccable, and the mood warm and mellow. Good conversation comes naturally in such a setting, which is perhaps why the celebrated "Round Table Luncheons" were held here in the 1920s by Dorothy Parker and Robert Benchley and Alexander Woollcott, and why current-day celebrities are always being interviewed here by the newspapers and magazines (wasn't that Mike Nichols you just passed on your way into the dining room?). But good food also comes naturally here, like everybody's favorite, the roast prime ribs of beef au jus with Yorkshire pudding, $16.50. Also recommended: poached rainbow brook trout stuffed with shrimp mousse and hollandaise sauce, $10.75; and the curried shrimps with rice and chutney, $12.95. You can have a cocktail (or afternoon tea) at a cozy sofa in the lobby, take lunch or dinner in the Rose Room, lunch and pre-theater dinner in the Oak Room, and enjoy a splendid after-theater buffet (including a superb dessert buffet) in the cozy Victorian lobby.

The Algonquin serves lunch every day from noon to 3 p.m., tea from 3 to 5 p.m., dinner every evening from 5:30 to 9:30 p.m., and after-theater supper, Monday through Saturday, beginning at 9:30 p.m. An important note for motorists: Parking is free for dinner guests, even if you come for pre-theater dinner at 5:30 and don't pick up your car until 1 a.m. Parking is also free for Saturday luncheon guests, from noon to 5 p.m.

New York's most celebrated artistic "salon" is the venerable **Russian Tea Room**, located "slightly to the left of Carnegie Hall," at 150 West 57th St. (tel. 265-0947), and as famous for its loyal following of musicians, dancers, and performers as it is for its borscht, caviar, and blinis. It's an incredibly warm and cozy place, always heady with excitement (could that have been Bernstein—or Nureyev—over in the corner?) and good talk and the aroma of those marvelous Russian favorites. Here's your chance to feast on steaming bowls of borscht (perfect on a cold New York winter day), delicate blinchiki (crêpes stuffed with cottage cheese and preserves, and topped with sour cream), rich beef Stroganoff, shashlik Caucasian, or the unusual pelmeny Siberian (dumplings of chopped beef and veal, floating in consommé with dill, mustard sauce, and sour cream) to mention but a few. Desserts are special, and we often have hot tea, served steaming in a glass, and some kissel (cranberry puree) or kasha à la Gurieff (hot farina with fruit sauce), or halvah. Dinner is prix-fixe at $26.75. Lunch entrees are à la carte, from $10 to $13. Lunch is served from 11:30 a.m. to 4:30 p.m., dinner from 4:30 to 9:30 p.m., and after-theater supper from 9:30 p.m. to 12:30 a.m. On Sunday, it's dinner only (table d'hôte), from noon to 1 a.m. It's fun to arrive at the Russian Tea Room about 6 in the evening to see the people who make this place so special; or come after the performance and join them as they reminisce about the high notes or the grand jetés over a glass of vodka or a bowl of borscht.

Long before there was a Lincoln Center, artistic-minded New Yorkers were enjoying the fine art of eating at **Café des Artistes,** 1 West 67th St. (tel. 877-3500). But ever since Lincoln Center opened just around the corner, it's become more popular than ever with people who love music, dance, and theater—as well as good food, served in a stylish atmosphere. Back in the late 1930s and early 1940s, the Café commissioned a young artist named

Howard Chandler Christy to paint murals of young maidens, clothed in nothing but their smiles, dancing and prancing through the forest—the work was done in exchange for free meals. Ten years ago the murals were restored, and now they are a lively topic of conversation if you happen to sit up in the bustling front dining room (a quieter, less formal dining room near the bar in back offers no murals, but more privacy for conversation). The menu is huge and eclectic. You might start with a plate of cold salmon in four variations, or from the char-cuterie, a dish of sweetbread headcheese with cucumber, or a crudité of fresh vegetables (appetizers run $5 to $9). At both lunch and dinner, you may order a prix-fixe meal consisting of soup or salad, a changing special of the day, an ice cream dessert, and coffee: $14.50 at lunch, $22 at dinner. On the regular menu, dinner entrees run from $15 to $22; lunch dishes, from $9 to $15. Some of our favorites include the smoked leg of lamb perked with a fresh tomato chutney, calf liver with onions, and a tasty melange of bay scallops in a sauce with shallots, walnuts, and herbs. You might, however, wish to eat lightly here, and save your strength for the dessert course: for the true gluttons among us, $13.50 buys a piece of every pie, cake, and pastry on the menu; and believe us, the mocha dacquoise, chocolate mousse, coffee pecan pie, carrot cake, and such are worth waiting for. More disciplined souls can have fruit and cheese plates instead. Café des Artistes is known as one of the "in" places for executive breakfast meetings, and it's also fine and fun for Sunday brunch, similar to lunch, with the addition of egg dishes and even more extensive dessert list than usual.

Café des Artistes serves dinner Monday through Saturday from 5:30 p.m. to 12:30 a.m., on Sunday from 5 to 11 p.m.; lunch, Monday through Saturday from noon to 3 p.m.; break-fast, weekdays from 7:30 to 9:30 a.m.; Sunday brunch, 10 a.m. to 4 p.m.

Regional Cooking

Regional cooking—some call it the New American Cuisine—is very big now in New York gourmet circles, and one of the best places to experience it is **Carolina,** 355 West 46th St., between Eighth and Ninth Aves. (tel. 245-0058), in the heart of Restau-rant Row. Carolina is close to all the Broadway theaters, so you can dine here before or after the show; but it's worth seeking out whether or not you have tickets for two on the aisle. But do make reservations. The front room is brick with beige banquettes, a few tables, a small antique bar, and plenty of flowers for color and cheer. The overall look is spare, clean, tasteful. The cozy back room is our favorite, particularly festive at night with its palm tree and flowers, and candles that flicker under the center skylight. Regional cooking, of course, has its own twist and flavor, depending on whose house you're eating at and where it's located. At Carolina it means bourbon-baked ham with black-cherry sauce, calf liver in brown butter with vermouth and shallots, crab cakes (from $13 to $19); or from the wood fire, succulent barbecues of salmon or swordfish steak, red pepper shrimp, lamb chops or shell steak ($15 to $20); and finally, hickory-smoked ribs, sausages, chicken, and brisket of beef (from $10 to $14). If you like your food "hot," try the jalapeño chili soufflé as an appetizer; if you prefer it just "spicy," order the sausage in puff pastry. (The twist can be quite sophisticated, you see.) Appetizers run from $4.50 to $8, but are really big enough and filling enough for two to share. Corn pudding, potato pancakes, Carolina slaw, and gazpacho salad are tempting side orders that can also be shared ($2.25 to $3.50). Chocaholics can go wild with dessert: the bittersweet chocolate pudding, Carolina mudd cake, chocolate fudge cake, and hot-fudge sundaes are all mouthwatering. So much for that diet. Tomorrow is another day. Prices and entrees are basically the same at lunch.

Carolina serves lunch Monday through Friday from noon to 3 p.m.; dinner, Monday through Saturday from 6 p.m. to midnight, on Sunday from 5 to 10 p.m.

French Treat

One of New York's oldest French bistros and still one of its most deservedly popular, **Pierre au Tunnel** charms everyone who passes through its doorway at 250 West 47th St. (tel. 582-2166). So do Jacqueline and Jean-Claude Lincey, the daughter and son-in-law of Pierre and Jane Pujol, the original owners, who now run this family business. White napery, good wine, courteous waitresses, and flowers at the entrance set a convivial mood. Complete dinners cost from $16 to $19. You could begin with a plate of hors d'oeuvres variés, proceed to a hot onion soup or a cold vichyssoise, then on to classics such as scampi Escoffier or mignonettes de boeuf bordelaise. If it's Friday, don't miss the bouillabaisse à la Marseillaise. Our favorite dessert here is the mousse au chocolat. Lunchtime prices are lower, from $8 to $14 à la carte, for dishes like calf liver sauté, tête de veau vinaigrette, or broiled lamb chops.

Pierre au Tunnel serves lunch from noon to 3 p.m. Monday to Saturday, dinner from 5:30 to 11:30 p.m. regularly, from 4:30 on Wednesday and Saturday. Closed Sunday.

Don't wait until you're going to the theater to have dinner at **René Pujol**, 321 West 51st St., between Eighth and Ninth Aves. (tel. 246-3031). But if you do want to make an 8 o'clock curtain, make an early reservation, so you can leisurely enjoy the complete dinner, priced from $20 to $25, depending on your entree. Bare brick walls, a working fireplace, wood beams, low ceilings, and a carpeted floor all result in comfortable, attractive surroundings in which to savor a first-class French meal. The complete dinner includes an appetizer—pâté, quiche, or marinated mushrooms are all good—plus a soup, either vichyssoise or soup of the day. After these two courses, you're ready for poached salmon with hollandaise, steak with green peppercorns, veal scallops in cream sauce, chicken in a Calvados cream sauce, or whatever you choose as an entree. And all of these delectable selections will be accompanied by vegetables and a salad. Now for coffee and dessert: crème caramel or chocolate mousse are the usual fine choices, and at René Pujol, they are unusually good. A complete lunch is served for $16 with all the same trimmings; the only real difference is that the list of entrees is a bit shorter and a mushroom omelet has been added—otherwise, it's the same wonderful food. There is an extensive wine list.

René Pujol is open for lunch Monday through Friday from noon to 3 p.m., and for dinner Monday through Saturday from 5 to 11:30 p.m. Closed Sunday.

One of the newer French bistros in the theater district, **La Vieille Auberge**, 347 West 47th St., between Eighth and Ninth Aves. (tel. 247-4248), has quickly won itself an appreciative local following; you'll appreciate it too if you enjoy an aura of quiet charm, very good French food with a few nouvelle touches, and a complete dinner for under $20. The feeling here is of dining in someone's home. A brick wall with sconces for dim lighting and tables covered in white linen set the mood, and the dessert display will make you anxious to be seated and begin partaking. Delicious appetizers like celery rémoulade, quiche, vichyssoise, and several terrines are all included in the price of lunch and dinner ($10.75 to $12.75 for lunch, $14.75 to $19.75 for dinner). We chose the delicately flavored poached bass au beurre blanc for our main course; also well recommended are the mignonette of beef, the filet of sole, and the excellent cheese soufflé (lunch only). Salad is extra, but those desserts that you eyed on the way in—mousse au chocolat, tarts, crème caramel—are as good as they look and worth waiting for. Coffee is extra.

La Vieille Auberge is open for lunch Monday through Friday from 12:30 to 2:30 p.m.; for dinner Monday though Thursday from 5:30 to 9 p.m., on Friday and Saturday until 11:30 p.m.; closed Sunday.

Making the Scene

Where does the trendy crowd hang out on the Upper West Side? So powerful is the lure of **Ruelles**, 321 Columbus Ave. at 75th St. (tel. 799-5100), that even members in good standing of the East Side singles set cross their usual boundary line of Fifth Avenue to get to this bistro with its enclosed sidewalk café, central bar, and opulent decor: an elaborate glass chandelier, old-fashioned fans, many plants, antique photographs of nudes all set against deep mauve walls. The food is pretty good too, and if you'd like to be "off camera" and away from the mob, a table on the balcony might do you fine. Entrees like steamed mussels meunière, lemon grilled chicken, and pasta primavera are modestly priced, from $6.75 to $14.95 (for steak). Lunch features many similar dishes in the $5 to $7 range. And Sunday brunch is both lively and filling: $9.50 buys dishes like challah french toast with fresh fruit and pure maple syrup, smoked trout with horseradish cream sauce, and all the coffee you can handle.

Ruelles serves dinner every day from 6 p.m. to midnight, lunch from 11 a.m. to 4 p.m. Monday through Saturday, brunch on Sunday from 11 a.m. to 4 p.m. The kitchen closes at midnight every night, but the bar stays open until about 3 a.m. on weekdays, until 4 a.m. on weekends for the wee-hours nightcap set. And Lincoln Center's not far away.

Old New York

Part of the charm of coming to **Sally's Turn of the Century**, 565 West 23rd St. (tel. 929-4432), is the remoteness of the area (Eleventh Avenue, indeed!); the other part is entering the front door. You're in a 19th-century saloon where the polished wood and the etched glass sparkle in the soft light; you're in the restored ground floor of an old waterfront hotel. It's all part of the exciting renaissance of the Chelsea area. Here at Sally's, the dining room is separated by a door from the lively bar up front, and it has a feeling of calm and spaciousness. Walls are hunter green with hunting prints and flower prints on the wall; bentwood chairs, white tablecloths, and green brass chandeliers lend a cozy charm. As you relax and lap up the atmosphere of old New York, order the smoked trout appetizer ($5), or try the bamboo steamed vegetables, done al dente with a flavorful Oriental sauce ($4.50 as an appetizer, $8.50 as a main dish, and very popular with vegetarians). Main courses begin at around $9 for pastas like linguine with clam sauce or meat tortellini with sundried tomatoes and go up to $14.25 for medallions of veal sauteed with pine nuts and fresh sage. We sampled an excellent filet of salmon steamed with a julienne of leeks and carrots in a mustard cream sauce and, the special for that night, a filet of sole in a creamy champagne sauce. Desserts are excellent, expecially the Fra Angelico cheesecake with hazelnut flour ($3.50). Sally's provides entertainment in the evening (singers, duos, big bands, gospel singers, comedians on various nights), and in summer, a lovely outdoor café. A charming spot.

Sally's serves lunch from noon to 3 p.m., dinner from 6 to 11 p.m. Tuesday through Friday, Sunday brunch from noon to 4 p.m., and Saturday and Sunday dinner from 6 to 11 p.m.

Argentinian-Italian

If you've ever been to Argentina, you know that a lot of Italians live there, so it's not too strange to find **La Tablita**, 65 West 73rd St. (tel. 724-9595), whose owners hail from Argentina, offering a sampling of both worlds on their menu. This is one of the high notes of the Columbus Avenue circuit, much appreciated by concert-goers who want hearty food before or after Lincoln Center, just eight blocks away. Warm and friendly, with brick and stucco walls, a glassed-in garden, a real fireplace, tango music, and Argentinian paintings and artifacts everwhere, La Tablita is both casual and charming. And the value is excellent, since main courses, although they run from $9 to $23, are all accompanied by a tangy green salad and a crusty loaf of Italian bread, along with pasta and vegetable side dishes. If you want more, you can have tasty empañadas (meat pies) or spicy sausages as appetizers, and wonderful desserts like doubledouble chocolate cake (a personal favorite) or warm Argentina crêpes called panqueqes. Seafood and fish dishes are fresh and well prepared, and so is the pasta; for those who want an authentic Argentinian treat, the parillada—a mixed grill of charcoaled

In Search of Sushi

So strong has the New Yorker's passion for Japanese raw fish delicacies of sushi and sashimi become that sushi bars are popping up in our town as often—well, almost as often—as they do in Tokyo. Should you want to get in on the craze, to savor the tender delights of, perhaps, tekkamaki (tuna filet wrapped in rice and seaweed rolls), uni (sea urchins wrapped in seaweed), homuchi-hombu (herring roe and seaweed), the solution is simple. Take yourself to one of the sushi citadels mentioned below, get yourself a seat at the counter, and make friends with the chefs, who are busy artfully arranging the delicacies. Confess ignorance and ask them to guide you to their freshest and tastiest morsels (if they don't speak English, fellow diners will offer advice). Beer goes wonderfully well with sushi and sashimi (the latter a variation of sushi, usually with vegetables instead of rice), and so, of course, does a bit of sake. Tea is always safe. Order carefully, as prices can mount up. Depending on your appetite, lunch might cost anywhere from $7 to $12.50; dinner, around $15 to $20 or more.

Some of our favorite sushi bars are, on the East Side: **Hatsuhana of USA,** 17 East 48th St. (tel. 355-3345); **Kurumazushi,** 423 Madison Ave., between 48th and 49th Sts. (tel. 751-5258), which has received top ratings from demanding critics; **Sushi Ginza,** 4 East 46th St. (tel. 687-4717); **Takesushi,** 71 Vanderbilt Ave. (tel. 687-5120); and, on the West Side, **Sushiko,** 251 West 55th St. (tel. 974-9721). Downtown, try **Mie Japanese Cooking Shop,** 196 Second Ave. near 12th St. (tel. 674-7060), in the East Village. Most sushi bars serve lunch from noon to 3 p.m. and dinner from about 5 p.m. on.

short ribs, sweetbreads, kidney, sausage, and the like—is a must. There's wine and a full bar. Lunch offers similar entrees, priced slightly less.

La Tablita is open from noon to 1 a.m. every day.

The time to come to **Mamma Leone's,** 239 West 48th St. (tel. JU 6-5151), is when you are truly hungry. Mamma's claim to fame rests now, as it has since 1906, on her old-fashioned habit of feeding massive portions to insatiable appetites. Although Mamma's complete dinner runs from $13.95 to $24.95, a bit more than it was back then, it's still one of the best buys in town . . . considering. As soon as you are seated (and unless you make a reservation that will take some time), you are brought a big hunk of cheese and a loaf of Italian bread, plus tomatoes, celery, and peppers—and that's before you start to order! Then comes the huge antipasto, followed by a steaming plate of pasta (the homemade lasagne is our favorite), followed by main dishes like chicken cacciatore or veal cutlet parmigiana or a whole roast chicken or filet of sole, followed by crunchy, deep-fried, and sugar-dipped bugie, followed by the vow not to eat again for at least three days. Steak and lobster dinners are at the high end of the price range, and there's an à la carte supper menu from 9:30 p.m. on. Kids can have a special dinner for $7.95. Lunch is fun too, for it's then that you are challenged to eat all you can of the "heroic" Buffet Italiano luncheon, at $8.95. The atmosphere at Mamma's, like the menu, is overgenerous: there are numerous rooms, filled with fountains and statuary and paintings and theater folk and celebrities and hungry New Yorkers and starving tourists and . . . Mamma Leone's serves lunch from 11:30 a.m. to 2:30 p.m. Monday through Saturday; dinner, from 3:30 to 11 p.m. daily, from 2 to 10 p.m. on Sunday.

Continental and Choice

It's a funny place for a restaurant, but **Kaspar's,** 250 West 27th St. (tel. 989-3804), is thriving. West 27th Street between Seventh and Eighth Avenues is actually the "campus" of the prestigious Fashion Institute of Technology, so the place is often crowded with fashion celebrities and would-be celebrities; it's also an ideal place to eat if you happen to be going to nearby Madison Square Garden or the Roundabout Theater. The tables are covered in white at night and are widely spaced so that you can hear yourself talk; the bar is a pleasant place to sit and wait for one if there's a crowd. The menu is imaginative at both lunch and dinner. Lunch entrees, which run from about $5.50 to $10.50, range from burgers and ratatouille omelets to delicious concoctions like shrimp and scallops, Thai curry, or grilled chicken adobo, with soy and garlic. Dinner entrees, priced from $8.50 for pasta, top out around $14.95 for a roast rack of lamb provençal (first class!); en route you can have Philippine-style escabeche, Thai beef salad, or ris de veau (fresh sweetbreads) Calvados. And there are also many daily specials centering around fresh shellfish and imported fish like Dover sole, brill, pike, and perch. A lovely house salad, along with a vegetable and potato or rice, is served with your meal. Home-baked desserts and pastries are wonderful. Plants and fresh floral arrangements, photographs and framed artwork, pleasant young waitresses, and soft background music (piano and bass) on Wednesday, Thursday, and Saturday nights (no cover or minimum charge), all add up to an attractive, casual, relaxing place to eat top-notch food.

Kaspar's is open every day except Sunday from noon to 4:30 p.m. for lunch, and from 4:30 p.m. to midnight for dinner.

Indian Adventures

New York's Indian restaurants, once tiny holes-in-the-wall catering to the Indian colony and adventurous young people, have lately gone glamorous; eating Indian is definitely "in" these days. The showpiece of them all is **Raga**, 57 West 48th St. (tel. 757-3450), a branch of India's Taj hotel chain. This midtown palace that occupies the site of the old Forum of the Twelve Caesars, decorated in the most elegant Indian fashion yet to hit New York, boasts thick, richly colored striped carpeting, lush silk banquettes, and antique Indian musical instruments on the walls. Service is solicitous and selections are above the ordinary run of Indian fare, featuring seldom-seen choices like appetizers of crab Goa or Bombay oysters. Dinner entrees range from about $8 to $16, and there are several tandoori specialties. Live music accompanies dinner except on Sunday.

Nirvana, 30 Central Park South (tel. 486-5700), is an Indian penthouse close to heaven, festooned with reams and reams of colorful hand-appliquéd fabric, forming a dramatic tented ceiling. Broad windows offer treetop views of Central Park. In the evening, Nirvana is one of the city's most romantic hideaways. Food is consistently good and often innovative, featuring excellent lamb curry and a rare fish called pompet. Tandoori dishes go from $6.95 to $13.95, business and executive lunches from $9.95 to $14.95, and theater dinners from $15.95 to $17.95.

EAST SIDE: Moving crosstown to the East Side, there is an equally impressive selection of restaurants, but of a slightly different nature and ambience.

The French Way

Le Veau d'Or, 129 East 60th St. (tel. TE 8-8133), has long been hailed as one of New York's best French bistros. Its robust hearty, bourgeois fare is responsible for drawing what seem to be unmanageable crowds night in, night out. And no wonder:

food and service are impeccable, and you can have a complete meal, from pâté to fromage, for the price of the entree, averaging $18.80 to $25. Rarely have we been disappointed in any of the house specials—and that includes the filet of sole amandine, the veal kidneys with mustard sauce, the sauteed veal à l'Indienne, and the spring chicken in casserole "Grand'-Mère." You may begin with appetizers like artichoke vinaigrette or boeuf en gelée, have onion soup or cold vichyssoise, and end with lovely desserts like crème caramel or pêche Melba. This is not the place for a quiet, hand-holding dinner—it's too crowded and tends to get noisy. For more relaxation, come at lunchtime, when it's not quite as frantic; complete lunches go from $12.90 to $18.

Le Veau d'Or is open Monday through Saturday, serving lunch from noon to 2:30 p.m., dinner from 6 to 10 p.m.; closed Sunday.

Even a brief visit to Provence does wonders for the palate and spirit, but a trip to **La Colombe d'Or**, 134 East 26th St. (tel. 689-0666), is the next best thing. The great majority of New York's French restaurants are Lyonnaise, but this one is strictly Provençal, from the traditional print fabric used for chairs, banquettes, and waitresses' aprons to the ratatouille and soupe de poisson on the menu. The foods of southern France are marked by an imaginative use of garlic and tomatoes, and, of course, seafood is a highlight. Provence is the home of bouillabaisse, and La Colombe d'Or's version does not disappoint. You might start a Provençal meal here with one of the homemade pâtés, which range from a coarse country variety to creamy pork rillettes; for a lighter beginning, try spinach dressed with olive oil, sesame, and garlic. Soups are so hearty and filling that only the biggest eaters should start with one of these. Main courses include a hearty winter cassoulet, a robust white bean stew with sausages and a variety of meats. Coq au vin, a rich Provençal beef stew, and sirloin of lamb with a delicate herbed sauce are favorites. A tempting dessert cart offers a luscious array of homemade pastries.

La Colombe d'Or provides a livelier, more aggressive fare and a sunnier ambience than most French restaurants. Open for lunch weekdays from noon to 2:30 p.m. with entrees from about $7.50 to $15, and for dinner Monday through Saturday (closed Sunday) with entrees from about $9.75 to $22.50.

You don't want a sandwich; you do want a glass of wine. **Bienvenue**, 21 East 36th St. (tel. 684-0215), is a little French restaurant that you dream about when your feet get tired while shopping. The red, white, and blue awning and picket fence welcome you at the outside, and the same tricolor motif and warm ambience continue within. Bienvenue is the kind of restaurant that's hard to find in midtown, with its good food, pleasant atmosphere, and moderate prices, so try to arrive close to noon or at about 1:30 p.m. at lunchtime to avoid standing in line with everybody else who's discovered it. Have an omelet, a quiche, or spinach salad with mushrooms for about $5.50 to $6; or a grilled steak, a beef stew, sliced lamb, or broiled fish filet (depending on the specials of the day) for $8 to $10, with vegetable and rice included. Appetizers and desserts are about $2.50 extra, not really worth the price for a budget-conscious diner. However, in the evening, appetizer, soup, salad, dessert, and coffee are all included in the $14.95 complete dinner; à la carte entrees run $8.75 to $14.50. The marinated mushrooms and the pâté both make good beginnings; next comes vichyssoise or soup of the day. And now for the big decision: will it be chicken Cordon Bleu, coq au vin, scallops, filet of sole, duck, or steak au poivre? They're all done very well. It wouldn't be a French restaurant without chocolate mousse or crème caramel—we prefer the latter—and a hot cup of espresso.

Bienvenue is open for lunch Monday through Friday from 11:30 a.m. to 2:30 p.m., and for dinner Monday through Saturday from 5:30 to 10 p.m.

Swiss Surprise

It's a little bit of the Swiss Alps transplanted to New York. Chalet Suisse, 6 East 48th St. (tel. 355-0855), has white stucco walls, wooden beams, waitresses wearing native costumes, and beautiful and authentic Swiss food—the makings of a perfect evening. You can choose from either the à la carte menu or the prix-fixe dinner at $30. At a recent dinner, both the cheese-and-onion pie and the cervelat salad (smoked pork and beef sausages) were very good. So were the breaded veal cutlet à la Holstein and the escargots bourguignonnes among the entrees, and the Swiss apple tart for dessert. For neuchâteloise (cheese) fondue, $15, order from the à la carte menu. And for dessert, what else but the classic chocolate fondue! It's $10 for two, and a delight. The lunch menu is completely à la carte, and prices range from $13.50 to $23 for steak. Open Monday to Friday for lunch from noon to 2:30 p.m., dinner from 5 to 9:30 p.m. Closed Saturday and Sunday.

A Japanese Favorite

The atmosphere is ah-so-harmonious over at **Nippon,** 145 East 52nd St. (tel. 355-9020 and 758-0226), one of the first and finest of New York's Japanese restaurants, where everything—from sculptures to the indoor garden to the wood used in the booths to the kimonos worn by the waitresses—is authentic, done in classical Japanese manner. So, too, is the food, which includes some rare Japanese dishes as well as those most appealing to American tastes. For a complete dinner, try the tempura (deep-fried fish and vegetables), $17,80; or the teriyaki (steak marinated in a sweet Japanese sauce), $19.50; or chicken sukiyaki, $16.80; and beef sukiyaki, $18.80. All these dishes come served with miso soup or consommé, rice, pickled vegetables, various side dishes, green tea, and desserts. À la carte entrees include shabu shabu (prime ribs and fresh vegetables); hama nabe clam casserole, and a yosenabe seafood casserole. It's fun to order a jug of warm sake to go with your meal. Lunch is also pleasant, and prices are a bit lower. If you wish to sit Western style—i.e., on a chair—be sure to make a reservation at both lunch and dinner. Otherwise, your choices will be floor seats in one of the numerous tatami rooms off the main Western-style room, or at the tempura and sushi bar up front where you can watch the chef prepare your order.

The Nippon serves lunch from noon to 2:30 p.m. Monday to Friday; dinner from 5:30 to 10 p.m. Monday to Thursday, until 10:30 p.m. on Friday and Saturday; closed Sunday.

Pasta Perfection

Contrapunto, 200 East 60th St. (tel 751-8686), has to be the best thing that's happened to Third Avenue since the invention of Bloomingdale's. Located right across the street from that famed shopping emporium, Contrapunto is also the best thing to happen to the noodle since Marco Polo came back from China. Two sides of this stylish, second-story trattoria are totally glass, so your view is of Third Avenue, just above Cinema Row. Everything in the room, which seats 60, is snow white: walls, napery (white tablecloths under glass), sparkling track lighting. Gorgeous flower arrangements in Chinese urns and fresh flowers on every table are the only splashes of color. The kitchen is in full view at one end of the room; in front of it is an oak table laden with fresh produce from which the chefs draw. To the right is the dessert and gelati counter, under an antique sign that reads

Dining at the City

Food can make even cold glass and steel lovable, as **The Market at Citicorp Center,** Lexington Ave. at 53rd St., demonstrates. A multilevel international bazaar of restaurants and retail food shops surrounds a stunning sky-lit atrium, well stocked with tables and chairs where you may eat (bring your own or buy some light food and carry it to the tables), often watch free entertainment, lounge, or just plain people-watch. For indoor dining try:

Avgerinos (tel. 688-8828) a dazzler of a Greek taverna with haunting Greek music dishes out the lightest of spinach pies and dolmades (stuffed grape leaves), a classic moussaka, wonderful souvlakis, and other traditional favorites. Dinner entrees, including salad, vegetables, and rice, run $9.95 to $12.50.

Market Coffeeshop (tel. 935-1744) is a winner in the pastry department for something luscious like chocolate mousse cake or mocha cheesecake. A few imaginative salads and sandwiches on pita bread, as well as ice cream drinks, round out the small menu.

Nyborg and Nelson (tel. 223-0700) famous for the finest Scandinavian herrings, salads, and pâtés. The restaurant serves open-face sandwiches from $2.85 to $4.35, plates from $4.95 to $7.25.

Auberge Suisse (tel. 421-1420) is a sleekly decorated, intimately lit Swiss restaurant serving, in addition to cheese fondue at $22 for two, specialties from all of Switzerland's diverse regions. Entrees run about $10 to $17.50.

Les Tournebroches (tel. 935-6029) is a tiny pink gem of a restaurant where one can view the huge rôtisserie (the turning spits or *tournebroches*), on which such delicacies as carré d'agneau and various brochettes—of seafood, grilled sausages, kidneys, etc.—are done to just the right turn. Entrees range from $10.50 (for half a chicken) to $19 for filet mignon. Don't miss the pâtisserie—tarts made of the freshest raspberries, oranges, or strawberries, or le dessert du jour—perhaps crème caramel.

Charley O's (tel. 752-2102) dispenses American food, good and hearty, with Texas-style chili a specialty. You can get a quick standup sandwich lunch at the bar weekdays, or enjoy a leisurely brunch on weekends, $5.95. Entrees run from $6.50 to $13.

Alfredo's (tel. 371-3367), a U.S. branch of Rome's most famous restaurant, offers a full menu of pastas (you can get a pasta dinner from $5.95 to $7.95) plus a large variety of chicken, veal, and other Italian dishes, from $8.50 at lunch, $9.50 at dinner. Sunday brunch, from noon to 4 p.m., is a hearty feast for $8.95.

Healthworks (tel. 838-6221) is a mecca for dieters and health food fans. Salads are between $3 and $4.95; homemade quiches and casseroles are $4.95.

"Pure Ice Cream, Made By Electricity." All of this gives the feeling of being not so much in a restaurant as in a very friendly and warm home. The waiters and waitresses are cheerful and efficient, and the Italian-Portuguese manager, Tony, is truly a genial host.

Contrapunto's theme is to serve as "counterpoint" to other restaurants serving pasta, and they carry it off with class. The menu lists 11 creations of either fresh or imported pasta; and since they're all so good, you might do best to come here with a group and try a little bit of several. We like the cappelli bergino (angel-hair pasta enlivened with dried red tomato and artichoke); the papparedele boscaiola (a wide ribbon pasta with fresh mushrooms); and best of all, the tagliarini conga d'ora (a thin ribbon pasta with julienned vegetables). Pastas run between $9.75 and $13.75. Other specialties include a very good grilled T-bone of veal served on a nest of spinach and pignoli nuts ($16.75) and a whole Cornish hen, grilled and roasted with a white-wine and bay leaf sauce ($10.50). Let your group also share some flavorful appetizers, like the insalata caprese, a cold salad of smoked cheese, tomatoes, and onions ($6.50). And when it comes to dessert, no one should have to choose between creamy homemade gelatis of praline or white chocolate (the flavors change every day), mocha cheesecake, or a luscious dry chocolate cake, so don't—you and your friends should have them all. Start your meal with some light champagne or wine, end with a good espresso or cappuccino.

Contrapunto serves lunch from noon to 3 p.m. Monday to Saturday; dinner from 5 to 11 p.m. Monday to Saturday, Sunday from 4 to 10 p.m.

GREENWICH VILLAGE, THE LOWER EAST SIDE, SOHO, AND POINTS SOUTH:
Here, again, another switch in ambience. With 14th Street as the northern boundary, a step into the Village, the Lower East Side, and Soho reveals a casually relaxed dining scene.

Under the canopy which announces **Marylou's**, at 21 West 9th St. (tel 533-0012), is a short flight of stairs going down to the basement of an elegant old Greenwich Village brownstone. Low ceilings, dim lighting, fireplaces, carpeted floors, and pale-peach tablecloths are some of the ingredients in the home-like coziness here. The garden room opens on to a garden where you can eat in warm weather. (For a moment, you may feel as if you've crashed a private dinner party.) Back to reality. The menu arrives. Clams and oysters on the half shell, cold mussel salad, smoked trout are all good for starters. Fish entrees range in price from $7 to $15 and include shrimp gumbo, trout or filet of sole almondine, seafood brochette, and bouillabaisse for two. Lobsters are priced according to size. Although this restaurant is known primarily for its fresh fish (Marylou is part owner of a fish market), chicken, veal, calf liver, and steak ($9 to $15) are all excellent and well prepared. Entrees are served with rice or potatoes and vegetables; the house salad is $2.50 extra. Desserts are about $3 more, but we wouldn't consider skipping them. Marylou's pastry chef bakes every day. How does warm apple pie or double chocolate layer cake sound? Or lemon mousse so light it can't be fattening? Or "angel cloud," as light as its name and unlike any rice pudding you've ever had? The lunch menu offers most of the dinner entrees at lower prices and adds hamburgers and omelets ($4 to $5) plus seafood salads (about $8). Sunday brunch is $8.95, and that includes a Bloody Mary.

Marylou's serves dinner Monday through Thursday from 5:30 to 11 p.m., until 2 a.m. on Friday and Saturday, until 10 p.m. on Sunday. Lunch Monday to Friday is served from noon to 3 p.m. Sunday brunch is from noon to 4 p.m.

Country French

Keep **Le Bistroquet,** 90 Bedford St. (tel. 242-8309), in mind if you're going to one of the downtown off-Broadway theaters; it's just a short, two-block walk from Seventh Avenue and many of the smaller playhouses. In fact, keep it in mind whether you're going to the theater or not; it's a wonderful little place with a crowd of regulars who wouldn't be happy if they knew we were giving their secret "find" away. Call ahead for reservations because of its size. The tables are white, the chairs green; the banquettes are covered in a delightful, flowered country print, and decorative plates hang on the walls. With flowers and candles on the tables and big windows with lots of small panes that look out on the corner of Bedford and Grove Streets, Le Bistroquet has the aura of a country inn that you just happened to stumble upon in the city.

Artichoke hearts sauteed with prosciutto or king crabmeat mousse with avocado are both highly recommended starters (both are $4). On the regular menu, the rack of lamb or beer-batter shrimp served with orange sauce are favorites of ours.

Specials always include veal, fish, chicken, and sometimes rabbit: prices are between $11 and $17. Salmon steak with a cream dill sauce, brook trout with a lemon-soy sauce, veal chop in an artichoke cream sauce, and breast of chicken Cordon Bleu are all typical of an evening. And all the entrees are served with a fresh garden salad with a dressing of your choice, rice or potatoes, and a fresh vegetable. The apple cake, the chocolate torte, the flan, and the pies are all baked on the premises; they are also all quite special.

Le Bistroquet serves dinner only, Tuesday through Sunday from 5 to 11 p.m.

Italian Standbys

Mention the name **Bondini's** and eyes light up: anybody who knows fine northern Italian cooking has only the highest praise for this charming Greenwich Village restaurant at 69 West 9th St., just off Avenue of the Americas (tel. 777-0670). Anselmo Bondulich, who is both owner and chef, has created a dining room of great refinement, with mirrored walls and ceiling, fine oil paintings, fresh flowers, and a graceful balcony area. And the food reflects that refinement: the freshest of ingredients, prepared and presented with skill and style. For $22.50, sample the scope of the menu in the House Dinner (5:30 to 7:30 p.m.). Start with soup or pasta of the day; choose among eight entrees including broiled whole baby chicken, shrimp brochettes, and broiled steak, accompanied by vegetables, salad, a dessert and coffee. On the à la carte dinner menu, expect to pay $5 or $6 for appetizers, $12 to $14 for pasta, $13 to $19 for meat, poultry, and fish. At lunch, entrees run $5.50 to $9.50. You might want to start with a tangy antipasto of roasted fresh peppers and anchovies or steamed mussels in white wine. Among the pastas, spaghettini al pesto and the linguine ai fruitti di mare are both first-rate. Or you might choose scampi ragusa (with garlic, rosemary, and tomatoes), lobster Fra Diavolo, saltimbocca alla Romana, steak with cognac and peppers, or very special veal chops for your main dish. Can you handle dessert after all that? Bondini's pastry chef makes a terrrific double-devil chocolate cake and a soothing zabaglione al marsala to go along with your espresso or cappuccino. The wine list is well selected and well priced. At the intimate cocktail lounge up front, a pianist will be playing soothing, sophisticated music Tuesday through Saturday from 7:30 p.m. on.

Bondini's serves lunch Monday to Friday from noon to 3 p.m., dinner Monday to Saturday from 5:30 to 11 p.m. or midnight; closed Sunday.

For almost 50 years, people have been traveling for blocks and miles to eat at **Joe's,** 79 MacDougal St. (tel. 228-2710). It's one of the best known restaurants in the Village for first-class southern Italian food. The gray walls, the black-and-white tiled floor, and the white tablecloths result in a clean, spare look. The three small rooms with their widely spaced tables provide a nice feeling of privacy for diners and seem to encourage lingering over coffee and wine. A lovely way to begin a meal here is with the antipasto—cold or hot ($5 and $6, respectively)—which can be shared and nibbled on while you decide on an entree. Joe's menu lists almost 20 different pasta dishes to choose from, ranging in price from $8 to $9. One of our favorites is the spaghetti with olive oil, garlic, anchovies, and olives. Veal, chicken, shrimp, and clam dishes, from $9 to $13, are expertly spiced and sauced; especially good are the shrimps in white wine and the saltimbocca alla florentina. Lobsters are also available in a variety of styles, and priced according to size. Eggplant alla parmigiana, which could be a side dish (to share) or a perfect lunch, is around $8. Joe's makes a wonderful hot zabaglione for dessert ($2) which someone at your table should try.

Joe's is open Wednesday through Sunday from noon to 11 p.m. for lunch and dinner. Closed Tuesday.

Spanish

To many aficionados, there is no better place for Spanish food in all New York than **El Faro,** an out-of-the-way restaurant at 823 Greenwich St. (corner of Horatio St.) in the Village (tel. WA 9-8210), but it's worth the effort to get to. For years, this restaurant has been packed with its fans, so make a reservation before you go, and then be prepared to wait. All entrees are à la carte, all served with Spanish rice or Spanish potatoes and salad, and the most sensational are the seafood dishes: the paella à la Valenciana, with lobster, of course, $14.50; the crabmeat with green sauce, $18.50; and the shrimp à la diablo, $10.50, are all memorable. Have a pitcher of sangría, or some imported Spanish wine, to go with your meal. Prices are cheaper at lunch. The salad dressing is so good that you'll probably want to take home a bottle. El Faro is thoroughly unpretentious, with no attempt at decor to relieve the Formica-table-and-bare-walls look, save for a few murals, but this, interestingly, is an atmosphere itself. At any rate, it's the food and not the ambience that counts here.

Lunch is served from 11 a.m. to 3 p.m. every day but Sunday; dinner from 3 p.m. to midnight, Friday and Saturday to 1 a.m.

Open the door on **Un Rincon de España** at 226 Thompson St. (tel. 260-4950) and, sure enough, you're in a little corner of Spain, complete to the bullfight paintings along the wall, the wrought-iron candlesticks on the white tables, the tiles bordering the tiny bar, and the Flamenco guitarist giving out with plaintive melodies. The Village regulars keep this place jammed, not only for the *muy autentico* mood, but for the top-notch food. Salad with a spicy house dressing arrives as soon as you sit down, and while you're dipping your crusty french bread in the sauce and sipping a glass of wine, go ahead and order the mejillones a la Carlos—mussels in a pungent garlic sauce ($4 at lunch, $5 at dinner) and enough for two. Seafood, fish, and meat entrees are priced in the $12.75 to $17.25 range, with an outstanding paella Valenciana (again, enough for two), $9.75 at lunch, $11 at dinner. Mariscadas—seafood stews—are another specialty of the house, and for those who dare, the broiled octopus is considered among the best in town. Desserts? Nothing special, but sip your coffee slowly and drink deep of the very special mood.

Un Rincon de España serves dinner only, from 5 to 11 p.m., Friday and Saturday until midnight, Sunday from 1 to 11 p.m.

The same management runs Un Rincon de España downtown at 82 Beaver St., open 11:40 a.m. to 9 p.m. Monday to Friday, and Saturday from noon to 11 p.m. There are two shows of flamenco dancing Saturday at 8 and 10 p.m., downtown only (tel. 344-5228).

Regional American

Regional American cooking is all the fashion in New York at this moment, and **Texarkana**, 64 West 10th St. (tel. 254-5800), with its Gulf Coast specialties brought here by the Cajun chef and owner, Abe de la Houssaye, is one of the more fashionable examples of the trend. The handsome, stylish young crowd begins gathering around 9 p.m. in the unusual bar. The highly polished, untrimmed sections of a very tall tree look more like a horizontal sculpture than the top of the bar. Make a reservation for about 9 p.m., and reserve at least one portion of the suckling pig served with cornbread and jalapeño dressing ($23), because when you come in and see it turning on the spit in the fireplace, you'll be sorry if it's all spoken for. You could come earlier, when the place is much quieter, but the pig will not be ready then. You can sit near the bar, near the fireplace, or on the more peaceful balcony.

Don't debate about the appetizer: have the pickled shrimp ($6). And while you wait for that to arrive, nibble on the free goodies like pickled okra or coleslaw or whatever comes your way. Someone in your party should have the gumbo of the day (fish, chicken, or beef, and priced accordingly); it's always dense and wonderful. And side dishes such as "dirty rice" with giblets and peppers ($3.50) or fried okra ($2.50) are recommended for sharing (sharing is part of the scene here—food and friends). There is always a long list of specials with poetic names like "Stolen Blackened Fish" ($18) or "Carpetbagger Steak" (a tenderloin of beef stuffed with caviar and wrapped in bacon), $22. On the regular menu, with entrees priced from $12 to $23, try the barbecued lamb chops with jalapeño jelly and barbecue sauce; or fresh gulf shrimp sauteed with lemon, garlic, and scallops; or southern fried chicken served with honey butter and Cajun mustard; or catfish with homemade tartar sauce. And for dessert, pecan pie, of course. Texarkana also has a late supper between midnight and 4 a.m. with appetizer, tastes from the dinner menu, and omelets; and a very good Sunday brunch at $12.50, including a drink.

Dinner is served from 6 p.m. to midnight, seven days a week; late-night supper until 4 a.m. Tuesday through Saturday; Sunday brunch from noon to 4 p.m.

Jewish-Roumanian on the Lower East Side

You don't have to be Jewish to love **Sammy's Famous Roumanian Steak House**, 157 Chrystie St., on the Lower East Side (tel. OR 3-0330), but it sure helps. Who else could understand the zany humor ("Oi vey, he just saw the bill," cracks the M.C. "Say Kaddish for the bill"). Who else could appreciate the food, fragrant with garlic and chicken fat, or the *freiliche* atmosphere that reminds you of your cousin Irving's noisy, long-forgotten Bar Mitzvah? Surprisingly, however, many of Sammy's most devoted patrons are not Jewish. "Do you have to be Japanese to like Japanese food?" asks owner Stanley (there is no Sammy) Zimmerman. "People come because they love the food and the friendliness, and they know they can relax here." All of this is so. Sammy's is a one-of-a-kind restaurant, a happening, a seven-nights-a-week show for which no tickets are required, as heart-warming as it is sometimes heartburning. Ordinary folks and celebrities all love this place, perhaps because of Stanley, who appears to be a close personal friend to almost everyone in the restaurant. Many of New York's top politicans dine here regularly. The decor is wall-to-wall people, especially on weekends. Don't come to Sammy's for a quiet, sedate evening. Come for a party and bring all your relatives.

Oh, yes, the food. It's Jewish style without being kosher, and Roumanian, which in this case means Roumanian-Jewish, and refers mostly to such dishes as a very flavorful Roumanian tenderloin, mush steak (the eye of the rib), and a sausage called karnatzlack—for garlic eaters only. Sammy's eggplant salad with fresh green peppers is authentic and delicious. As soon as you sit down, a bottle of seltzer, plus huge bowls of sour pickles, sour tomatoes, and roasted peppers, are brought to your table to munch along with bread and challah. We could happily make a meal on the appetizers alone—chopped liver, grated radish and chopped onions with chicken fat, broiled chicken livers, and unborn eggs—all rich, greasy, unforgettable. A bottle of chicken fat is put on the table, just in case you like it greasier. (Appetizers run $2.95 to $3.95.) Try the mushroom barley soup—one of the 50 best dishes in New York, according to *Vanity Fair* food writer Mimi Sheraton (who also raves about the tenderloin steak).

Main dishes might include flanken with mushroom barley gravy, stuffed cabbage, broiled veal chops (excellent!), half a broiled spring chicken, or the Roumanian tenderloins (prices run from $6.95 for chicken fricassee to $18.95 for prime rib steak). Side dishes are memorable: mashed potatoes with *grieven* and schmaltz, potato latkes with applesauce, kasha varnishkes. What's for dessert? "Jewish mousse," says Stanley, chocolate pudding with heavy cream. You could also have strudel, rugelach, stewed prunes. But you really don't need dessert after all this. They'll replace your bottle of seltzer and bring out a bottle of Fox's U-Bet Chocolate Syrup, plus a container of milk; mix your own egg creams at the table. (Egg creams are a famous Lower East Side drink, so named because they have neither eggs nor cream in them, just in case you didn't know.)

Now you can sit back and enjoy the entertainment. Tuvia Zimer, a joke-cracking Israeli musician is at the piano Wednesday through Sunday ("Your stomach isn't feeling so hot? Take two egg creams and call me in the morning"); on Friday, Saturday, and Sunday he is joined by a soprano and tenor from the

New York City Opera. And on Monday and Tuesday, when the mood is much quieter, Reuben Levine plays the violin. There is a cover charge of $1.95 per person on Friday, Saturday, Sunday, and holidays.

Sammy's serves dinner every night from 4 p.m. to midnight, "Jewish time." That means maybe a little earlier, maybe a little later. It is closed only on Yom Kippur.

Soho Specials

Coming to Soho is a weekend ritual for many New Yorkers. On a sunny day in spring, summer, or fall, strolling down West Broadway is like attending a series of dress rehearsals. Mimes and jugglers, musicians and clowns perform on the street corners; everybody seems to be in costume of one kind or another; the whole world seems to be a festival. **Central Falls,** 478 West Broadway (tel. 533-9481), adds a touch of culture to all this frivolity. It's actually an art gallery/restaurant/bar which has live classical music at Sunday brunches: the Cantabile Trio performs on violin, cello, and flute from 1 to 4:30 p.m. When the windows are open and the sounds drift out to the street, you will wish you were inside sitting at one of the tables, having buttermilk pancakes with sausage, steak and eggs with pan-fried potatoes, brioche french toast, or eggs Benedict, perhaps. All the brunch entrees are from $6 to $10.50; desserts such as mocha pot de crème, hazelnut cheesecake, and crème brûlée go from $3 to $4.50. High ceilings, tall, elegant Corinthian columns, and lush greenery in a long, spacious room—it's a perfect place for listening to music, viewing art, and eating good food on a Sunday afternoon.

Lunch and dinner are pleasant here too (no music, but the paintings and good food remain). The range goes from hamburger to filet of sole and filet mignon. Entrees run from $5.50 to $13 at lunch, from $6.50 to $19.50 at dinner. Central Falls is open seven days a week: lunch is served Monday through Saturday from noon to 4:30 p.m.; brunch on Sunday is from 11:30 a.m. to 4:30 p.m.; dinner is from 5 p.m. to 1 a.m. daily; the bar is open from noon to 2 a.m. Reservations are suggested for Sunday brunch.

Once your eyes have adjusted to the dim light in **Berry's,** 180 Spring St. (tel. 226-4394), and you can read the menu, you'll discover that you're in a small, European-style bistro. It can be noisy for brunch and dinner, particularly on weekends when there is always a congenial crowd at the bar, but it's fun. And there are a few tables in the back room if you want to get away from it all. At any rate, once you've tried the food, international in style, you'll be pleased. Entrees are fairly priced between $10 and $15 at dinner and are served with a fresh vegetable and either sauteed new potatoes or rice. (A side order of salad is $2.) Berry's menu changes every three weeks for dinner, every day for lunch, but you can always count on a seasonal fish poached or broiled to perfection. Calf liver with shallots, cooked just the way you like it, is often on the menu; we recommend it. At lunch the fish is $6; the liver, $8; and there is usually a salad platter and an omelet for about $5. At dinner, appetizers are available from $2 to $5; our favorite is the salad chinoise—Chinese noodles, straw mushrooms, and broccoli in a sesame oil dressing. Our favorite dessert, served at both lunch and dinner, is an irresistible Grand Marnier trifle. Berry's famous french toast (made with a brioche) is served on weekends for brunch ($4).

Berry's is open for lunch Tuesday through Friday from noon to 3 p.m.; brunch on Saturday is from noon to 3:30 p.m. and on Sunday from 11 a.m. to 4 p.m. Dinner is served Tuesday through Thursday from 6 to 11:30 a.m., on Friday and Saturday from 6 p.m. to midnight, on Sunday from 5 to 10:30 p.m. Closed Monday.

At South Street Seaport

The South Street Seaport is an adventure—in looking, in shopping, in just mingling with happy crowds enjoying the waterfront festivites. How nice, then, that it also has some of the most enjoyable dining in the city right at hand. Case in point: **The Coho**, premier dining facility at the Seaport, a handsome, triple-tiered restaurant perched atop the Fulton Market Building, 11 Fulton St. (tel. 608-0507), whose glass walls provide panoramic views of the East River and the Brooklyn Bridge for lucky diners (ask for a table with a view when you make your reservations). When the weather is warm, 400 diners can be seated on the outdoor terrace; the rest of the year, 350 can dine inside. Pink pastel tablecloths, fluted napkins, comfortable banquettes, and tables spaced well apart, an attentive staff, and impeccable yet friendly service create a glamorous setting in which to partake of very fine, very fresh fish, purchased right next door at the Fulton Fish Market.

The best way to go here is to order any of the fish fresh that day—it could be Coho salmon or red snapper, tilefish or Boston scrod—and have them prepare it to your liking, either sauteed, broiled, poached, or fried. Prices run from $10.95 to $17.50; a two-pound or larger lobster, steamed or broiled, is $12.95 the pound. Start your meal, perhaps, with the satiny-smooth Fulton Market fish chowder; it's all fish, no potatoes ($3.75); or with succulent Littlenecks, Long Island Bluepoint oysters, or cherry-stone clams from the raw bar ($4.25 to $5). The waiter will tell you about the interesting specials of the day: we sampled a flavorful mako shark that had been marinated in a whiskey soy sauce with scallions and sesame seeds. Salads, like tomato and mozzarella with fresh basil dressing (delicious!), are extra ($3 to $4). All main courses are served with a loaf of freshly baked semolina bread, a choice of potatoes or rice, and a vegetable. You may not think you have room for dessert, but don't give up now: desserts here are spectacular. We are hard put to choose between the chocolate velvet mousse cake (heavenly) or the chocolate walnut pie (better than any pecan pie you've ever tasted). If you're in the area at lunchtime, you can join the Wall Street crowd in a well-priced three-course executive lunch at $12.95; or on weekends, partake of a $9.95 brunch that includes a drink, seafood-based quiches and omelets, and beverage. Happy Hour takes place from 4 to 7 p.m.; all drinks are $2.50, and hot hors d'oeuvres are free.

The Coho serves dinner from 5 to 9 p.m. Monday through Thursday, until 11 p.m. on Friday and Saturday, and on Sunday from noon to 8 p.m. Brunch is noon to 3 p.m. on Saturday and Sunday.

Tribeca Treats

City Hall people and the downtown business crowd keep **Laughing Mountain Bar & Grill**, 148 Chambers St. (tel. 233-4434), hopping during the busy lunch hour. When dinnertime comes it's much more peaceful, and that's a good time to sample some superior continental cooking in an atmosphere that might be described as quietly elegant. The room is quite simple, with rose-colored walls, wooden tables, and parquet floors. A secluded skylit area in back is the perfect place to carry on a secret romance. Splendid vases of fresh flowers are an integral part of the decor.

As for the food, it is nouvelle American, changes with the seasons, and is expertly prepared. The taste treats unfold as you sample the appetizers: a flavorful cream of carrot soup, tangy cold noodles in sesame sauce, a wonder of an Oriental salad with just the right crunch to it, topped with roasted cashews and dressed in a faintly mysterious mustard sesame oil dressing; at $5, it was more than enough for three of us. Appetizers, which are generous, run from about $2.50 to $4. The bread basket is certainly one of the best in town; everything in it is baked right in Laughing Mountain's own kitchen and includes an Irish soda bread and raisin bran muffins. Watch out, or you'll be tempted to fill up on this and scarcely have room for the entrees. There are specials every night, like a delicate tile fish done with capers, croutons, rosemary, and lemon butter, or poached salmon in a not-too-rich hollandaise. On the regular menu, imaginative dishes like roast duck in green peppercorn sauce, sea bass in black bean and ginger sauce, shrimp with fresh mangos and jalapeño, run about $10 to $12. Pastas and omelets are modestly priced, from $5.50 to $7. Side dishes of seasonal vegetables come with your entree. Our favorite among the desserts was the chocolate coffee cake with a strong hint of rum, which goes very well with cappuccino, espresso, or even chamomile tea. There's a full-service bar for stronger stuff.

Lunch at Laughing Mountain is modestly priced: entrees like chicken in soy sauce and ginger, puff pastry filled with seafood in béchamel sauce, and fish of the day, all served with homemade bread and salads, run about $5.50 to $6.50. Sunday brunch is pleasant, with live guitar music and lots of good egg dishes.

Laughing Mountain is open daily from 11:30 a.m. to 4:30 p.m. for lunch, from 5 p.m. to 1 a.m. for dinner.

Modest: Dinner Around $18

WEST SIDE: The West Side dining scene gets better all the time. Here are some of our favorites:

The Neighborhood Crowd

There's a very relaxed feeling at **Teacher's,** Broadway at 80th St. (tel. 787-3500), a hangout for many of the city's artists, writers, and other members of the intelligentsia who live on the West Side. Since it's just about 15 blocks (a short bus ride) from Lincoln Center, it makes sense to enjoy a delicious, reasonably priced meal here before or after a Lincoln Center event. Walk past the big mahogany bar up front and you'll find a dining room with natural-wood walls, butcher-block tables and booths, and a feeling that manages to be both intimate—so you can really sit and talk—and yet lively. The paintings and photographs on the walls were all done either by customers or by the aspiring artists and performers who wait on table with good cheer and courteous attention.

Teacher's specialties are the work of its artistic Thai cook, Sam for short, who turns out a lightly spiced chicken gai yaang, marinated and broiled in a special sauce and served with a cucumber salad, a hotter Thai beef salad, and a flavorful pork sate Indonesian, served on a skewer with a peanut-butter sauce, all from about $4.95 to $6.95. For those whose taste runs to French food, there are five dishes on the blackboard every night, including the likes of bouillabaisse and duck à l'orange; and they always have two broiled fresh (never frozen) fish dishes every night. These are superbly done, and cost from about $8 to $12. Teacher's is also known for its tasty spinach-and-bacon salad (if you find sand in it, your meal is on the house!), great appetizers like guacamole and toasted tortillas or homemade country pâté, and luscious desserts of which the praline ice-cream cake and the apple pound cake are standouts. Lunch is a bargain, from $3.25 to $5.25. Come on Sunday between 11 a.m. and 4 p.m. and indulge in one of the liveliest brunches in town—eggs Benedict, eggs rancheros, caviar and sour cream, and the like, from $3.95 to $6, with a cocktail thrown in for good measure.

If Teacher's is too crowded, walk one block north to **Teacher's Too,** an exact duplicate of the original restaurant at Broadway and 81st St. which has the added blessing of a summer sidewalk café. The menu here has a few more Asian specialties—scrumptious! Better yet, phone either place for reservations: Teacher's at 787-3500, Teacher's Too at 362-4900. Both restaurants are open Sunday to Thursday from 11 a.m. to 1 a.m., until 2 a.m. on Friday and Saturday.

After your meal, saunter next door to Zabar's, the city's prime appetizing emporium (open practically all the time), and just try to resist the heady aromas of fresh breads, wursts, cheeses, spices, and . . .

Julia's, 226 West 79th St., just east of Broadway (tel. 787-1511), is a knockout of a new restaurant that's been playing to happy crowds since its opening in 1983. Not only is the food exceptional, but Julia's is so quaint and provincial looking—with its tiny, year-round garden (enclosed by a skylight atrium in winter), with with fresh flowers at every table—that you feel you might be at a small café in, say, the south of France. And while there are French, Italian, and American accents to the menu, better to call the food "market cuisine": owner Arthur Meola and his chef (and his mother Julia, for whom the restaurant is named) work with whatever is fresh (never frozen, not even herbs) in the market. The results are wondrous. Among the appetizers ($2.75 to $3.75), don't miss the fritter of goat cheese with salad, a true taste explosion—light and crispy on the outside, mouthwateringly soft on the inside. Another house specialty—have it as a main course at lunch or as an appetizer at dinner—is the grilled chicken or veal sausage called boudin blanc, served with a delicious chunky applesauce. The sausages, like many other dishes, are done on a big charcoal grill which imparts a luscious flavor. For dinner, you can have grilled steak with steak butter and french fries, grilled lamb chops with thyme, fresh fish of the day grilled on an open flame, with very delicate sauces that allow the flavor of the food to speak for itself. Grilled meats are $7.95 to $15.95; fish is $7 to $15. Two or three pastas from a rotating selection of 35 are offered every day, and they too are different: how about pasta with bacon and sun-dried tomatoes, or linguini with anchovies and garlic in oil? (Pastas run $7 to $8.) Lunch is modestly priced, with burgers, omelets, sausage, and the like under $5.

Don't even think of skipping dessert here: Aunt Carmela's cheesecake, made from a family recipe, is a lemony, very light ricotta cake; and the coffee toffee pie is sinfully rich and worth every calorie.

Julia's is open every day from 11 a.m. to 2 a.m., for lunch, brunch, dinner, and supper (remember it after a concert at Lincoln Center).

Shelter, 2180 Broadway, corner of 77th St. (tel. 362-4360), is a delightful café, with a very simpatico, laid-back atmosphere. You can sit in the charming glass-enclosed café if you choose, or move inside to the lively bar-lounge area and the dining room with its dark woods, plants, and European posters. The menu is well priced, with most dishes from $5.75 to $8.95—and that includes some of our personal favorites, like the whole grilled baby chicken with wild rice, broiled bay scallops, roast duck with Grand Marnier or plum-ginger sauce, and barbecued spare ribs. You might start your meal with a tasty fresh mozzarella, tomato, onion, and basil salad, or a hearty soup. Pasta selections are varied and authentic. Burgers, club sandwiches, curried chicken salad, and other light fare are always on the menu. And the fresh fruit pies and layer cakes are great for dessert. Lunch features similar specialties, and Saturday and Sunday brunch are of particular value, since the price of your entree ($4.95 to $7.95) includes a drink, juices, an appetizer, and beverage.

Shelter is open daily from 11:30 a.m. to 4 o'clock in the morning.

Classy Bargains on 72nd Street

One of the Upper West Side's busiest thoroughfares boasts two handsome restaurants, both under the same management, that are among the classiest bargains in town. If your taste runs to barbecued chicken and ribs, then Dallas Jones Bar-B-Q is your cup of tea; if you prefer pasta, both Eastern and Western styles, try Noodles, just across the street. Either way, you'll be served tasty food in handsome settings at prices that went out of style years ago.

Arrive early, or you'll have to wait in line (they do not take reservations) at **Dallas Jones Bar-B-Q,** 27 West 72nd St. (tel. 873-2004). The crowds are drawn by the beautiful room—a two-level space with flowers and candlelight, soft chairs, modern art on the walls—the band music on weekends and piano other nights, and the food: expertly charcoal-grilled chicken and ribs, at prices from about $2.95 to $8.95. Side orders of vegetable tempura loaf and onion loaf, huge enough for several famished eaters (about $3), should not be missed, and desserts are outrageously good. Crowded, noisy, and lots of fun, Dallas Jones Bar-B-Q is open every day from noon to midnight or 1 a.m.

Noodles, 40 West 72nd St. (tel. 873-3550), is a different kind of charmer—soft, quiet, with spacious seating, candlelight, solicitous service, an atmosphere that makes you want to sit and linger. Against a Mediterranean kitchen background—white stucco walls, beamed ceiling, red-and-white checkered tablecloths—you can dine on noodles from either the East or the West, which means Oriental and Italian dishes at ridiculously low prices: most entrees are $3.95, $4.95, or $5.95—just a few are in the $7.95 to $9.95 category. Our favorite here is the cellophane noodles, sauteed with mixed vegetables and egg, a Korean specialty, but also very good are the soba noodles—that's buckwheat noodles in Japanese broth with crispy tempura vegetables. Among the Italian entrees, we like the linguine with white clam sauce, the pasta primavera, and for an appetizer, a generous antipasto that is almost a meal in itself ($5.95). The special chopped house salad at $3.95 would delight any health-food fan. Especially nice is the basket of delicious hot garlic bread brought to your table as soon as you are seated, and kept refilled without your having to ask. That, plus a glass of wine, will keep you contented until you get your food, which is all cooked to order. The dessert menu is limited pretty much to homemade strudel (try the blueberry cheese!), and there's cappuccino and espresso to top things off.

For those seated before 6:30 p.m. Monday to Saturday (before 6 p.m. on Sunday), there's a special pre-theater dinner for two at an unheard-of $10.95: that includes choice of soup or salad, any entree except seafood dishes and specials ($3 more), garlic bread, beverage, and dessert.

Noodles serves dinner only, from 5 p.m. to 1 a.m. on Friday and Saturday, 5 p.m. to midnight Monday through Thursday, and on Sunday from 4 to 11 p.m.

Figuring that you can't have too much of a good thing, the same people who run Shelter have three other restaurants around town, all with similar ambience, menus, and prices. Close to the Lincoln Center area, at 269 Columbus Ave., between 72nd and 73rd Sts. (tel. 873-9400), there's **Ruppert's.** Its 40-seat outdoor café will allow you a prime vantage point from which to watch the people parade on Columbus. Indoors, you'll enjoy the delightful mood of an 1877 saloon restored to its turn-of-the-century Victorian atmosphere, so pretty with its mirrors and mahogany, big bar, forest-green leather banquettes. Dinner items like grilled butterfly leg of lamb with shallot butter, shrimp in a beer batter, curried chicken salad, and fish and pastas of the day run between $5.95 and $14.95. A nice choice at lunch, which will cost between $4.95 and $7.95, is the seafood salad, a marvelous mixture of shrimp, clams, mussels, and calamari.

Over on the East Side, there's the original **Ruppert's,** 1662 Third Ave. at 93rd St. (tel. 831-1900), a big favorite with the Upper East Side crowd: and farther downtown, at 30th St., still another **Shelter,** 540 Second Ave. (tel. 684-4207).

At Lincoln Center

Practically an annex to Lincoln Center, and just across the street from it, the **Ginger Man,** 51 West 64th St. (tel. 399-2358), one of the first English-style pubs in town, has for over 20 years been the place to go for a bite after the opera or theater or ballet. Over omelets and burgers and rich desserts, you can mingle with everyone from audience members to superstars. The Ginger Man is a good place for lunch, pre-concert dinner, and Sunday brunch, as well as light supper or snacks. Watch the crowd go by from the enclosed sidewalk café outdoors, or move indoors into one of the several dining rooms, each with tables widely spaced for comfort and privacy, and with special charms: some have real marble fireplaces (working), one even has a balcony.

Dinner specials change every day, but you can always count on finding roast duck with fresh apples and cognac, rack of lamb with garlic and white wine sauce, spinach salad with ham, mushrooms, and fresh watercress, on the regular menu; prices run from $10.50 to $19.95 (for shell steak). For lunch you could have sandwiches and hamburgers, omelets, soup and salad, or entrees like broiled filet of sole, calf liver au poivre, or lamb brochettes—from $6 to $12. All desserts are homemade, cost around $4, and vary from day to day; try the lemon and lime mousse or the upside-down apple gingerbread, if they're available. Sunday brunch is a treat at $9.95, prix-fixe.

The Ginger Man is open for lunch Monday through Saturday from 11:30 a.m. to 5 p.m., for brunch on Sunday from 11:30 a.m. to 4 p.m., and for dinner Monday through Saturday from 5 p.m. to midnight, on Sunday from 4 to 11 p.m.

You don't need tickets for the Metropolitan Opera House to hear some beautiful singing at Lincoln Center. Just have dinner at **The Maestro,** 68 West 65th St. (tel. 787-5990), and while you're dining on very good continental cuisine, you can also hear impromptu performances by Metropolitan Opera stars, Broadway talents, or the staff of the Maestro itself—all of it presided over by Maestro Larry Woodward, who sits at the grand piano, playing, singing, and orchestrating the evening of impromptu performances. It all seems very casual—as if you just happened to be having friends over for dinner who had great voices. The setting is a sophisticated one, done in soft pinks and grays, the large room broken up into intimate dining areas, with murals of musicians on the walls. It's the kind of place where you'll want to linger and talk.

As for the food, entrees run about $12 to $15, and include an excellent poached red snapper, a tasty shrimp bamboo (marinated in a cognac and soy sauce), excellent grilled lamb chops, and veal scaloppine. Don't miss the friand de brie (melted brie in a light pastry) for an appetizer, or the chocolate mousse cake with mocha sabayon for dessert. Maestro serves lighter fare at lunch, including sandwiches and omelets; it has a lavish Sunday buffet brunch, served against a classical music background, prix-fixe at $13.95. And it's so pleasant after Lincoln Center, when you can rehash the performances over burgers or croques, omelets, desserts, or even champagne and caviar.

The Maestro is open daily, serving lunch Monday to Saturday from 11:30 a.m. to 4 p.m., dinner Monday to Sunday from 5 to 11 p.m., late-night supper Wednesday to Sunday from 11 p.m. to closing, and Sunday brunch from noon to 4 p.m.

Also very popular at Lincoln Center is the **Saloon,** 1920 Broadway at 64th St. (tel. 874-1500), a bustling and attractive place, with an invitingly spacious sidewalk café open in nice weather, and a menu that has something for just about everyone's taste, whether it be a burger or an omelet, fresh fruit salad with crème fraîche or a hot salad of wild mushrooms and fresh salmon, or roast chicken with black olives. Prices begin at $4.95 for burgers, with most meat and fish entrees from $9.25 to $15.95, and specials of soup, main dishes, dessert, and wines every day. They'll see that you get to your Lincoln Center event promptly if you tell them you have a curtain to make. And after the concert, plenty of luscious desserts, a variety of coffees, teas, and mineral waters, and an extensive wine list make this a perfect place for discussing the niceties of the performance. Yes, they do have roller-skating waiters.

The Saloon is open every day from 11:30 a.m. until 2 a.m. for food, until 4 a.m. for libations.

The best bargain in the Lincoln Center area has to be **The Milestone,** 70 West 68th St., just east of Columbus Ave. (tel. 874-3679), a cozy, homey place run by a family who take great pride in the cooking, the service, and the friendly atmosphere. There are several pretty rooms, one with a fireplace, another with a skylight, another a garden room and bar. The menu is a mix of Italian and continental dishes priced from about $9 to $10.50. Italian dishes change every week, but often include chicken Sorrento, pasta carbonara (pastas are very fresh and sauces are imaginative), chicken or veal parmigiana. Fish and seafood dishes are beautifully done; shark filet Provençal, for one, is a favorite. Entrees come with vegetable or starch, and salad is extra. There are usually raisin pumpernickel rolls from a famous local bakery on the table, and desserts are made in the Milestone's own kitchen: hot butterscotch sundae and walnut chocolate-chip pie are two of our favorites.

The Milestone does not accept reservations, so get there early unless you want to wait. Dinner is served from 5 until 10:45 p.m.

Tuesday through Friday, on Saturday from 4:30 p.m. Closed Sunday and Monday.

Mexican

Since it's right in the heart of the theater district, **El Tenampa,** 304 West 46th St. (tel. 664-8519), has become somewhat of a hangout for theater folk: one well-known Broadway star used to eat in the kitchen here. It's fun, too, if you're on your way to the theater, and even more fun after the theater crowd clears out and you can spend a whole evening pretending you're in Mexico. This cozy little colonial-style place, cheerfully decorated, is a husband-and-wife operation, with the friendly Marco Holderbaum, an auto-racer by passion and restaurateur by profession, and his wife Olivia cooking up marvelous traditional dishes. Go with all sorts of combination plates ($7 at lunch, $8 at dinner), or try some of the specialties like pollo mole poblano (chicken with Mexican chocolate sauce) or chiles nogada estilo Pueblo (peppers stuffed with cheese and covered with cream and nut sauce), around $7 to $8. Be sure to tell the waiter whether you want your food mildly seasoned, moderately seasoned, or positively mouth-burning: he'll oblige. We can't resist the spicy appetizers like nachos and quesadillas, a good glass of wine or beer to cool it all off, and some refreshing fried bananas with honey for the finale. Lunch, priced even more modestly, is served weekdays only, noon to 3 p.m., dinner, every day from 5 to 11:30 p.m.

You might not think of going all the way to Ninth Avenue and 18th Street for Mexican food, but knowing that you can eat all you want for $6.95 in a charming atmoshpere is more than enough incentive to hop in a cab and head for **La Cascada Café,** 132 Ninth Ave. (tel. 255-6529). The setting is delightful: flickering candles on white tablecloths, large terracotta Mexican tiles covering the floor, even a waterfall behind the bar. And the $6.95 "all-you-can-eat" deal means you help yourself to as much as you like of tacos, enchiladas, tostadas, burritos, tamales, mussels à La Cascada, with extras of chips, sauce, rice, and beans, plus a glass of sangría. It's served from Tuesday through Sunday, and believe us, it's good. Of course there's another menu, also well priced, and with many excellent specialties. It's fun for two of you to start with the mixed Mexican appetizer ($6.95) and sample all the available first courses. For your main dishes, priced from about $6.25 to $10.95, you'll do well with chicken Zapata (chicken with green tomatoes, white wine, and garlic), the lobster and shellfish in broth called mariscada, and the pollo mole poblano (chicken in Mexican chocolate sauce). Margaritas, piña coladas, and banana daiquiris can precede your meal, sangría can accompany it, and chocolate decadence cake can add the final touch. Saturday and Sunday brunch means omelets with guacamole and cheese and the like, eggs "your style," burgers, and salads, all served with a drink and coffee for $6.95—the magic number here.

La Cascada is open seven days a week for dinner from 5 to 11:30 p.m., Saturday and Sunday for brunch from noon to 5 p.m.

Seafood

We sometimes wonder if New Yorkers—or at least New York seafood lovers—could continue to survive without **Paddy's Clam House**, 215 West 34th St. (tel. CH 4-9123). Since 1898, it's been drawing huge crowds, manages to keep its prices ridiculously low, and sends everybody home happy. They must be doing something right.

Paddy's, however, is no place for romantic dawdling over your meal; ravenous seafood lovers are always waiting for a table, and the atmosphere is far from intimate. It *is* the place for delicious, absolutely fresh fish, beautifully prepared and promptly dispatched to your table. The atmosphere is noisy, friendly, and lots of fun, with no frills at all. Lunch is a bargain at Paddy's: for around $5.45 you can have a fish or clam chowder appetizer, and entree of fresh fish that changes every day, french fries or boiled potato, dessert, and coffee. There's a similar dinner special every night for about $7.99. Other crowd pleasers include a broiled lobster dinner, broiled scampi with garlic butter, and varied seafood combinations, all at prices much lower than elsewhere. Many kinds of pies for dessert; beer and liquor are available.

Paddy's is open from 11 a.m. to 9:30 p.m. Monday through Saturday, and from noon to 8 p.m. on Sunday and holidays.

Some Theater District Favorites

An extremely popular, usually jam-packed Italian restaurant in the heart of the theater district is **Johnnie's,** a small and intimate place at 135 West 45th St. (tel. 869-5565). If you have to wait for a table, you can do so comfortably in the friendly bar, and if you're planning to dine before the theater, we suggest you make reservations. In addition to the à la carte menu, Johnnie's offers an old-fashioned bargain dinner for about $9.95, and hearty and complete it is. You begin with minestrone, piping hot and thick with fresh vegetables. For your main entree, you have a choice including chicken parmigiana, sausage and peppers, baked ziti, and chicken liver sauté. There's rum cake, tortoni, or spumoni for dessert, and coffee, too, for the one price. Lunch at Johnnie's is another bargain: daily specials, served with soup, dessert, and beverage, average $7.95. Lunch is served from 11:30 a.m. to 3 p.m. Monday to Friday; dinner, from 3 p.m. to 1 a.m. daily (on Sunday, noon to midnight).

There's a little restaurant in the theater district that's so good you'll often find a line out on the street waiting to get in. That's **King Crab,** 871 Eighth Ave. at 52nd St. (tel. 765-4393), and what those hungry folks are waiting for every evening from 5 p.m. on is delicious fresh fish (generally broiled) and seafood here at reasonable prices, served by friendly young people in a warm and artistic atmosphere. The splendid old marble bar was once the soda fountain at the old drugstore that King Crab replaced: antiques, paintings, Tiffany-type lamps, old wood carvings, and flowers lend a graceful touch. Our favorite specialties of the day here are red snapper, salmon steak, or bluefish, served with saffron rice or baked potato, vegetables, and salad, $5.95 to $8.50. There are always seafood selections like shrimp, scallops, and Alaskan king crab legs (from $8.95 to $14.95), an excellent clam chowder, big whole-wheat rolls on the table at lunch, garlic bread at dinner. On no account should you pass up dessert: the chocolate and praline cheesecakes, baked by Montana Palace, are among the wonders of New York. Lunch is an especially good buy: fish of the day, with rice and vegetables, is just $3.95. The owner and chefs at King Crab all hail from Thailand; that, we've found, usually means superior cooking and caring. King Crab serves lunch from noon to 3:30 p.m. weekdays, dinner every day from 5 p.m. to midnight.

For more of the King Crab type of culinary magic, try **K.C.'s Place,** a sister restaurant at 809 Ninth Ave. at 54th St. (tel. 246-4258). It's worth a visit here just to see the artful decor: a large green grasshopper lamp floating on the ceiling, warm chocolate-brown walls, tulip-shaped gaslight lamps (with real fire), mirrors, Tiffany-style lamps, stained-glass murals, a chandelier of shells, tropical foliage set in enormous urns—a fascinating juxtaposition of period pieces, objets d'art, and Victoriana. Amid all this splendor, it might be hard to concentrate on the menu, so relax—everything is good, fresh, and well priced. Entrees of fish of the day, ranging from $7.45 for brook trout to $8.25 for striped bass, include salad, a vegetable, and rice or potato, as do such seafood specialties as Alaskan king crab legs at $10.95, or bouillabaisse for two at $22. Thai entrees, $5.95 to $9.75, include a sauteed vegetable plate for vegetarian types, chicken gai yaang, and a fiery deep-fried whole sea bass with hot sauce. Sunday brunch, around $5.25, is a filler, with two Bloody Marys (or screwdrivers, wine, or beer), and such dishes as steak and eggs, eggs Benedict, and the like.

K.C.'s Place is open daily, serving lunch every day but Saturday from noon to 4 p.m., dinner every day from 4 to 10:30 p.m. There's another K.C.'s Place at 45 Lexington Ave., between 24th and 25th Sts. (tel. 532-6402), on the East Side, which is closed on Sunday.

Looking for a new dining adventure? Try **Empañadas Etc.,** 257 West 55th St. (tel. 247-3140), where a delightful bit of Argentina awaits you. Empañadas, in case you never knew, are a national snack for the Argentinians, little crescents of puffed pastry stuffed with various fillings, and eaten in combination with other dishes at a meal, or alone, standing up or on the run. Empañadas to go are available at the take-out counter, but we suggest that you sit down and relax in the very pretty setting with its fountain and tiny garden, and have a real meal. Dinner allows you to mix and match any empañada with either soup or salad and a main dish of, perhaps, pastel de choclo, mixed grill, créole shrimp or pork chops, all for $10.95 to $12.95, including french fries. More modestly, for around $6, you could have a pasta dish, a generous salad plate, or a hearty Argentine-style omelet called a tortilla. At lunchtime, it's mix-and-match empañadas with a variety of soups, stews, or salads, from $3.75 to $6.95. At either meal, don't miss the desserts: balcarse (meringue cake with peaches, walnuts, whipped cream) and dulce de leche (a sweetened, caramellike milk) can only be described as, ah . . . an experience. There are imported wines from Argentina, Chile, and Italy, plus beers, sangría, herb teas, espresso, and cappuccino.

Empañadas Etc. is open daily from 11 a.m. to midnight.

Fondues and Fromage

It's a cheese-lover's idea of Paradise, and even if you don't know your Emmenthal from your Esrom, we think you'll still enjoy a visit to **La Fondue,** at 43 West 55th St. (tel. 581-0820). Owned by one of the largest cheese importers and retailers in the city, La Fondue is a brick-walled, provincial-looking French place, crowded and noisy at the busier times of the day, with small, too-close-together tables, like so many of the restaurants dispensing food in New York. But if you come late-ish for lunch, or on a weekday for dinner, you'll really have the time and comfort for enjoying the quality food. There are three kinds of fondues—the classic Swiss cheese fondue, $6.85; the prime filet mignon fondue, $12.95; and a heavenly chocolate fondue, $3.95 —plus a variety of cheese and sausage boards, excellent quiches and croques, even le cheeseburger, all modestly priced à la carte. Pasta primavera with pesto and fish dishes are new on the menu. Five-course dinners have plenty of cheese choices (from quiche Lorraine to cheddar cheese soup to fondue to cheesecake), and most are under $14. For non-cheese-eaters, there's prime broiled filet mignon, sirloin, chicken, and burgers. Lunch is all à la carte, with plenty to eat from $5.25 to $8.95. Cider, beer, and wine, plus Swiss grape juice are available, as well as cocktails. On your way out, you can stop at the retail store and take some cheese— or a fondue pot—back to your hotel! La Fondue is open seven days a week, from noon to midnight, on Friday and Saturday to 12:30 a.m., and on Sunday to 11 p.m.

The Chelsea Contingent

As neighborhoods change, so do the restaurants in them. New places are blossoming all over Chelsea, an old neighborhood that's going through a major facelifting. Restaurants here tend to be more relaxed and less expensive than their counterparts uptown. A case in point is **Moran's Chelsea Fish House,** 146 Tenth Ave. at 19th St. (tel. 929-9379), an Irish bar more than a century old that's been made into a most appealing seafood house. The huge old mahogany bar is still here, along with a blazing fireplace, Tiffany-type lamps, a mahogany breakfront with old glass, a pressed-tin ceiling, a mix of nautical and Irish artifacts here and there. The overall atmosphere is charming, complete to the colleens who wait table, their brogues fresh from the old country. We like the big room in back, where you can sink into the atmosphere and ponder the daily blackboard specials, deciding whether to have, perhaps, poached salmon, a broiled seafood combination (scallops, shrimp, sole, and clams on a bed of rice in the lightest of cream sauces—wonderful!), soft-shell crabs, or tempura shrimps, deep-fried and wrapped in bacon. Most run between ($9.50 and $12.50). On the printed menu, you can't go wrong with the fried seafood plates and the linguini Moran—shrimp, scallops, and mussels, both around $9.50. Raspberry linzer torte, key lime pie, and chocolate walnut pie are the star desserts here, a bit too sweet for our taste. But the Irish coffee is a winner—so are the drinks, and so is the place. A new garden and patio are making it nicer than ever.

Moran is open seven days a week, serving basically the same menu at lunch and dinner, from noon to midnight.

Palm trees in pots and conch shells on the walls, latticework dividers and whirling ceiling fans, mirrors which reflect the predominant tropical colors of blue and green—all are part of the scheme of things at **Claire**, 156 Seventh Ave., between 19th and 20th Sts. (tel. 255-1955). Or you might say the theme of things, which is Key West, where the owners have another restaurant of the same name. The island theme carries over into the food some of the time (Bahamian conch chowder, pompano, red snapper, Key West grouper, and key lime pie, for example), but is much broader than that, including continental and even Thai specialties—thanks to the Thai chef, you might have Thai beef salad marinated in hot chilis and exotic Thai spices ($6.95) as an appetizer, or the broiled Cornish game hen with gai yaang sauce ($8.95) as a tasty main course. Appropriately, fish dominates the menu. Cold mussels with New Orleans-style rémoulade sauce and ceviche of fresh tuna with dill and capers ($4 and $5, respectively) are also good choices for starters. Two of our favorites among the entrees are broiled Norwegian salmon with cucumber-dill sauce, and monkfish with capers, pimientos, and pesto; served with rice and vegetables, fish dishes run between $10 and $15. Key lime pie seems to be the obvious dessert to order, but the Grand Marnier mousse, Mississippi mud cake with whiskey sauce, and a variety of chocolate confections are also mouthwatering. Claire is also one of the nicest places in New York for lunch; it's sunny, colorful and elegant, and prices are a few dollars less for similar entrees as at dinner. Omelets, burgers, and sandwiches run about $5. Claire is stylish and fun, and the well-dressed Seventh Avenue crowd that patronizes it obviously adores it; were it not for the high noise level (unmitigated by the bare wooden floor) we would give it an unqualified rave.

Claire serves lunch Monday through Saturday from noon to 4 p.m., Sunday brunch from noon to 4 p.m., and dinner from 5:30 p.m. to 12:30 a.m. daily.

No need to go to New Orleans for authentic Cajun and Créole cooking, now that **Cajun** is in town, at 129 Eighth Ave. at 16th

St. (tel. 691-6174). The genial host-owner, Herb Maslin, is about as authentically Créole as anyone born in Brooklyn could be, but when he retired from an engineering career a few years back, he spent a good bit of time in New Orleans researching the local cooking and came back with a concept and a cuisine that always keeps this neighborhood restaurant packed. The combination of tasty food, unfashionably low prices, and authentic Dixieland jazz bands Wednesday through Sunday nights is obviously a winner. The atmosphere is all Bourbon Street: the front bar area has red stucco walls and wrought-iron grillwork; the back is a long room with posters and murals on the wall, oilcloth tablecovers—nothing fancy, but very warm and cosy. The country cooking of the Cajun people is skillfully mixed with the more sophisticated French and Spanish influences on the menu here. Shrimp and oyster dishes are among the specialties of the house, so you might want to start, for example, with fresh shucked oysters on the half shell ($7.95 for a delicious dozen), spicy broiled shrimp in the shell ($4.75), or oysters Rockefeller ($3.95 for three). Don't miss the steaming gumbo soup of the day. Menu prices run from $5.95 to $8.95, and these include meaty barbecued spare ribs, stuffed eggplant with oysters, gougonettes of sole, and our personal favorite, the shrimp Tchoupitoulas, the chef's own Créole-style creation of shrimp, mushrooms, and artichoke hearts in a tangy garlic and white wine sauce (terrific!). Two or three specialties running between $9.95 and $12.95 are offered every night. Desserts are unforgettable: it's hard to choose between the Créole bread pudding with its creamy whiskey sauce, an authentic southern pecan pie, and deep-fried, crispy sweet beignets. Of course the coffee is blended with chicory; stronger beverages include Sazeracs, brandy milk punch and Ramos gin fizz.

Cajun's menu is the same at lunch, and that might be just the time to experience a "po-boy"—New Orleans's sophisticated answer to the hero sandwich. Cajun's Sunday champagne brunch is probably the best buy in town: $5.95 complete for soup, entrees like New Orlean's pain perdu (french toast with Canadian bacon) or smoked turkey Rochambeau, served up with coffee, champagne, and a Dixieland jazz quartet. It's on from noon to 4 p.m.

Cajun serves lunch Monday through Friday from noon to 3 p.m., dinner Monday through Thursday from 6 to 11 p.m., on Friday and Saturday to 11:30 p.m. and on Sunday from 5:30 to 10:30 p.m. There is no cover or minimum at any time.

One of the nicest things about the Chelsea renaissance has got to be **Rogers & Barbero,** 149 Eighth Ave., between 17th and 18th Sts. (tel. 243-2020). It's won bravos from the food establishment as well as from the neighborhood people and theater-goers en route to the nearby Joyce Theater. Tables are well spaced for conversation in the lovely blue- and-white art deco dining room. American regional dishes are among the specialties here, so you might have pan-fried trout in cornmeal, a hearty pot roast, or southern fried chicken. Some unusual items with a nouvelle touch are the herbed pork loin with apple butter demiglâcé; chicken in parchment with jalapeño, tomato, and apricots; and calf liver with hot maple garlic vinaigrette. Most entrees run from $9 to $13. Among the appetizers, which run from $3.95 to $6.75, we like the tomato fritters with basil hollandaise sauce and the skewered shrimp with a sweet red pepper puree. For lunch you can have anything from a BLT to fresh fish, from shirred eggs with Novia Scotia salmon to a minute steak, from $5 to $8. The late-night supper menu runs the gamut from hamburger platters and omelets to T-bone steak. And Saturday and Sunday brunch is a special treat: flapjacks, sausage, and apples, blinis, and American caviar are served up along with the shirred eggs and omelets, most entrees in the $5.50 to $6.25 category. At any of these meals, you can enjoy the "Seriously Chocolate Cake" for true chocolate fanatics, a hearty banana split, or a refreshing raspberry mouse. Then it will be time for a cappuccino or an espresso.

Rogers & Barbero serves dinner nightly from 6 p.m. to midnight, and late supper from midnight to 1 a.m. Lunch is on Monday through Friday from noon to 3 p.m.; Saturday and Sunday brunch from noon to 4 p.m.

Jewish Dairy Foods

The classic Jewish dairy dishes—blintzes, potato pancakes, kashe varnishkes, and the like—are no longer known only in cities like New York; cultural assimilation and food technology being what they are, blintzes are now frozen and sold in supermarkets as far away as Honolulu! And by a kind of reverse process, the famous dairy restaurants of New York are dwindling in number. Only a few are left, but happily, one of the best of these is found right in the heart of the busy midtown area: that's the 56-year-young **Farmfood Vegetarian Restaurant,** at 142 West 49th St. (tel. 719-1650). It's a big, busy, noisy place, and if you're in a hurry you can sit up at the counter and feast on a big bowl of soup (it may be borscht or schav or the great cabbage soup the day you're there) and black bread. Take one of the tables in the big back room for more relaxed dining. No meat is served at Farmfood (roasts and cutlets are made from nut meats), and no animal fats are used, but there are plenty of fish and cheese dishes. Many of the famous Jewish classics—cheese kreplach, potato pirogen, blintzes, kashe varnishkes with mushrooms—are here, priced around $5 to $7 or under. A full meal will probably run between $9 and $12. Since you're in the heart of smoked fish country, you might want to try a lox omelet, a chopped herring salad, or a plate of smoked whitefish. The Farmfood people are also health oriented and have long attracted health-food addicts with huge, fresh salads. The menu changes daily, but everything you eat here will be fresh, tasty, and old-fashionedly inexpensive.

Farmfood is open from 8 a.m. to 9 p.m. on weekdays, until midnight on weekends, except on Friday when it closes at 3 p.m. In keeping with rabbinical laws, the restaurant is closed on Saturday but reopens after sunset.

The uptown star of the sour-cream circuit is the **Famous Dairy Restaurant,** 222 West 72nd St. (tel. 874-8607), which is not far from the Lincoln Center area, and is fine for a blintz and a strudel before the Philharmonic. Every meal is accompanied by a basket of irresistible assorted rolls (fattening!), and the reasonably priced pastries are homemade and delicious. All meals are strictly kosher.

Should you find yourself downtown, bargain hunting on the Lower East Side (an activity we heartily recommend), you can have a great dairy-vegetarian-fish meal at **Ratner's,** 138 Delancey St., between Norfolk and Suffolk Sts. (tel. 677-5588). Prices are moderate and the food is fresh and delicious. Don't miss the pastries!

Note: Any of these restaurants is a fine place to make the acquaintance of that New York phenomenon, the Jewish waiter, who is often more temperamental, if less haughty, than a French maître d'. You may practically have to shout across a crowded room to get his attention (he is continually in motion), but be persistent. He is apt to be bossy and may want to make your selections for you, but be resolute. Actually, he is really a Jewish mother and only wants to help; he'll feel terrible if you don't enjoy your meal and eat it all up. So eat.

Two Popular Bistros

Over in the French neighborhood (Ninth Avenue in the 50s) is a small, attractive, and enormously popular restaurant heavily frequented by the local French population and knowledgeable New Yorkers who want a good and inexpensive French dinner. We refer, of course, to **Brittany du Soir,** 800 Ninth Ave. at 53rd St. (tel. 265-4820). Everything is à la carte. We could make a meal just on their delicious homemade soup, the potage fermier, the wonderful french bread, and a carafe of red wine. On the main courses, we usually take the moules marinières, mussels in wine sauce ($11 at dinner, $9.50 at lunch), but we can also vouch for the filet of sole ($10.25 and $8) and the noisette of lamb ($13 and $10.75). Dinner entrees are accompanied by salad, vegetables, and potato. Desserts range from a simple cheese with french bread to a lovely mousse. Entrees at lunch, served from noon to 2:45 p.m. weekdays, go from $6 to $11.25. Dinner is served Monday through Thursday from 5 to 11 p.m. , on Friday and Saturday until 10 p.m.

Not far from here, at 311 West 51st St., is **Tout Va Bien** (tel. 974-9051). This small, one-room French bistro, complete with red-checkered tablecloths, is a family affair, and its faithful clients have been coming here for years to partake of good, solid home-cooking—none of that fancy nouvelle stuff here. Entrees are reasonable priced—at dinner, the likes of coq au vin, boeuf bourguignon, frog legs, salade Niçoise and Cornish game hen range from $7 to $9; at lunch, they're about $1 cheaper. Hors d'oeuvres are excellent, especially the pâté maison and the haricots blancs avec onions (white beans with onions). Bouillabaisse is available on Friday at $15. Desserts include spumoni and tortoni, as well as the most expected French offerings like pêche Melba and poire Hélène.

Tout Va Bien is open for lunch Monday through Saturday from noon to 2:30 p.m., and for dinner from 5 to 11:30 p.m. Monday through Saturday. Closed Sunday. Tout Va Bien—it's all okay.

Soul Food

Since it's not too easy to find a really good soul-food restaurant in Manhattan south of Harlem, it's a treat to discover **Jack's Nest** at 59 West 56th St. near Sixth Ave. (tel. 399-0003), a casual place, popular with family groups. Here, in large and comfortable surroundings, you sit in big booths and feast on delicious southern fried chicken, hickory-smoked barbecued ribs, chicken smothered in gravy, whiting, croakers, or porgies, smoked ham-hock, or, of course, chitlins (pig intestines), all with your choice of black-eyed peas, candied yams, collard greens, plus corn bread, etc., and all at prices to quiet your soul: $5.25 to $6.95 at lunch, $8.75 to $10.25 at dinnertime. And although the portions are more than filling, such good home-cooking almost cries out for second helpings, which are available at reduced rates. For that special celebration, you could have the chitlins and cham-pagne, $11.25 at dinner, a rather royal Carolinian treat. Desserts include an exceptionally mouthwatering sweet-potato pie. Open every day from 11 a.m. to 11 p.m., until 2 a.m. on Friday and Saturday.

THE EAST SIDE: There are many interesting eateries up and down the main thoroughfares and little sidestreets of the East Side—and the fancy location does not necessarily mean fancy prices.

Mexican

No need to fly to Mexico City for a great meal—the afi-cionados consider **El Parador,** 325 East 34th St. (tel. 679-6812), on a level with the best anywhere. El Parador is done in a Mexican colonial motif, but it's so jammed with people that you probably won't notice the decor; they do not accept reservations, so be prepared to wait on line weekends. But you will notice the food: it's excellent. Mexican standbys like enchiladas, tacos, bur-ritos, and tostadas are $10.50, and hefty combination plates are a bit more. Fancier dishes, like the superb pollo Parador (one of the three Spanish dishes on the menu, steamed with onions and heady with garlic), the mole poblano (chicken in a spicy choco-late sauce), and the camarones en salsa tomatilla (shrimp in a mild green sauce), command fancier prices, from $11.75 to $13.75. The appetizers (around $4.50 to $6.50) are almost as good as the main dishes: we find it hard to choose between the guacamole, the ceviche (whitefish marinated in lime juice), and the nachos. The classic Mexican and Spanish desserts, flan and natilla, are here, as well as mango and guava shell preserves. And of course you'll want a cooling pitcher of sangría or some Carta Blanca or Moctezuma XX, imported Mexican cerveza, to go with the hot and spicy delicacies. El Parador serves dinner only, from 5 to 11 p.m. every night except Sunday.

French Fun

It's always open, it's always fun, and the food does not disappoint at **Brasserie,** 100 East 53rd St., in the Seagram Building (tel. PL 1-4840), one of midtown's most popular informal restaurants. The decor is brightly French Provincial, the menu a combination of French and Alsatian dishes, plus some French-American hybrids like fromage burgers. *Le déjeuner, le diner,* and *le souper* menus are mostly à la carte: Prince Igor (caviar) omelet, $6.25; choucroûte à l'Alsacienne, $9.75 (a house specialty); onion soup, $3.50; steak hambourgeois avec sauce champignons, $8.50. Complete dinners too, with entrees like roast duckling with orange sauce for around $17.95, served with hors d'oeuvres or soup, vegetables, dessert, and beverage. Lunch, with main courses like quiche Lorraine and eggs Benedict, goes from about $7.75 to $8.75. Lunch is from 11 a.m. to 5 p.m., dinner from 5 to 10 p.m., and supper from 10 p.m. to 6 a.m., perfect after an evening's entertainment. Open every day, 24 hours a day.

Créole Cooking

To celebrate Mardi Gras all year long, make reservations at **La Louisiana,** 132 Lexington Ave., between 28th and 29th Sts. (tel. 686-3959). The walls are as sandy and peachy in color as some of the houses in New Orleans, and the plants are as green as those in the gardens of that famed city. The bar is tiny, really a service bar, so you will want to have your drink at your table. Crudité de boeuf, paper-thin slices of fresh raw beef served with a mild sauce and a wickedly hot mustard, is certain to make you want another drink and feel as if you're in a southern climate; smoked breast of chicken with horseradish cream and a pepper sauce is another unusual treat for an appetizer; both are $4.50. Proceed on to the gumbo de jour, priced according to its ingredients, always authentic, thick, and outrageously tasty. You did want southern food, didn't you? There's southern fried chicken, southern fried steak, pork scallops with homemade butter, and catfish (grain fed, and don't ask how they do that), pan-fried and served with homemade tártar sauce—all these dishes are under $14. All entrees are served with rice and vegetables in vinaigrette. As for dessert, who can resist pecan pie at a place that specializes in southern food?

La Louisiana is a sister restaurant to Texarkana in Greenwich

Village, described above. It's open for dinner Monday through Saturday from 6 to 11:45 p.m.

Fancy, Unlimited

We doubt if there's another place in New York—or anywhere else for that matter—quite like **Serendipity.** Located at 225 East 60th St. (tel. TE 8-3531), a block behind Bloomingdale's, Serendipity is a way-out kicky country store that sells Tiffany shades and cinnamon toast, Hebrew eye charts and Zen hash, frivolous hats and frozen hot chocolate drinks. The prettiest people lunch and meet here for afternoon tea and after theater, over the marble-topped coffee tables, and while the food is on the whimsical side, there are times when fantasy is more fun than meat and potatoes. Personally, we have long found Serendipity to be one of the city's happier happenings. The "Serious Food" side of the menu features very good casseroles (curried chicken, burgundy beef, shepherd's pie), omelets, a foot-long chili hot dog, hamburgers, and the enticing Ftatateeta's toast. Zen hash and a variety of open-faced vegetable sandwiches are there for those on natural-food trips. Dishes go from about $4 to $7.50. But we wouldn't dream of coming here without indulging in the desserts: perhaps the heavenly apricot smush or the frozen mochaccino or the lemon ice-box pie or the dark-devil mousse. . . . Not to mention the glorious espressos and hot chocolates and spicy teas and chocolaccinos—but come and see for yourself. Serendipity is open Sunday to Thursday from 11:30 a.m. to 12:30 a.m., Friday to 1 a.m., Saturday to 2 a.m.

Czechoslovakian

A trip uptown to eat at **Csarda**, 1477 Second Ave., at 77th St. (tel. 472-2892), allows you to work in a little sightseeing with a good meal. For this is New York's Yorkville neighborhood, longtime home to thousands of Germans, Hungarians, Czechs, and Ukrainians. Now the population is changing as the high-rise, high-price apartment buildings of the Upper East Side move relentlessly north and east, but there are still plenty of Mittle-European beer halls and cafés, intriguing butcher shops, and fragrant spice and cookery emporiums to wander through (Paprikas Weiss, one of the best, at 81st St. and Second Ave., stays open until 6:30 p.m. for pre-dinner browsers). Almost all of the restaurants are good here, but Csarda is one of the best. The dining room is small and square, cheery with whitewashed walls bedecked with hand-painted plates, colorful rugs, and native costumes. As soon as you sit down, the menus and a dish of cucumber salad arrive at your table to whet your appetite. Traditional appetizers like stuffed cabbage, brains and eggs, and stuffed pepper are about $4, and too good to miss. Entrees run $9.50 to $11.75, and come with appropriate side dishes. One of the house specialties is a roast chicken with chicken liver stuffing under the skin; other good choices are the roast pork with sauerkraut, the veal paprikash with nokerl, and the crispy roast duck. Pilsner Urquell beer, brewed since 1292 in Pilzen, goes nicely with this type of food. (Wines and other beers are available, but no liquor.) Do save room for dessert. The strudels are all made here, and are served warm with powdered sugar; so are palacsintas, the Czech version of crêpes suzette.

Csarda is open Monday through Friday from 5 to 11 p.m. for dinner; on Saturday and Sunday from noon to 11 and 10 p.m.

Another family-run ethnic restaurant in the same neighborhood is **Vasata**, 339 East 75th St., between Second and First Aves. (tel. 650-1686). The setting is very comfortable, something right out of the old country—and so are many of the guests. Vasata has been popular with a Central European crowd for many years. Whitewashed brick walls are decorated with ceramic plates; crisp white cloths cover the tables. Czech cooking, we were told (and you will be too, if you question your waiter) is a combination of Russian, Hungarian, German, and Austrian cuisine (at the end of the meal you won't have to be told that it's rich and filling). The traditional appetizers—marinated herring, homemade pâté, headcheese with onions—are all here, priced modestly around $3.25. Entrees go from $6 to $11, and that includes the side dishes, like dumplings, potato salad, and sauerkraut. Main dishes include three kinds of veal schnitzel, pork chops, shish-kebab, fresh calf brains, and of course, the ever-popular roast duck. During the winter you can feast on roast goose (no need to wait for Christmas!) and on winter Thursdays you can usually get some form of game. Now for the desserts: poppyseed cakes, chocolate tarts, apple strudel and those wonderful palacsintas (here stuffed with either apricot preserves or chocolate sauce) are hard to resist.

Vasata is open Tuesday through Saturday from 5 to 11 p.m., on Sunday from noon to 10 p.m. Closed Monday.

Czechoslovakian warmth and largesse are also found in abundance at **Ruc**, 312 East 72nd St. (tel. 650-1611), as pretty as it is homey, with a pink, beige, and sienna motif heightened by brick arches, crystal chandeliers, hand-painted porcelain, folk paintings on the wall. There's more of this European atmosphere in the smaller Wintergarden, with hanging flower baskets and chandeliers that look like plants. And when the warm weather comes, around mid-May, as many as 150 people can be seated in the sunny, tree-filled, three-level garden. Indoors or out, however, you'll be treated to homemade, absolutely delicious food served in large portions. Specialties of the house are boiled beef with dill sauce (an unbelievable gift to your taste buds), roast loin of pork, roast Long Island duckling, and wienerschnitzel. Along with your main course comes beef and liver dumpling soup or cream of cauliflower soup, plus salad, vegetables or potato, desserts, and beverage. The price range for these complete dinners is a trifling $9.50 to $14, surely one of the best bargains left in New York! Although all of the homemade desserts are good, the apricot-filled palacsinta outshines them all. There's a small, well-priced wine list and wine available by the glass as well.

Ruc is open Monday to Friday from 5 to 10:30 p.m., on Saturday and Sunday from noon to 11 p.m.

Bargains Around the Clock

For some of the most generous meals in town at some of the most generous prices, it's hard to beat the **Green Kitchen,** First Ave. at 77th St. (tel. 988-4163), still going strong after almost half a century under the same family management. There are lots of comfortable booths inside amid the plants and Tiffany-type lamps, but it's fun to pick a seat at the glassed-in sidewalk café and watch the Upper East Side world saunter by as you dine on very good Greek and fish specialties at prices that went out of style years ago. You might try the eggplant moussaka with a small green salad or the boiled striped bass at $6.25; the price for this and other entrees (from $3.95 to $12.95, for steak) includes, amazingly enough, not just a complete plate, but a complete meal: soup, salad, vegetables, potato or rice, and homemade desserts. The side dishes are standard, the main courses excellent. Splurge a little bit and order the extraordinary Black Forest cake for an extra $1.50; it's baked right on the premises, as are all the pastries and the luscious soft bread that is brought to your table as soon as you sit down. Not only is the Green Kitchen easy on the pocketbook, but it also stays open every day, 24 hours a day, so it's perfect in the midst of the day of sightseeing or at the end of a night on the town.

The Natural Life

A gourmet natural-foods restaurant, a cut above the usual, is **Zucchini**, 1336 First Ave. at 72nd St. (tel. 249-0559), which offers lots more than zucchini: dinner in this attractively decorated little room with oak tables and antiques, plants, changing art exhibits, and (praise be) classical music in the background, is quite special. Best of the entrees—which include spanakopita, ratatouille Provençale, fish of the day (from about $5.50 to $9.50)—is the chicken India, an exquisite dish of tender chucks of chicken topped with a light curried cream sauce with a hint of ginger. Salad, pita bread, brown rice, veggies, and tofu or melted cheese accompany most entrees. Soups are homemade and fresh (cream of zucchini is excellent) and their chocolate cake, with its subtle almond flavor and a slice of lemon on the side—is truly something to shout about. Zucchini serves dinner from 5 to 10:30 p.m., lunch (quiches, soups, noodles, rice, and beans, etc.) from 11 a.m. to 4:30 p.m. daily.

Orchids to You

After you've had a meal at **The Orchid**, 81 Lexington Ave. at 26th St. (tel. 889-0960), you may want to send the people there a bouquet of flowers—or at least a corsage. The Orchid is that kind of rare place that serves excellent food in a pleasant yet unpretentious atmoshpere and keeps the tab refreshingly low. The room is intimate, darkly lit, done in black and white with the dark paneling that was here when the place was an Irish bar a quarter of a century ago, still intact. But the menu is very new—nouvelle American, in fact—with many imaginative touches which, in this instance, taste as good as they sound (not always the case in many restaurants). Dinner entrees, which range from about $10.95 to $14.95, always include a fish of the day, a sauteed sprout and vegetable dish, and a pasta; barbecued spare ribs, lemon chicken, chili, and beef stew are other regular favorites. No problem at all if all you want is a burger or salad—they're on the dinner menu, too. Appetizers are especially good, particularly the homemade strudels, soups, and bisques (everything is made from scratch; nothing canned is ever used). Lunch features a strudel of the day with tossed salad, lots of good omelets (our favorite is the caviar, sour cream, and scallion), burgers, and salads. Wonderful desserts like chocolate mousse pie and walnut pie should not be overlooked at either meal.

Specials change daily for lunch, dinner, and Saturday and

A Trio of Top Delis

New York has long been famous for its Jewish delicatessens, but the genuine article is no longer so easy to find. True mavens advise: avoid all imitations and head directly for any of these three places, where the traditions of succulent corned beef and spicy pastrami, greasy gribenes and calorific chopped liver (rice with chicken fat) are still honored. On the East Side, the new **Kaplan's at the Delmonico,** in the Delmonico Hotel at 59 East 59th St. (tel. PL 5-5959), is as its name implies, the classiest of the lot, and the closest replacement to the late, lamented Reuben's. High marks go to the deli sandwiches, as well as to such oldtime favorites as chicken or beef in the pot, Roumanian tenderloin, stuffed cabbage, and potato latkes. Prices range from about $5.25 to $9, for sandwiches and main dishes. On the West Side, the shrine for deli lovers is right near the shrine for music lovers: **Carnegie Delicatessen,** 854 Seventh Ave. near 55th St. (tel. 757-2245), has practiced, practiced for years to turn out some of the juiciest and most flavorful corned beef on ryes in New York. Main courses are also tasty, and prices are similar to Kaplan's. The best prices (about $1 less per sandwich) can be found downtown at the long-beloved **Second Avenue Delicatessen,** 156 Second Ave. at the corner of 10th St. (tel. 677-0606), where you may have to stand in line to sample the superlative chopped liver, the complete and delicious meals from about $8 to $12.50 A new café room, named after Molly Picon and decorated with memorabilia from her career, adjoins the plain main dining room. The meat is kosher, and portions are generous.

Sunday brunch—one of the most unusual in town in that, in addition to very good brunch fare (french toast with fruit salad and sausages or eggs Benedict and eggs au gratin, for example), the fixed price, $9.95, includes unlimited selections of Bloody Marys, screwdrivers, wine, coffee, and tea.

The Orchid serves weekday lunch from noon to 5 p.m., Saturday and Sunday brunch from noon to 4 p.m.; dinner daily from 5 to 11:30 p.m., until 12:30 a.m. on Saturday, when there's live music.

GREENWICH VILLAGE AND POINTS SOUTH: Perhaps the largest variety of inexpensive restaurants is in this area. Along with your food, enjoy the unique ambience that makes the Village so special.

Italian Favorites

The bargain meal is still available in Italian restaurants that have been sustaining Villagers and visitors for years. We have a quartet of favorites here where prices are very moderate—most entrees run from $7 to $12—and the food very good in the grand old southern Italian tradition. You'll do very well at any of the following: **Grand Ticino,** 228 Thompson St. (tel. 777-5922); **Rocco's,** 181 Thompson St. (tel. 677-0590); **Villa Mosconi,** 69 MacDougal St. (tel. 673-0390), and **Villa Eda,** 131 Bank St. (tel. 924-3787). For delicious northern Italian food in this era, try **Trattoria da Alfredo,** 90 Bank St. (tel. 291-2930) and its sister restaurant, **Tavola Calda da Alfredo,** 285 Bleecker St. (tel. 924-4789). Have desserts at these restaurants or, even better, visit one of the famous Italian caffès of the Village—ideal for a cappuccino on ice or a piping hot espresso, great places to sit, talk, play a game of chess, read the papers—or just watch the world whirl by. Our favorite caffes on MacDougal Street are **Caffe Dante** at no. 79 and **Caffe Reggio** at no. 119. **Caffe Lucca,** at 228 Bleecker St. is more spacious than these and another pleasant place to linger, and so is **The Peacock,** 24 Greenwich Ave.

Steaks

Generations of hungry Villagers have soothed their appetites for steak at one of the most pleasant and unpretentious of restaurants, the **Blue Mill Tavern,** 50 Commerce St. (tel. CH 3-7114). Almost hidden amid century-old houses in a quaint and quiet part of the Village, it is still within walking distance of many off-Broadway theaters. Come in for a drink and sit at the bar, or arrive for lunch or dinner and sit in the main room where beige walls, small tables pushed together, and white tablecloths outline the warm simplicity of this place. The menu has slight, occasional changes, but you can always count on the small steak at about $9, it's excellent, well seasoned and done to perfection, and adequate for all but the largest of appetites. Other good choices are the sea trout at $9, the chopped sirloin at $5, and the sirloin at $12. All meals come with salad or vegetables, and home-fried potatoes, all served family style, so this is a place where you can really save those dollars.

Blue Mill Tavern is open for dinner Monday through Thursday from 5 to 10:30 p.m., until 11:30 on Friday and Saturday. Closed Sunday.

Real charcoal-broiled steaks are a rarity in New York (many steakhouses use gas-fired briquettes), and it's hard to believe that you can still get them for a reasonable price at the **Derby Steakhouse,** at 109 MacDougal St. (tel. 475-0520). This pleasant restaurant, with its brick walls, floor of multicolored tiles, captain's chairs, booths, and well-worn banquettes, has been going strong for some 25 years now: "the steaks that made them famous," they say, are the club and sliced steaks at $11.50. Filet mignon and sirloin at $15 are the highest priced items, but there's plenty you can eat for $9.95—ham steak, barbecued spare ribs, chicken, beef tips, fresh fish of the day. Try the barbecued shrimp as an appetizer, or the spare ribs, but keep in mind that the main-course portions are plentiful and served with a baked potato and salad. You may be too full to have a piece of the homemade walnut pie.

The Derby Steakhouse is open for dinner only, from 5 to 11:30 p.m. Monday through Saturday, from 4 to 11 p.m. on Sunday.

Mexican

Mexican Village, 224 Thompson St., in the heart of the busy Village scene (tel. 475-9805), is one of those restaurants that's *always* busy, even on a cold winter weeknight when everyplace else is practically empty. Its popularity has continued for over 20 years, and with good reason: not only is the atmosphere *muy simpático* (lots of wood and brick, a beamed ceiling, Mexican glass lanterns), but the food is authentic and good, and reasonably priced. To the traditional Mexican favorites, they often add new dishes not offered in New York before, like four kinds of steaks done in distinctive native styles or a classic seafood dish of shrimps and scallops simmered in a piquant vegetable sauce, called mariscos Vera Cruzan style. Be sure to ask about the daily specials. There are terrific appetizers too—guacamole, nachos, chilled avocodo soup, cactus salad. Most combination plates and main dishes, like chiles rellenos, run $5.75 to $7.50. Vegetarians can enjoy the Mexican vegeteria offerings: meatless enchiladas supremas (cheese and avocado stuffed in flour tortillas and baked in a sour cream and tomato sauce), as well as vegetarian tacos, enchiladas, and burritos, averaging $6 to $7.25. The chile sauces on the table are hot, so use them sparingly; to cool off, you can always order some iced mint tea or a bottle of Carta Blanca cerveza—the ideal accompaniment to a Mexican meal. It's pleasant to linger over your tequila while you're waiting for the delicacies to emerge from the hole-in-the-wall kitchen, presided over by a native chef. Open every day from 4:30 p.m. to midnight, until 1 a.m. on weekends.

One of the newer Mexican restaurants in the Village, **El Coyote,** 774 Broadway at 9th St. (tel. 677-4291), is one of the most popular. The food here is as much Tex as it is Mex, which is just fine with the loyal crowd that hangs out at the bar and in the big room, colorful with bullfight paintings against white stucco walls, tin lanterns, Mexican artifacts. Meals are decently priced, with most main courses around $6 to $10, and that includes our favorites, enchiladas suizas (stuffed with chicken and topped with sour cream and green sauce) and a flavorful vegetarian casserole. Arroz con pollo lends a Spanish note to the menu. Combination plates are big and hearty, and run from about $5.50 to $7 at dinner, about $2 less at lunch. Mexican restaurants are not generally noted for their desserts, but El Coyote is an exception, especially when it comes to the homemade pecan and banana cream-pies. Muy deliciosas.

El Coyote is open every day, serving lunch from 11:30 a.m. to 11:30 p.m., to 12:30 a.m. on Friday and Saturday.

East-West Success

Dine like a real in-the-know New Yorker at the Lower Manhattan "in" spot—**Hisae's Place,** 35 Cooper Square, near the Public Theater (tel. 228-6886). Throngs fill the place every night, and with good reason. The decor is comfortable and casual—pale salmon walls, gray carpeting, white accents. An eclectic establishment, Hisae's offers market-fresh ingredients in Oriental style, although not strictly Oriental preparations. You can, for example, feast on exciting East-West combinations like whole brook trout dressed with ginger or shrimp enlivened with black beans and vegetables for about $10. Or you could go Italian with tortellini stuffed with prosciutto or cheese-and-spinach ravioli. Enormous appetizers include a mound of scungilli salad or a seasonal treat like crunchy asparagus with real bleu cheese dressing. A platter of raw vegetables with dipping sauce precedes appetizers. Portions are large, so order sparingly or bring a big appetite. Sushi fans can begin their meal with tidbits from the sushi bar.

Everybody comes to Hisae's, from local types to serious food lovers. Hisae's Place is open for dinner only, from 4:30 p.m. to midnight, Friday and Saturday to 1 a.m., with entrees from $6.95 for chicken Hawaiian to $9.95 for shrimp, and $11.95 for steak and shrimp.

Hisae's popularity has spawned several offshoots. The newest and most handsome is **Backstage at Hisae's,** 318 West 45th St., in the theater district (tel. 489-6100), a highly styled modern setting in tones of black and polished brass, with Japanese accents, wonderful floral arrangements, exquisite plates, and red napery. The menu is a bit more continental here, with distinctive house specialties like fresh duck smoked over mesquite, flounder en papillote, rack of lamb with rosemary and mustard. A pianist entertains most evenings. As at all of the Hisae's, there's a sushi bar and wonderful desserts like hazelnut sour cream coffee cake, a double-double chocolate cake, and a 14-layer mocha mousse. Prices are higher here, with entrees from $7.95 to $18.95. It's open daily from noon to 1 a.m. (to 9 p.m. on Sunday). **Hisae's West,** 20 West 72nd St. (tel. 787-5656), not far from Lincoln Center is about halfway between Hisae's Place and Backstage at Hisae's in formality and price. It's open daily from 5 p.m. to midnight. All three are memorable.

Seafood

If you like your seafood good and fresh and served in the warm and cozy atmosphere of a neighborhood pub, then you're sure to like **Sailing,** at 282 Hudson St. (tel. 691-1988), in the burgeoning new Hudson Square area downtown. Not far from Soho, it's a great lunch or dinner spot if you've been gallery hopping. Windows gracefully etched with nautical scenes, a gleaming oak interior, and an old-world crafted bar that stretches across the side of the room set the mood. Owner Judy Berstell will greet you and make you feel right at home. Two of Judy's house specials—cold calamari salad and chewy, deep-fried calamari— are among the appetizers ($3.25 and $3.95), and are positively addictive. Very fresh clams and oysters on the half-shell will be opened to order; in season, you can have steamed mussels. To go with these good beginnings, there are special drinks, like piña coladas, strawberry daiquiris, frozen margaritas, and sangría. The menu is the same both at lunch, when a lively crowd from the nearby printing and graphics shops takes over, and at dinner, when the mood is quieter. The food is always excellent and very well priced. Burgers are available all day long, and so are omelets, barbecued chicken, and chile. The seafood entrees, from $5.95 to $9.95 for the likes of shrimp scampi, mussels posillipo, and Boston scrod, are excellent—and there's usually a lobster special for under $10! Judy brings in different desserts every day, so you might treat yourself to a slice of chocolate silk pie (outrageous!), a chocolate walnut mousse cake, or key lime pie. You can dine outside in warm weather.

Sailing is open Monday to Friday from 11:30 a.m. to 2 a.m., on Saturday from 5:30 p.m. to 2 a.m.

Health Foods for Gourmets

Brownies, 21 East 16th St., at the top of the Village (tel. AL 5-2838), is the kind of endearing place that has devotees rather than customers. Some are devoted health-food types, some devoted vegetarians, some devoted dieters—but most are just devoted to good food. And that's what you get plenty of here at the most reasonable prices high quality will allow, served either at a long, busy counter up front, in the country-style, antique-filled dining room in back, or in the no-smoking dining room on the side. The atmosphere is tea-roomy warm, the service pleasant and to-the-point.

Sam Brown (there really is a Brownie), who's been at this stand for over 45 years, is finicky about using natural ingredients (whole-grain flours, vegetable oils, ultra-fresh spices, honey instead of refined sugar), never saves leftovers, and is constantly creating new and delicious recipes for the likes of African couscous or breaded vegetable cutlet or chopped liver that tastes just like grandma's—except that it's made of vegetables. Although meat is taboo here, fish is not, and every night, in fact, Brownies offers a choice of five fanciful fresh fish specialties at $7.25 to $11.95, served with soup or salad, carrot cupcake or baked whole-wheat donut, and beverage. On the extensive à la carte menu, there are many salads, sandwiches (including tasty stuffed pita platters), vegetarian and fish entrees. For budget watchers, the imaginative "Lunch 'n Later" specialties (served from 11 a.m. to 8 p.m.) are big winners at just $5.75. Brownies, by the way, is something of a celebrity hangout. Danny Kaye, for one, is frequently in attendance at his own special corner. And wasn't that Zubin Mehta joining him over the Oriental chow chow? Brownies is open weekdays until 8 p.m., Saturday until 4 p.m.; closed Sunday.

After your meal, saunter around the corner to Brownies gourmet and health-food store at 17th St. and Fifth Ave., stocked with an international array of healthful goodies plus home-baked and mouthwatering cakes and cookies. Copies of Brownies natural-foods cookbook are available. Children, by the way, adore both eating here and visiting the retail shop; there's so much to look at—and even the candy bars are nutritious!

Chinatown

Manhattan is dotted with Chinese restaurants, and you can have an adequate Chinese meal almost anywhere in the city. But we think you should make the trek down to Chinatown, not only to combine a little sightseeing with your meal (see details in Chapter V), but because the city's best, most authentic Chinese kitchens are to be found here. And now the restaurants are more enticing than ever before, thanks to the thousands of new immigrants streaming in from Hong Kong, who have brought with them a demand for the authentic cuisine of the many and varied regions of China. A case in point is the **Great Shanghai,** 27 Division St. (966-7663), a large, crowded, typically decorated restaurant, specializing in Soo-hang food, one of the most delicate of Chinese cuisines, which originated in the southern part of China along the Yangtze River. The innovation here is the Oriental fondue, a cook-it-yourself affair. As simmering broth in a large pot is brought to your table and placed on a gas burner. You order a variety of small meat, fish, and vegetable dishes—the ones we like best are the fish balls, squid, and the paper-thin chicken—which you cook yourself in the broth, dipping them into the steaming brew with a wire mesh basket. The waitress brings a tray of condiments and mixes you a sauce—hot or mildly spicy, as you designate. We thought it was wonderful. And our total bill for this feast, for two people, was $15.60.

Since the owners of the Great Shanghai are also in charge at the **Peking Duck House Restaurant,** 22 Mott St. (tel. 227-1810), also excellent, there's another great choice here: the Peking duck dinner, an extraordinary bargain at $10.95 per person, for at least two. It includes steamed dumplings and spring rolls as appetizers, beancurd and vegetable soup, half a Peking duck or sliced chicken with orange flavor, and fried bananas for dessert. Come here at lunchtime, 11:30 a.m. to 3 p.m. daily, for dim sum. Come here anytime, any day, between 11:30 a.m. and 10 p.m. for terrific Chinese food.

The food of the mountain-living Hakka peasants of southern

China is another relative rarity in Chinatown; at this writing, there were only three restaurants serving it. Our favorite among these is the **Home Village Restaurant,** at 20 Mott St. (tel. 964-0380). Eat here and you can tell your friends you dined on sauteed pig's stomach and dried squid, for example, or deep-fried fresh pig intestine, and came home to tell the tale. For a true culinary adventurer, Home Village is fascinating. The dining rooms are pleasant enough, on two levels, and can be very crowded and noisy until about 9 in the evening, when the large Chinese families go home. After then it quiets down, and the waiters will have more time to assist you in choosing from almost 200 items on the menu. If you can get a Chinese friend to go with you, wonderful—if not, keep the waiter explaining.

As an appetizer (but not listed as such), the deep-fried meatballs are a good choice, and so is the minced chicken and sweet corn cream soup. Main dishes offer a huge selection to choose from: we've done well with the sauteed chicken with ginger and scallions, the baked prawns, the fried crabs with black bean sauce, the roast duck, and the bean curd with meat and giblets. As in any Chinese restaurant, it's best to bring a group of friends and try a little bit of everything, but be sure to plan your own meal, without falling back on the all-inclusive "house dinners." Bring your own beer, which goes well with Chinese food, and cash—no credit cards are accepted. But don't worry. At the most, your bill will be $10 or $12 per person, often less.

The Home Village is open daily from 9 a.m. to midnight, to 1 a.m. on Friday and Saturday.

Another place the devotees swear by in Chinatown is **Hong Fat,** at 63 Mott St. (tel. WO 2-9588), a shrine to the wide noodle, that is always open, always crowded, and cheap. Noodle soups are hearty, too, at **Wonton King,** 72 Mott St. (226-4290).

For a real experience in Chinese eating, choose a dim sum lunch at either **Hee Seung Fung,** or **H.S.F.** as it is familiarly known, 46 Bowery (tel. 374-1319), or **Silver Palace,** 50 Bowery (tel. 964-1204), two of the most "in" establishments in the city at this moment. Dim sum, in case you hadn't heard, is the umbrella term for dumplings and other exotic morsels that are served early in the day, always accompanied by pots and pots of tea. The correct procedure for a tea lunch is to choose whatever appeals to you from the carts and trays that are constantly whisked by your table (dim sum never offers a menu). Your bill is tallied by counting the number of empty plates you've amassed. It's perfectly proper to linger over tea lunch and continue eating until you're thoroughly sated. You'll be seated communal style with lots of other diners, all eating happily away. Both places are jammed on weekends. Individual selections at both average about $1.30 to $2.25 each. H.S.F. serves dim sum from 7:30 a.m. until 5 p.m.; at Silver Palace, the dumpling hours are 7:30 a.m. to 4 p.m. *Note:* H.S.F. now has an uptown location at 578 Second Ave. at 32nd St. (tel. 689-6969).

Vegetarians can usually find something to eat at a Chinese restaurant, but at **Vegetarian Paradise,** 48 Bowery (tel. 571-1535), the vegetarian is king. Here vegetarians may dine on "prawns" in black bean sauce (really baby corn), sweet-and-pungent "pork" (tofu), or vegetarian "roast duck" (made of tofu skins). Best of all, the food is absolutely delicious and the prices are tiny. Buddha's lo mein is a winner at $3.80, so is the lemon "chicken" at $4.95, and the large variety of soups—hot and sour, seaweed, snow cabbage with bean curd—are almost big enough for a meal. There are just a few plain tables, and you may have to wait to get in. It's open every day but Wednesday from 11:30 a.m. to 10 p.m.

On the Waterfront

An ideal stop if you're touring the downtown New York area or visiting the South Street Seaport, **Sloppy Louie's,** down in the Fulton Fish Market at 92 South St. (tel. 952-9657), is one of those places that is practically a New York institution, like the Brooklyn Bridge or the Staten Island Ferry. Its prices are cheap, its seafood is wonderful, but perhaps best of all it is still as unadorned and unpretentious as it was over 50 years ago when Louie took over (there has been a restaurant in this building since 1811). The recent restoration/preservation done in this block by the South Street Seaport has made Louie's a little more comfortable, but not changed the style very much: everyone still has a grand time, sitting at long wooden tables, feasting on succulent plates of hot fish, and brushing shoulders with the Wall Street executives, fish market truckdrivers, and others who throng the place. The main attraction is, of course, the fish, Everything is à la carte, from $7.50 to $14.95, but the entrees come served with potatoes and vegetables, so they are almost a meal in themselves. A good plan is to ask the waiter what's in season before you order. The shad roe, when they have it, is delicate and lovely, and also good are the Florida red snapper, the oyster fry, and the New Orleans shrimp créole. We are especially partial to Louie's famous bouillabaisse, a huge, steaming concoction, just as good as the last time you tried it in Marseilles, $7.95. The big, hearty bowls of fish soup, like Maine lobster soup and Long Island clam chowder, are also a treat. Everything at Louie's is, in fact, good and absolutely fresh, since the fish comes right from the market and only the choicest selections are bought. The freshest of lobsters are served at very fair prices. Liquor is not served, but you can bring your own bottle of wine.

Louie's is open daily from 10 a.m. to 10 p.m.

Tops at the South Street Seaport for terrific fresh seafood, a lively and casual atmosphere, and cheery service is **Roebling's**, on the Mezzanine Level of the Fulton Market Building (tel. 608-3980). Since it occupies almost the entire balcony of the Fulton Market, it's a great place to sit and watch all the busy goings-on at the shops and stalls on the ground level. Tables are well spaced for comfort and conversation. The atmosphere is casual, and the 70-foot bar over in one corner always attracts a lively crowd, especially on Friday afternoon when Wall Street folks quit work for the week.

Roebling's chefs are young masters: their food is elegant and imaginative. And the price is not exorbitant. Start, as we did, with cultivated mussels in a robust white-wine-and-tomato sauce, great for dowsing with bread ($4.95). The salad of smoked mozzarella, prosciutto, and roasted peppers ($4.75) is another winner; so is the four-leaf salad ($2.50). Your waiter will announce the special catch and the pasta of the day. Ordering from the regular menu, at least one person in your party should sample the Norwegian salmon with a delicate-yet-tangy sauce of ginger, garlic, and Japanese mustard; another could have the broiled bay scallops in port wine or the grilled lamb chops—very nicely done—with sage and garlic butter. Most entrees run from $9.25 to $12.95, and are accompanied by a vegetable and rice or potato. Lunch offers similar items at lower prices, with the addition of hamburgers and some imaginative omelets; a similar menu is served for Sunday brunch. Whenever you're here, though, be sure to ask for the special dessert menu. We'll sing the praises of the coffee toffee pie, the Bailey's Irish chocolate walcan (a combination of walnuts and pecans) pie, and almost anything else Roebling's dishes out.

Roebling's is open daily from 11:30 a.m. to 5 p.m. for lunch, from 5 p.m. to midnight for dinner.

How long since you've had a real English pub lunch? Homesick Englishmen and Anglophiles had better hasten to the **North Star Pub,** at 93 South St. in the South Street Seaport (tel. 509-6757), for what some visitors from the British-American Chamber of Commerce have called "the best pub lunch in or out of London." North Star is a bit of Victorian England, what with tables and wall sconces imported from London, five English beers on draft, another five in bottles, and such tasty touches of home as fresh fish battered in Guinness stout and beer, Cornish pasties, game pies, savoury plates, and of course, fish and chips. Prices for these snacks run $4.25 to $6.75. Come for lunch, afternoon snacks, or drinks. There'll probably be a party of some sort going on, so a jolly good time will be had by all.

The North Star Pub serves food daily from 11:30 a.m. to 11:30 p.m., drinks until later.

Perfect for lunch after you've toured the South Street Seaport is a newer addition to this neighborhood, the **Bridge Café,** 279 Water St. at the corner of Dover St. (tel. 227-3344), just under the Brooklyn Bridge. It's on the first floor of an old clapboard house, now painted a deep red, but a coat of paint is about the only visible sign of remodeling that's been done in many a year, and this is all part of the charm. A long, dark bar, red checkered tablecloths, clay pots filled with flowering plants sitting in the windows, wainscotting on the walls—all add to the decor of this waterfront bistro/restaurant. The congenial group that works here makes you feel at home; and the prices make you relax. At lunch, a bowl of hearty, homemade soup—it might be lentil, pea, or black bean—along with a sandwich, makes a fine repast for $5.25. The fish of the day usually costs about $6.95 to $7.95; it's as fresh as you can get and well prepared. (The blackboard menu changes every day.) There are unpredictable specials at dinner too, but also a printed menu on which entrees are priced from $8.75 to $14, and include such goodies as fried sea scallops with a tangy red pepper salsa, chicken breasts with goat cheese, prosciutto, and sage, and roast duck with green peppercorns. Entrees are served with vegetable and potato; salad is extra. Seafood appetizers are tasty, and so are desserts like the pear ginger pie and the ricotta cheese pie; they seem to go fast, so you might want to reserve your favorite when you order your entree.

The Bridge Café does not accept credit cards. It is open daily, from noon to 3 p.m. for lunch, from 6 p.m. to midnight for dinner.

A Meal in Little Italy

For those who love lusty, truly ethnic Italian food, the greatest neighborhood in the city has to be Little Italy, a subway stop or two below Greenwich Village. The streets are lined with homey, family-style restaurants where they make the fried mozzarella, the lobster Fra Diablo, the clams in garlic sauce, the steak in hot peppers, and the fried zucchini the way they did back in Naples or Sicily, from whence most of the area's citizens descended. Come to lunch, after you've been touring downtown Manhattan, and join the local politicians and legal eagles (City Hall and the courts are just a few blocks away) wheeling and dealing over the steaming pastas. If you come for dinner on a weekend, be prepared to join the hungry throngs queued up in long lines, since most of these restaurants do not accept reservations. Prices are slightly lower than uptown, and you can probably get a good meal anywhere from $5.50 to $15. **Grotta Azzura**, 387 Broome St., is the most popular of the restaurants, and the one where the lines are longest. **Paolucci's**, 149 Mulberry St., has long been a personal favorite. Other delicious choices: **Angelo's**, 146 Mulberry St.; **Antica Roma**, 40 Mulberry St.; **Forlini's**, 93 Baxter St.; **Luna's**, 112 Mulberry St.; **Paolucci's**, 149 Mulberry St.; **Puglia**, 189 Hester St.; **Raffaela's**, 134 Houston St.; **Villa Pensa**, 198 Grand St.; and **Vincent's Clam Bar**, 119 Mott St., for the best Italian fish dishes anywhere. It's nice to walk around the streets a little bit beforehand, poke your head into the grocery stores and smell the marvelous cheese and sausages, perhaps listen to a strain of a Caruso record. Finish your evening with a heavenly pastry and espresso at any of the wonderful Italian coffeehouses that line the streets: two of our favorites are **Café Roma**, 385 Broome St., and the oldest "pasticcerria" in the country, **Ferrara's**, 195 Grand St., where in summer, you can sit at the sidewalk café and pretend, perhaps, that you're on the Via Veneto.

Soho

It's nice to spend a Saturday afternoon browsing through the galleries and boutiques of Soho (below Greenwich Village; see sightseeing chapter for particulars), and it's also fun to stop off and have a meal with the local colony of artists, musicians, and creative types who keep this area hopping.

"The Revolution in Mexican Food" is boldly printed on the menu of **Cinco de Mayo**, a new Mexican restaurant in Soho at 349 West Broadway, between Broome and Grand Sts. (tel. 226-

5255), a spearhead of a new movement among Mexican restaurateurs, weary of the same old Tex-Mex food, to present the authentic cuisine of the many and varied regions of Mexico. Just as American regional cooking and Chinese regional cooking are becoming popular in New York, so is the regional cooking of Mexico, with similar happy results. Cinco de Mayo is a handsome, stylish restaurant with a two-level dining room, aglow at night with candles on the tables and pale-pink tablecloths matching walls of the same hue. We like to start a meal here with the sauteed shrimp in mustard and jalapeño vinaigrette or the ceviche, fish marinated in lime juice with just a touch of green chile and coriander (appetizers are $3.95 to $4.25). There are two different regional specialties every day, so depending on what day you go, you might have pollo en pipian (chicken in a chile-and-pumpkin-seed sauce) from the Yucatán on a Tuesday, or picadillo criollo (ground beef with rice, black beans, and fried plantains) done in the Veracruz style, on Sunday. Available every day are the tasty budin de tortilla (tortillas layered with shredded chicken, cheese, chile sauce, and sour cream), and some unusual specialties from the grill: skewered sirloin with sausage, marinated shrimp, char-broiled pork chops, tortillas filled with char-broiled meat. Prices for all of these dishes average between $9.50 and $12.95. Lunch is quite similar, with prices about $2 lower per dish, and the pink cloths removed to reveal attractive chopping blocks. Desserts are fairly standard Mexican: flan, huevos reale (a custary cake), and batido de Kahlúa (a Mexican mousse).

Cinco de Mayo is open Tuesday through Sunday from noon to midnight. A South American harpist plays music nightly.

Spring Street Natural Restaurant, 149 Spring St. (tel. 966-0290), is a great big airy place where wooden tables, exposed brick walls with paintings by local artists, many plants, overhanging fans, and a relaxed atmosphere set the mood for dining on wholesome, unprocessed, really good food. Everything is homemade from all natural ingredients. There are many flavorful fresh fish and seafood dishes (salmon steak au vin with rice, shrimp in mustard sauce, mussels sauteed in spinach); gourmet vegetarian creations like leek casserole, zucchini tempura with parmesan sauce, bulghur croquettes with curry sauce; imaginative salads like the excellent tabbouli topped with tahini sauce and surrounded with lemons and cucumbers, a huge meal at around $4; unusual homemade soups (avocado, spinach, or cream of cauliflower); and mouthwatering desserts like carrot layer cake, cranberry pie, and praline cheesecake. Most entrees run $4 to $9. Sunday brunch, 11:30 a.m. to 4 p.m., is a special treat; try the delectable whole-wheat crêpes. You can have wine at your table or a drink at the big, friendly bar up front, crowded with local types. Open daily, from 11:30 a.m. until 2 a.m.

No need to journey to the Spice Islands, now that **Tamu** has landed in Soho, at 360 West Broadway, at the corner of Grand St. (tel. 925-2751). This lovely, two-tiered restaurant is a breath of the tropics, with batik fabrics, chairs of cane and bamboo, basketry lamp coverings, plenty of greenery. Have a drink on the balcony, lean back, relax—you could be on the other side of the world. You can try all sorts of Indonesian specialties à la carte at dinner (entrees from $8.95 to $13.95) or lunch ($5.50 to $9.95, a considerable saving), but we would definitely opt for the rijsttafel, the traditional Indonesian feast centered around rice and offering a variety of taste sensations—flavors of ginger and coriander, chili and lemon grass, intricately spiced but not too hot—in soup, salads cooked and raw, dishes of chicken, lamb, shrimp, beef, fish, plus pungent condiments. Your $30 for two at either meal calls forth the splendid 12-dish meal, plus a dessert of sweetly battered, deep-fried bananas, plus coffee.

Tamu is open for dinner Monday through Friday from 6 to 11:30 p.m., and for lunch and dinner on Saturday and Sunday from 1 p.m. to midnight.

Tribeca

Rachel's, 25 Hudson St. (tel. 334-8155), is the kind of place you like right away: a big attractive restaurant with a warm, hearty atmosphere, not at all pretentious, tables spaced comfortably apart; lots of people obviously having a good time; and reasonably priced and delicious food. And on weekends—cabaret, to boot. No wonder it's always busy; everybody from the singles crowd to large family groups (their tables can seat up to 12 comfortably), from the limousine set to blue-collar folks, find their way way downtown. The crowd is especially big on Sunday (be sure to make reservations) when Rachel generously serves up "New York's only all-day buffet," a lavish spread of seafood, roast sirloin, salads, soups, breads, even a Viennese dessert table: all for $9.95 (noon to 6 p.m.). Another big crowd pleaser is the nightly prime rib dinner, $12.95, including seafood bisque, baked potato, fresh vegetable, watercress and tomato salad. On the regular menu too there are many good things. Reasonably priced appetizers include some tasty stuffed mushrooms ($3.25) and a knockout loaf of onion rings, enough for two or three of you ($2.50). Main dishes begin at $5.95 for a hamburger platter; most are in the $7.95 to $10.95 category. We found the salmon steak with dill sauce delicious, as was the filet of sole stuffed with crabmeat; a special that night, baby scallops in a white wine sauce, was seasoned perfectly. Rachel's "famous baby back ribs" are very tender and not at all greasy. Home-baked desserts and pies are outstanding, especially the lemon Ginra cake (of sponge cake–like texture, with lemon filling), the cappuccino cake (mocha filling), and the hard-to-find-elsewhere key lime pie. After all this, it's perfect to lean back with an espresso—or maybe Irish coffee—and watch the show.

Rachel's is open from noon to midnight Monday to Friday, on Saturday from 5 p.m. to 1 a.m., and on Sunday from noon to 6 p.m. A dinner cabaret is held in "The Little Room" Wednesday through Saturday; showtime is 10 p.m., and there's a $5 cover and two-drink minimum.

Fast Foods, Friendly Prices: Meals from $3 to $7

Now we come to those places that seem to have been designed with budgeteers, visiting or otherwise, in mind. They are ideal for a quick, casual meal; they offer hearty, satisfying food, and in most you can put together a good meal for little price. Some are one-of-a-kind places, other are the popular chain restaurants that you'll find all over the busiest parts of town. Wherever you are, you won't be far from one of these nourishing dispensaries. (Consult the Manhattan phone directory for complete addresses.)

NATURALLY SPEAKING: Lois Lane's Ninth and Natural, 580 Ninth Ave. at 42nd St. (tel. 695-5055), is heaven for midtown natural-food fans. It's a bright and attractive café in the rear of a very good health-food store, and the food is tasty, nourishing, and very inexpensive. In addition to daily specials like tofu lasagne, enchilada bake, or tamale pies (all $5.50), the menu offers a very good tempeh "chicken" salad, nori rolls, tabbouli, huge sprout salads, fresh vegetable and fruit juices, and herbal teas. Most dishes are between $2.50 and $4. There's a delicious pie of the day too, and of course, tofutti desserts. Open weekdays from 7 a.m. to 8 p.m., on Saturday from 10 a.m. to 8 p.m.

We'd call the food at **Dennis'**, 91 Fifth Ave. (tel. 741-0770), "fast and natural." Dennis' is a big, casual place with green-and-white chairs and tables and, at first glance, might almost be a McDonald's; you order your meal here just the way you would at McDonald's, and computerized service speeds it along to you. But the results are different: no chemicals, additives, or preservatives are used. You might go with the "Inside Pizza" (a whole-wheat pita bread split and stuffed with veggies and melted mozzarella), pita stuffed wtih couscous, garbanzos, and salad, or with codfish and homemade cole slaw. Or savor the baked stuffed potatoes, the spinach noodles and cottage cheese, the homemade soups, fruit and vegetable juices, fanciful yogurts, and the carrot, orange, and walnut cupcakes. In cold weather, home-baked whole-wheat-and-honey donuts with steaming apple cider are a must. Prices are modest: most specials run around $3.50, but portions are small; if you're really hungry, two entrees might be necessary. Dennis' is open from 10:30 a.m. to 7 p.m. weekdays, 11 a.m. to 6:30 p.m. on Saturday, closed Sunday.

FROM THE MIDDLE EAST: There are six **Amy's** in town—in the Lincoln Center area at Broadway and 62nd St. and Broadway and 72nd St. (both open daily from 11 a.m. to 10 p.m.), across from Carnegie Hall at 147 West 57th St. (same hours), at 108 University Pl., at Broadway and 112th St., and at 28 West 40th St. (open five days from 11 a.m. to 6 p.m.)—and wherever they are, people get turned on to the delights of Israeli–Middle Eastern food, served cafeteria style at tiny prices. All of the Amy's are attractive, with brick walls and butcher-block Formica tables, and a tempting counter which dispenses wonderful sandwiches—an Amyburger (mashed chickpeas, vegetables, and spices), hummus, grilled feta cheese, baba ganoush, Amyleen (chopped meat, nuts, spices, and wine), hamburgers, fish filet, chicken filet, eggplant sticks, steak, and the like—served in toasted pita bread, from $2.15 to $3.10, as well as various combination platters of these ingredients at $3.25 to $5.95. Amy's dinner plates are excellent bargains, and they are served with all the Middle Eastern accompaniments. Prices may vary slightly at different locations.

AND FROM THE ORIENT: For fast food with style and nutritional value, use your noodle and head for one of the **Dosanko Larmen** restaurants. These are Japanese noodle shops that are exceptionally clean, attractively decorated, and feature only larmen (soft noodles and vegetables in broth) in several varieties, as well as gyoza (Japanese fried dumplings), priced from $3.90 to $5.20. Japanese-style deep-fried pork, seafood, and spare ribs are all $5.20. Service is brisk and friendly, the food is fresh and good. You'll find Dosanko Larmens at Madison Ave. and 48th St., 10 East 52nd St., 135 East 45th St., 329 Fifth Ave. (between 32nd and 33rd Sts.), 123 West 49th St., and still another at 19 Murray St., in the financial area, among some 15 locations.

OF BAGELS AND PIZZA: Since New Yorkers are absolutely mad about bagels, it's no wonder that the **Bagel Nosh** chain and several similar bagel-based operations have caught on like wildfire. Bagel Noshes are most attractive, self-service places, with loads of greenery, butcher-block tables, and a variety of bagels—like garlic, onion, pumpernickel, raisin—plus an even greater variety of toppings to put on them, from cream cheese to salami to burgers to brisket of beef. Prices run from about $1.15 to $4.25. There's a Bagel Nosh at Fifth Ave. and 35th St., another at Broadway and 71st St. (near Lincoln Center, with an enclosed outdoor café area, great for people-watching), one at 501 Seventh Ave. at 37th St. (near Macy's), and still another at Third Ave. at 38th St., plus several more. Most stay open early until quite late.

Pizza parlors are by no means a rarity in New York—there must be one on every other block—but we know of none that has such a fiercely devoted clientele as **Famous Rays Pizza** at 465 Avenue of the Americas (corner of 11th St.) in Greenwich Village. Rays pizzas have marvelously crusty bases, the thickest cheese toppings anywhere, and wonderful flavors—many aficionados have rated them the best in New York. Two pizza slices (it's hard to stop at just one—they're around $1 each) make a satisfying lunch and a wonderful snack anytime you're in the Village. A plain pizza pie is $12.75, and a special pizza with all the good stuff on it is $14.

MIDTOWN SOPHISTICATE: You're catching a show at Radio City Music Hall on Sixth Avenue or shopping on Fifth; you're weary and starving, but you want something nicer than a diner, simpler than a fancy restaurant: **Ceci's,** 55 West 51st St. (tel. 586-0050), is the place for you. Breakfast, lunch, and dinner are served six days a week for 13 consecutive hours, in a stylish hi-tech setting, with colored neon tubing and flickering light-bulbs for decor. The young executive crowd keeps this place packed, especially at lunch, so you may have to wait in line a bit, but it usually moves very quickly and, once inside, service is speedy. You can have eggs or omelets (primavera or cheese, bacon and tomato, $4.25) at lunch, or cold platters like shrimp on avocado slices, salade Niçoise, antipasto, and fresh fruit salad (around $5) anytime. For an early dinner before going to see the Rockettes on stage (you may also see them here between shows), try any of the pasta dishes, the chicken parmigiana, or chili—all $6 to $7. Ceci's is open from 7 a.m. to 8 p.m. weekdays, from 10 a.m. to 8 p.m on Saturday; closed Sunday.

AT THE WORLD TRADE CENTER: Before or after catching the view from the top of the World Trade Center, have a fine lunch or snack downstairs at the **Big Kitchen,** built on the site of the old Washington Market and one of the most imaginative fast-food dispensaries anywhere. Take your choice of the Delicatessen, which sells overstuffed sandwiches and barrel pickles; the Bakery, which uses no additives or preservatives, and turns out an enormous variety of fresh and fantastically good breads and pastries at low prices; the Oyster Bar; a health-food section, which serves salads, yogurt, and pita bread sandwiches; a barbecue area which roasts chicken and ribs on spits; and the Grill, which is known for its excellent freshly grilled burgers. You should be able to put a meal together here for anywhere from $3 to $7. Open weekdays from 7 a.m. to 7 p.m., weekends until 5 p.m.

Chapter V

SIGHTS OF NEW YORK: THREE ONE-DAY TOURS

IT OFTEN SEEMS to us that New York tourists fall into one of two categories. The first are the compulsive sightseers who feel that if they *don't* get to the top of the World Trade Center, visit the United Nations, have a meal in Chinatown, and take the boat to the Statue of Liberty, they might as well have stayed home. Then there is the other school, the lazy ones who like to know that the World Trade Center is *there* if they really want it, but are perfectly happy just walking around the city, absorbing the sights, the sounds, the sensations as they find them.

Our own feeling is that both have a point: the major sights of New York *are* exciting and important, and you should see as many of them as you comfortably have time and energy for. But you should also allow yourself plenty of time to let New York sink in by osmosis: to rummage through the Village antique store or watch the lovers stroll through Central Park or sip a martini at some cocktail lounge in the sky as the city shimmers below you. A holiday in New York, we think, ought to be made up of equal parts of doing and dreaming—with enough leisure for both.

But fitting everything in can be quite complicated, especially if you're here for just a short time. The quickest way to see the city is, of course, to take a guided tour: **Short Line Tours,** for one, offers some interesting excursions in glass-roofed buses (tel. 354-4740). Tours run by **Gray Line** (tel. 397-2600) are always reliable. You'll get plenty of information and an overall view of where you're at. For an even more overall view, plus a sensational thrill, take a helicopter trip. **Island Helicopters** (tel. 889-0986) leave every day between 9 a.m. and 5 p.m. from the Heliport at 34th Street and the East River and skim over the highpoints of New York—the Empire State Building, the Statue of Liberty, the United Nations. There are evening flights too, from 7 to 9 p.m. Prices begin at $20. No reservations are required. Closed Christmas and New Year's Day.

If, however, you have the time for the in-depth approach, the best way to see the city is to get out and walk. We have, therefore, devised three one-day walking tours (taxis, subways, or buses will get you to each area to explore quickly and economically) that you might use as basic guideposts for seeing the city. If you have more than three days, break the tours up: follow a suggested activity for the morning; spend the afternoon shopping or going to the Central Park Zoo or catching a matinee.

The first tour concentrates mostly on the sights in the midtown area and then takes you downtown to see the Statue of Liberty: it would be ideal if you have just one day in the city. The second tour sends you exploring the financial and shopping district of downtown Manhattan, takes you to the top of the World Trade Center, then directs you to the Staten Island Ferry, the United Nations, and proposes an evening dining and browsing in Chinatown. On the third day we suggest you see the city from the decks of a "round-the-island" boat, take in a few of the important museums, and explore the shops and sights of Greenwich Village. There are, of course, numerous other places that are important and fun to visit which we'll describe in other chapters. But we think that once you've completed the three main tours, you'll be able to say, "We've seen New York." And if you have children with you, you'd better *not* leave without having seen these sights: these are the experiences youngsters remember all their lives.

Note: You'll be doing plenty of walking, so be sure to wear comfortable shoes. You should also carry with you two maps, both free. The first, the **New York Visitor's Guide and Map,** is available (in six languages) at the offices of the New York Convention and Visitors Bureau at 2 Columbus Circle (59th Street). The bureau is open every day, also has all sorts of excellent free sightseeing information plus discount theater coupons, and will also answer questions by phone (tel. 397-8222). The second, a **map of the New York City subway system,** should be available at the Visitors Bureau, but can also be picked up at the information booths in both Grand Central Terminal and Pennsylvania Station any day between 7 a.m. and 10:45 p.m. If you're the type who plans ahead, you can write for a map to: Map and Schedule NYCTA, 370 Jay St., Room 823, Brooklyn, NY 11201 (send a stamped, self-addressed envelope). Bus or subway information is also available by phoning MTA at 330-1234.

The First Day
(The Empire State Building, Macy's, Rockefeller Center, Radio City Music Hall, then downtown to the Statue of Liberty)

THE EMPIRE STATE BUILDING: You might as well start this tour at the top: the top of the Empire State Building. You'll have plenty of company; some 1,500,000 visitors a year, from all over the world, make the pilgrimage to the world's once-highest building: 1472 feet above sea level, 102 stories high, a sleek, modernistic monument that well typifies the skyscraper city in its boldness, daring, dominance. The real excitement starts when you reach the 86th-floor Observatory; from the outdoor promenade deck, it's a 360-degree view, and if the day is clear, you can see as far as 50 miles into the distance. But the big show lies below you: Manhattan, an island of steel and concrete and glass rising out of the sea, looking from this height like a Lilliputian landscape until you start to pick out the landmarks: the lacy spires of the New York skyline, the Statue of Liberty, the United Nations, the green expanse of Central Park, the great ships heading out of the Hudson, bound for Europe. For a view from an even higher vantage, you can go up another 16 stories, to the 102nd floor and its spaceship environment. From either observation tower (this one is enclosed), the effect is spellbinding: you may forget to leave. But do get down to earth again, to explore at close range the wonders you've glimpsed above.

The Empire State Building, Fifth Ave. and 34th St. (tel. 736-3100), is open every day from 9:30 a.m. to midnight. Admission: $2.75 for adults, $1.50 for children.

While you're here, stop in at the **Guinness World Record Exhibit Hall** on the concourse level to see who and what broke all the records. This multimedia display is great fun for kids and adults alike. Open daily 9:30 a.m. to 6 p.m. with admission $3 for adults, $2 for children (tel. 947-2339).

MACY'S: Since you're already on 34th Street and you'll want to see Macy's sooner or later, you might as well catch it now. Walk just a block west from the Empire State Building to Herald Square and visit the world's biggest store. You can shop here for anything from hams to hammocks to haute couture; if you're lucky, you might catch an Irish Festival or a Mideast Bazaar or some other international fiesta of the kind that Macy's frequently presents. Be sure to visit "The Cellar" downstairs, a veritable street of little shops—a pastry shop, a candy shop, a produce area—selling gourmet foods and cookware from all over. There's even a branch of P.J. Clarke's famous bar-restaurant down here. Take the kids to "Growing Up on Five," a floor for children that completely outfits youngsters from infants to preteens and has a toy shop, shoe department, pet store, hair salon, and decorative fabrics store to boot. There's a natural-foods spot on the fourth floor. A personal shopping service can aid newcomers. After you've exhausted Macy's (could that be possible?), or yourself, you might consider Gimbels, next door. In between the two is the new Herald Center, an 11-floor, 200-store mall that re-creates the many neighborhoods of New York. Proceed or ignore, as you please, and then hop a bus going uptown on Sixth Avenue (Avenue of the Americas) to your next destination, Rockefeller Center, which runs from 48th to 51st Streets, observing the new office-building skyscrapers that line the avenue. Somewhere between Macy's and Rockefeller Center, you could schedule a stop for lunch (see Chapter IV on restaurants).

ROCKEFELLER CENTER: It's noted as one of the architectural marvels of New York—and of the United States, a high-water mark of urban design. Although it is one of the busiest, most heavily trafficked areas in the city, this 24-acre, 19-skyscraper complex gives the feeling of old-world gentility and beauty, thanks to the masterful use that has been made of open space. You'll appreciate this as you approach the Center from the best vantage point, the Channel Gardens, which begin between 49th and 50th Streets, across Fifth Avenue from St. Patrick's Cathedral and Saks Fifth Avenue. Depending on the season, the gardens will be abloom with chrysanthemums or lilies or roses or tropical plants, and you'll see scores of other tourists and natives stopping to sit on the benches and maybe munch a lunchtime sandwich here. On either side of the walk is a continental array of shops and services. Continue down the promenade to the central sunken plaza, the focal point of the complex. In winter, the plaza is an ice-skating rink, a Brueghel canvas in the heart of the city; in summer, an open-air restaurant. Directly behind the plaza is the massive statue of *Prometheus* by Paul Manship, with its fountain in back, and behind that the RCA Building soars skyward.

However, in order really to appreciate the intricacies of Rockefeller Center, you should take a guided tour, which also takes you to the private roof gardens and backstage at Radio City Music Hall. Tour groups leave frequently from the lounge on the main floor of the RCA Building from 9 a.m. to 4:45 p.m. daily except Sunday. The one-hour tour costs $4 for adults, $3.50 for students and senior citizens, and $2.50 for children under 12. The tour also includes admission to the Observation Roof, another stunning vantage point from which to view the vista of New York. If you've already seen the view from the Empire State Building, you will be forgiven for skipping this one, but better yet, come back some evening for a trip to the Observation Roof alone (admission is $3 for adults, $2.50 for students and senior citizens, and $1.15 for children), to see one of the original—and still the greatest—of the city's light shows. Or combine sightseeing with a romantic drink sky-high in the Rainbow Room, where the view is included in the price of your cocktail (see Chapter VIII on nightclubs).

RADIO CITY MUSIC HALL ENTERTAINMENT CENTER: Since you've already seen one of the world's tallest buildings, its biggest department store, and its biggest privately owned complex of office buildings, you might as well see the world's biggest theater—which, of course, is the famed Radio City Music Hall Entertainment Center. Recently restored to its 1930s art deco elegance, the 6000-seat theater is an architectural wonder, and its shows—concerts, spectacular presentations, and special events (no more movies)—run the gamut from family entertainment to pop singers, from *Snow White and the Seven Dwarfs* to Linda Ronstadt. Of course you'll see the Rockettes (America's most famous chorus girls) and enough spectacle—stages rising and disappearing out of the pit, fireworks, curtains of rain and steam—to make you suspect it must be the Fourth of July. Tickets, priced according to attraction, are available at the box office or from any Ticketron outlet (there are booths in Grand Central Terminal and at Madison Square Garden).

STATUE OF LIBERTY AND ELLIS ISLAND: Let's wind up your first day's sightseeing now with an exclamation point: a trip downtown to the Statue of Liberty, and its American Museum of Immigration. The Statue of Liberty is one sight in New York that no one, not even the most blasé, should miss. It's simple to get to: just make your way to the West Side IRT subway, take a downtown local train to South Ferry, and head for the Statue of Liberty boats; they leave on the hour from 9 a.m. until 4 p.m., with additional ferry service during July and August, and for a fare of $2 for adults, $1 for children 11 years and under, they will deposit you, in about 20 minutes, on Liberty Island, a short distance from the statue. You'll enjoy your visit more if you come early on a weekday, since the crowds get thick in the afternoons, and particularly on weekends and holidays. Repairs and refurbishing will take place inside the statue during 1985–1986, but the boats will be running, and the museum will be open as usual. (Phone: for museum information, 732-1286; for boats, 269-5755).

Every schoolchild, of course, knows the story of the statue: of how it was given to the United States by the people of France in 1886 to commemorate the alliance of the two countries during the American Revolution; how its construction became the ruling passion of the French sculptor Auguste Bartholdi, who raised funds in France and then designed the monument (Alexandre Gustave Eiffel, who built a rather famous tower in France, did the supporting framework); and how the people of the United States, reluctant to match the one-million-franc contribution of the French people, had to be prodded into it by an intensive campaign led by the *New York World*'s Joseph Pulitzer. Finally, the money was raised, and now it seems that the statue was always there, so magnificently does it blend into its site in Upper Bay, so splendidly does it typify the ideals and dreams on which the nation was built. Stepping from her chains, Liberty, a tablet commemorating the date of July 4, 1776, in her left hand, the torch of freedom held high in her right, has become the symbol, to thousands of immigrants and exiles from all over, of a new life, a new world. The story of these immigrants is eloquently told at the American Museum of Immigration, a new addition to the complex, located in the base of the statue. It's worth a look.

When you actually get to the statue, the statistics—the figure is 152 feet high, the pedestal another 150 feet, the arm 42 feet long, the head large enough for a man to stand in—become an awesome reality. There's an elevator to the top of the pedestal and, from there, a 12-story stairway to the top, which your kids will undoubtedly take. If you've got the energy to join them, you'll be rewarded with a magic view of the New York skyline.

Note: You won't get too close, but you'll also get a good view of the statue and the skyline from the decks of the Staten Island Ferry, another New York must that we'll tell you more about, below.

Another boat trip that you may want to make in this area is the one to Ellis Island, the portal through which more than 12 million immigrants entered the United States. Circle Line Ellis Island Ferry makes frequent May through October departures from Battery Park; fare for the 90-minute round trip is $2 for adults, $1 for children. On the island, you'll take part in a guided tour conducted by National Park Service personnel. Ellis Island is not much to look at, but it stirs poignant memories of the aspirations and disappointments of those who did—and those who did not—make it to the promised land.

Now that you've seen New York from the top, cased the biggest and the best, you deserve a rest. Plan a leisurely dinner and get yourself tickets to the best Broadway show in town.

The Second Day
(Downtown Manhattan, the World Trade Center, South Street Seaport, the United Nations, Ford Foundation Garden, and Chinatown)

DOWNTOWN MANHATTAN: If you are interested in history— or money—or architecture—or the sea—you will have to visit downtown Manhattan. Haunted with ghosts of the city's past, booming with construction and commerce of the present, an area rich in classical architecture and sleek, new futuristic office buildings, ringed by the sea that made its wealth possible, this oldest area of the city is so richly textured that you could spend days here without exhausting its possibilities. But even a morning's walk will give you a basic feeling of what created New York and still makes it tick. For youngsters, this area is a must. To start your explorations, take any downtown train to Wall Street (an express stop) on either the East or West Side IRT trains.

More than anything else, New York is a marketplace. Today it is the greatest one on earth. It has always been a marketplace. It was settled, back in 1626, not as a haven for political or religious freedom as most of the other colonies were, but as a fur-trading post for the Dutch West India Company. Peter Minuit, the governor of Nieuw Amsterdam, technically "bought" the island from the Manhattoes Indians for $24 worth of baubles; 22 years later the Dutch allowed the English to take possession and rename it New York without so much as a fight. But a little over a hundred years later, after a very big fight, the fledgling revolutionary government of the United States of America established its capital here and inaugurated its wartime hero, Gen. George Washington, as its president.

The city grew with the lusty young nation: thanks to the opening of the Erie Canal, it became one of the country's major marketplaces; after the Civil War, when the canal was no longer important, its ideal deep-water harbor attracted to it the commerce of many nations. The temples of finance and commerce grew up alongside the water's edge, and this is where they still are. A modest stock exchange had already been set up—under a buttonwood tree in 1792—but it was not until the New York financiers had been able to underwrite the Civil War that Wall Street took its place as the financial power of the nation—and, indirectly, of much of the world. Residential New York grew up and moved north, but the citadel of money and power remains. And this is where you begin your downtown tour: **Wall Street.**

The best place to start your exploration is at Broadway and Wall, in the quiet calm of **Trinity Church**, a graceful English Gothic beauty that was built by Richard Upjohn and completed in 1846. This designated National Landmark was once the tallest building in Lower Manhattan. In its tranquil cemetery lie buried a few parishioners who once lived in this area: Robert Fulton, Alexander Hamilton, and other early leading Americans. You can visit both church and cemetery daily from 7 a.m. to 6 p.m. An Acoustiguide tour is available.

After paying your respects to these early New Yorkers (or perhaps catching a free lunchtime concert, or one of the other noontime activities), proceed down Wall Street (there really was once a wall here made of tree trunks by the Dutch settlers to protect their city from the wilderness) and stop at the corner of Wall and Nassau Streets, at the **Federal Hall National Memorial.** The place is full of ghosts: it was on this site that John Peter Zenger won the trial that established the right of freedom of the press and it was here that General Washington took the oath of office as the first president, in 1789. A statue of Washington commemorates the event. The first American Congress met here and adopted the Bill of Rights. You'll occasionally find some kind of protest or demonstration being held on the steps, perhaps in response to the street plaque commemorating the Zenger trial and quoting his words: "Everyone who loves liberty ought to encourage freedom of speech." Mostly, however, office workers lounge on the steps to eat their lunch and get a bit of sunshine, quite oblivious to the history that was made on this site, or the fact that the current building (1842), first a Customs House, later a Sub-Treasury, now a museum, is considered perhaps the finest example of Greek Revival architecture in the city. Explore this Athenian gem in New York. Inside is a free museum of the Colonial and Early Federal periods, open from 9 a.m. to 5 p.m. Monday through Friday. Special programs—films, folksinging concerts, etc.—are often held here.

If Federal Hall is the shrine to history on Wall Street, the **New York Stock Exchange** corner Broad and Wall) is the temple to the gods of money. Appropriately, the building is done in "Renaissance-temple" architecture. Inside, in the Great Hall of the Exchange, are the member brokers, acting for clients all over the world, are buying and selling millions of dollars' worth of securities in an atmosphere that, to the uninitiated, looks like a pandemonium. To understand the subtle inner workings of the whole scheme, you can take a guided tour; they are offered every half hour on regular business days, between 10 a.m. and 4 p.m. at 20 Broad St. (free). Or just drop in, gaze at the ticker tape, and see what's happened to your shares of General Motors while you've been away. The Exchange is the second most popular tourist attraction in New York. The public is also invited to the Visitors' Gallery of the **American Stock Exchange,** 78 Trinity Pl., Monday through Friday from 9:45 a.m. to 4 p.m. (also free).

Those who are really turned on by money and banking might continue, now, a few blocks north on Broadway to 33 Liberty St., the site of the **Federal Reserve Bank of New York.** This formidable Renaissance palace actually has more gold than Fort Knox. To see what goes on here, take a guided tour through the gold vault and currency-handling operations. Tours are given at 10 and 11 a.m., and 1 and 2 p.m. during banking days, and reservations must be made at least one week in advance. Family groups may include children. You may write to the Public Information Department at the bank, or phone 791-6130 to request a reservation.

Now, here's chance to rest your feet a bit and see some exciting new outdoor sculptures at the same time. Where William Street, Liberty Street, and Maiden Lane meet is a tiny vestpocket park called **Louise Nevelson Plaza,** fitted out with trees, benches, and seven vertical sculptures by Nevelson called *Shadows and Flags.*

Head back to Broadway now and walk west one block for the highlight of your downtown excursion: a less-than-a-minute elevator ride will take you zooming to the top of the **World Trade Center,** the world's almost-tallest building. Here, at the Observation Deck on the 107th floor of the South Tower (Tower Two)—more than a quarter mile in the sky—you'll see perhaps the most spectacular view on earth. Below you is all of New York, its bridges, its monuments (now you can *see* the Empire State Building that you've just looked out of), the silent streets below, the rivers and their toy ships, and, on a clear day, a view that extends 50 miles in all directions. It's hard to say when the view is most dazzling—in morning sunlight or in evening splendor; dusk, when the lights are just beginning to come up on the darkening city, is particularly enchanting. The Observation Deck on the 107th floor is glass-enclosed; if you also go up to the promenade on the roof above the 110th floor, you'll be on the highest outdoor observation platform in the world. After you've seen your fill, have a look at the entertaining exhibit on the history of trade and a peek at the souvenir shop. Since anywhere from six to nine thousand people visit the Observation Deck on fine summer and holiday weekends, try to plan your visit for a weekday, when there will be only a few thousand of you. It's open from 9:30 a.m. to 9:30 p.m. daily, with an admission charge of $2.95 for adults, $1.50 for children and senior citizens (tel. 466-7377 for information).

Now that the Observation Deck has put you in the mood for gorgeous views, you may want to see a similar view and have a drink and hors d'oeuvres at the Hors D'Oeuvrerie section of the stunning Windows on the World Restaurant, perched above Tower One, the North Tower of the World Trade Center (see Chapter IV for details on the City Lights Bar and the Restaurant). Or stop for refreshment back on the ground, on the concourse level of the Trade Center, either at the Market Dining Rooms & Bar, built on the site of the old Washington Market, or at the Big Kitchen with its various food stalls (including a raw bar for seafood and a natural foods pantry), with modestly priced food for every taste. Check out the stunning new Vista International Hotel, and perhaps stop in for high tea or a cocktail at its relaxing lobby lounge. Inspect some of the monumental art at the World Trade Center, including a gigantic Joan Miró tapestry (considered one of his masterworks), hung against a 50-foot-high marble wall in the Mezzanine of 2 World Trade Center; Alexander Calder's *World Trade Center Stabile,* resembling three giant sails, at Church and Vesey Streets; and Louise Nevelson's sculpture *Sky-Gate New York,* which hangs in the Mezzanine of 1 World Trade Center. You can also have a peek at the changing exhibits at the United States Customs House, or stop in at the Visitors' gallery of the Commodities Exchange, on the ninth floor of 4 World Trade Center, to watch some fast and furious financial trading (open weekdays, 9:30 a.m. to 3 p.m., free). You can even do a bit of shopping. Any children in the crowd will enjoy a visit to a branch of F. A. O. Schwarz, New York's most famous toy emporium. And Alexander's, a department store with very good prices, especially on women's clothing imports, is well worth a quick stop.

If you're planning to see a Broadway or off-Broadway show at night, stop in at the branch of TKTS on the mezzanine level of 2 World Trade Center for half-price day-of-performance tickets. Hours are Monday to Friday from 11:30 a.m. to 5 p.m., on Saturday from 11 a.m. to 3 p.m.

Note: If you've scheduled your trip to the World Trade Center as a separate excursion, take the IRT Seventh Avenue subway local to Cortlandt Street, or the IND AA or E train to Chambers Street. Underground parking is also available.

Return to Broadway now and proceed south. You'll pass a branch of **John Wanamaker's,** all that remains of that once-famous New York emporium (the main building uptown was torn down some years ago) on your left, and you'll also see the Marine Midland Trust building at 140 Broadway, with Isamu Noguchi's enormous rectangular cube precariously balanced on one corner in front of it. 140 Broadway is one of the few new buildings in the area that has made any attempt at public art or sculpture; another is 1 Chase Manhattan Plaza, where Jean Dubuffet's whimsical "mushrooms" tower skyward. This is a particularly busy area of Broadway, where you'll often see street musicians playing to the lunchtime crowds. **Bowling Green Park,** where the Dutch burghers actually used to bowl, is ahead of you (it has been restored to look the way it did a century ago with London plane trees, wooden benches, and oldtime lamp posts), and so is the massive neoclassic former **Customs House,** with its imposing sculptures of Asia, America, Africa, and Europe, done by Daniel Chester French of Lincoln Memorial fame. (The building is currently being considered as a site for a multipurpose commercial and cultural center.)

Keep going now, on the other side of the street from Bowling

Green and Battery Park, until you come to the **Seamen's Church Institute**, 15 State St., a handsome modern structure which not only serves and houses merchant seamen, but is also a favorite lunch and supper spot for downtown office workers. You can join them in their lively new Mariner 15 Café with its glass wall overlooking the shipping activities of the harbor or at the carpeted and comfortable Mariner 15 dining room. Meals are well priced (under $5), and the food is good. Note the interesting ship's bells and maritime paintings outside the cafeteria and the free-form stairways with plaques hanging in the stairwells, somehow reminiscent of a ship's mast. Rest rooms, telephones, and a Visitors Center (showing changing exhibits of paintings and ship models) all help to make this a pleasant place to break your tour.

Next door to the Seamen's Institute, at 7 State St., is one of the few remaining examples of early Federal architecture in New York. Built by John McCoomb as a private town house in 1800, Watson House is noted for the colonnade that curves with the line of the street. It is now **Our Lady of the Rosary Church**, the shrine of Saint Elizabeth Seton.

Right behind State Street is Pearl Street, and at the corner of Pearl and Broad Street is one of New York's most famous historical houses. Built in 1719 as the home of Stephen DeLancey and converted into a tavern in 1763 by Samuel Fraunces, **Fraunces Tavern** was an establishment favored by George Washington. It became part of American history when Washington bade farewell to his officers in the Long Room here on December 4, 1783, after the American Revolution. It is now owned and maintained by the Sons of the Revolution in the State of New York as a museum with permanent and changing exhibits of the Revolutionary War and 18th-century American history and culture. You might catch the museum's audio-visual presentation of the early history of New York City, or attend some of their lectures and concerts (open Monday to Friday, 10 a.m. to 4 p.m.; tel. 425-1778 for information). On the ground floor is a restaurant, where the food is still excellent, and you could have a lovely lunch, in the company of illustrious ghosts.

Now make your way to the waterfront and begin walking up South Street, once dotted with ship chandlers' stores and other establishments having to do with sailing and the sea. The old South Street and Front Street, which runs parallel to it and where coffee-roasting houses once processed the fragrant beans right off the ships, have been totally taken over by giant office buildings. Those who mourn the old days on the waterfront have mixed emotions about the steel-and-glass monsters, but there is no denying that some are handsome. If you're interested in architecture, have a look yourself at the soaring columns of 2 New York Plaza or of **55 Water Street**, which we find the most impressive building here. We especially like the plaza on its northern side (although we would prefer some grass to all that concrete) that overlooks the highway. Here one can join the local office workers eating lunch at the chairs and tables outside, or just sit and watch the tugs and the whirlybirds and the harbor traffic, catch the marvelous ocean breezes, and dream a little bit about the vanished days of the tall ships, the giant clippers that came from all over the world to drop anchor at the port of New York, arching their bowsprits across South Street.

SOUTH STREET SEAPORT MUSEUM: To see what a very practical group of dreamers and visionaries are doing to commemorate the old days of South Street, walk a few blocks north now, and you'll soon come to the South Street Seaport Museum. The museum is an 11-block center that stretches from Piers 15 and 16 all the way over to Fulton Street, and it is dedicated not only to preserving New York's seaport heritage but also to encouraging city planners and builders to make the sea an intrinsic part of new construction—to create, in fact, a waterfront renaissance. Walk out on the piers, have a look at the water and the gulls swooping down, then board, if you like, some of the ships. The current fleet consists of, among others, the original *Ambrose Lightship,* which guarded the approaches to the Port of New York from 1908 on; the 376-foot barque *Peking,* one of the world's largest square-rigged sailing vessels; the *Pioneer,* a coastal schooner built in 1885; the square-rigger *Wavertree,* 1885; the *Lettie G. Howard,* a Gloucester fishing schooner built in 1893; and the *Major General William H. Hart,* a city ferryboat built in 1925. General admission to the museum is $3.50 for adults, $1.50 for children, free to members, and includes admission to the ships, the Seaport Museum's Gallery at 215 Water St., which features changing exhibitions, and the museum's educational programs, films, and lectures, which vary monthly. An additional charge of $1.50 is made for the museum tour, a 50-minute guided introduction to the ships, the streets, and the buildings of the seaport area.

For those who have the time, there's an even more delicious

possibility: a chance to take a cruise in the summer months into New York Harbor on the 99-year-old, 102-foot-long, two-masted schooner *Pioneer*. Her specific destination depends on wind and tides; passengers are limited to 40, and those who wish are invited to help sail the ship. The cost is $15 for adults for a two-hour trip, $20 for three hours; children under 12 are $10 and $15. A special Fourth of July Fireworks Trip (recommended!) is $40. The boat can be chartered for private events. Call 699-9400.

Another museum attraction is Bowne & Co., Stationers, at 211 Water Street, a re-creation of a 19th-century stationery shop whose antique letterpresses are used daily. Bowne carries fine paper products for sale, many of them printed in the shop itself. Other museum stores include the Edmund M. Blunt Book & Chart Store (nautical books and materials); the Seaport Shop (museum merchandise); Staple & Fancy Goods (antique gifts and decorative items); and the Container Store at Pier 16, in season (children's toys and accessories).

There's always plenty of activity going on at the South Street Seaport Museum, including summer-long free jazz concerts, films, readings, nautical events, classes, workshops, and special events. For further up-to-date information, call 669-9400.

The museum's ships and piers and its architectural focal point, the 1811 countinghouses called **Schermerhorn Row,** are part and parcel of the South Street Seaport area, a multi-million-dollar, multiphase project along the lines of Boston's Fanueil Hall Marketplace and Baltimore's Harborplace, which includes the new Fulton Market Building, devoted exclusively to food—provisioners, fine restaurants (see reviews of the Coho, Roebling's, and North Star Pub in Chapter IV) and "fast-food" menus from all over the world. Among the latter, we love to put a meal together from places like Ming's Bau House for great dim sum, Empañadas for Argentine meat and vegetable turnovers, Gaylord's Saffron for Indian tandoor cooking, and Jimbay for the enthralling taste sensations of Japanese sushi. (You should be able to eat for under $6.)

As part of the first phase, completed in late July of 1983, 75 shops and restaurants are open every day of the year, many of them from early morning to well past midnight. So anytime you come by, it's fun to browse at places like Brookstone for one-of-a-kind gadgets, Captain Hook's for nifty marine antiques, Caswell-Massey for George Washington's favorite cologne, Sarah Bernhardt's cucumber cream, and other authentic, oldtime apothecary items. By the summer of 1985, the glass-and-steel Pier Pavilion on Pier 17 will stretch out into the East River, offering still more food specialties and shops, and public promenades with a magnificent view of the Brooklyn Bridge.

Want more? Take the family to see *South Street Venture* at the Trans Lux Seaport Theater, an hour-long film spectacular with dazzling multimedia visual and sound effects that depicts the history of the area in colorful style. The kids will love it. Admission is $4.50 for adults, $3 for children (phone 608-7888 for hours).

THE STATEN ISLAND FERRY: Backtrack a little bit now, and proceed a few blocks south, in the direction you came from, and you'll find yourself at the next part of your tour, the Staten Island Ferry.

If you've covered even half the places we've told you about downtown, you're probably pretty tired. The ideal way to rest your feet, recoup your energy, and catch a few more "sights" at the same time is to take a trip on the Staten Island Ferry. The cost is 25¢ for a round trip for an enthralling, hour-long excursion into the world's biggest harbor. Most of the Staten Island commuters will be sitting inside reading their papers, but do join the sightseers out on the deck, where you can view the busy harbor traffic: tugs and railroad barges, garbage scows and jaunty yachts, freighters and great liners on their way to ocean cruises. En route, you'll pass close to the Statue of Liberty, and also catch glimpses of Governor's Island and of Ellis Island which, up until 1954, was the gateway to America for millions of immigrants. When the boat arrives at St. George, Staten Island, debark, walk through the terminal, and catch the next boat going back to Manhattan. This is really the best part of the trip, for now you can pretend you are coming in from Europe and catching your first sight of the fabled New York skyline looming up there ahead of you. If you have time, try a ferry ride at night, when the skyline is even more dazzling. On a hot summer night, the ferry beats air conditioning by a mile and it's practically a haven for young lovers who find riding back and forth all night the cheapest date in New York.

Pause now for a leisurely lunch (or have a snack on the ferry or in the St. George terminal) and make your way uptown to 45th Street and First Avenue, the entrance to the United Nations.

UNITED NATIONS: Downtown Manhattan is where New York history was made; the United Nations is where world history happens every day. An international enclave on the East River, bounded by 42nd Street on the south and 48th Street on the north, it is headquarters for almost 6000 men and women from all over the world who carry on the work of the Secretariat and the General Assembly.

Just *being* at the United Nations has an excitement about it that exists nowhere else. You could have a lovely visit just walking around, observing the sculptures and artworks donated by the member nations (in the garden, for example, a massive sculpture of a Soviet worker beats a sword into a plowshare), shopping in the downstairs stores (more about these later), and observing the lively international crowd, but do take time to attend one of the General Assembly or other meetings and/or to take a guided tour. Tickets to the meetings are given out in the lobby of the General Assembly building just before they start, on a first-come, first-served basis. There is no charge. To find out in advance what meetings will be held, phone PL 4-1234 between 9:30 a.m. and 5 p.m. Once you gain admission, you can plug in your earphones and listen to the debates—sometimes quite lively—in either English or French or Chinese or Spanish or Russian—the official languages of the U.N. Guided tours begin about every ten minutes, from 9:15 a.m. to 4:45 p.m., and cost $3 for adults, $1.75 for college and high school students, $1.25 for junior high and elementary school students (those under 5 are not permitted). The tours are a wonderful introduction to the history and activities of the U.N., and also give you a chance to explore the varied collections of art and sculpture. There are also tours for non-English-speaking guests.

You could easily browse away a few hours downstairs at the United Nations. Our favorite spot here is the Gift Center, where beautiful and tasteful handicrafts from many of the member nations are sold. On a recent visit, for example, we found pewter ware from Norway, beautifully painted nesting dolls from the Soviet Union, silk scarves from India, brassware from Iran, carved figures from Nigeria. The collection of ethnic dolls is enough to win the heart of any little girl on your list. Stamp buffs should stop in at the United Nations Postal Service, the only spot on the globe (besides the United Nations office in Geneva) where you can mail cards and letters bearing U.N. postage stamps; these stamps, which deal with the work of the U.N. and its agencies, are issued about five times a year. And don't neglect, during your visit to the U.N., to look for the nearby Delacorte Geyser in the East River, which spouts between the hours of noon and 2 p.m.

If you arrive early enough, have lunch at the United Nations in the Delegates Dining Room. It's open to the public Monday through Friday, between 11:30 a.m. and noon and from 2 to 2:30 p.m., on a first-come, first-served basis. Although you probably won't see any delegates (the room is reserved for them between noon and 1 p.m.), the view of the East River and the United Nations gardens is one of the best in town.

While you're in the U.N. neighborhood, it would be a shame not to cross the street and have a look at the **Ford Foundation** building, designed by Kevin Roche and occupying the block between 42nd and 43rd Streets. Considered one of the rare modern architectural masterpieces of New York, a structure built with humanistic concerns for its employees and its environment, it is especially notable for its splendid indoor garden—a glorious, 12-story, 160-foot-high hothouse. The noted architectural critic of the *New York Times,* Ada Louise Huxtable, called the building "a splendid, shimmering Crystal Palace" and its garden "probably one of the most romantic environments ever devised by corporate men." Don't miss a quiet few moments here. The garden is open weekdays from 9 a.m. to 5 p.m. Phone 573-5011 for information. Art lovers should walk a few blocks (or take the crosstown bus) to Park Avenue and 42nd Street to view the splendid sculpture court and small museum, a branch of the **Whitney Museum,** in the Philip Morris World Headquarters. It's open daily, from 11 a.m. to 6 p.m. Free.

CHINATOWN: The final part of this sightseeing sojourn takes place at night. Head down to Chinatown, have dinner at one of the many intriguing restaurants there (see Chapter IV for suggestions), and after you've feasted on the likes of wonton soup and moo goo gai pan and sin koo har kow, spend the next hour or so just walking around the streets. There's plenty see here: this is Hometown, U.S.A., to about 6000 Americans of Chinese descent, and on weekends, thousands of relatives and friends who've moved elsewhere come home to visit. Thousands of new residents, from the mainland and Hong Kong, add to the density of the neighborhood. They pack the tiny winding alleys and streets, and so do the tourists, for this is one of the most exotic and appealing sections of the city. (If you happen to be in New

York for the Chinese New Year, usually early in February, you're in for a great treat: parades in the streets, fireworks, an Oriental Fourth of July.) There is a **Chinese Museum** at 8 Mott St. (tel. WO4-1542; open from 10 a.m. to 6 p.m. daily; admission is 75¢ for adults, 50¢ for children on weekdays, but $1 and 75¢ on weekends and holidays), which the kids will like a lot. We are always quite satisfied just window-shopping, looking at exotic Chinese herbs like ginseng in the pharmacies, bamboo sprouts, thousand-year-old eggs and lily roots in the groceries. Poking around the gift shops is delightful. Many wares from the People's Republic have now made their way into what was once exclusively a Nationalist Chinese stronghold: try **Chinese Native Products** at 22 Catherine St., for one. Pick up an ivory carving of a fan, maybe even a Mao cap, and then go back to the hotel to relax and sort out the day's impressions. Tomorrow, we promise, a gentler pace.

Note: Chinatown begins just below Canal Street, on the Lower East Side. The main street is Mott. Take either the Lexington Avenue Subway or the BMT to Canal Street and walk to Mott.

The Third Day
(A Cruise Around the Island, the *Intrepid* Sea-Air-Space Museum, the Metropolitan Museum of Art, the Museum of Modern Art, Greenwich Village, and Soho)

CIRCLE LINE: We promised we'd let you relax a bit more today, so let's spend the morning aboard a boat. You will, however, have company, for this particular vessel is the Circle Line sight-seeing boat that makes a three-hour, around-the-island tour of Manhattan, and it is one of the most popular attractions in town—and one of the best. We recommend it to those who've never seen the city and to those who've seen everything two dozen times; it's one of the best inventions for cooling off in the sultry New York summer.

The unusual thing about this trip is the perspective it gives you; the buildings that you've already seen at close range suddenly look quite different when viewed from the sea. Your orbit around the island begins at Pier 83, at the foot of West 43rd Street, takes you down into Upper Bay where you'll see the Statue of Liberty and Ellis Island, then up along the East River, as the Brooklyn Bridge, the Manhattan Bridge, and the former

Lower Manhattan

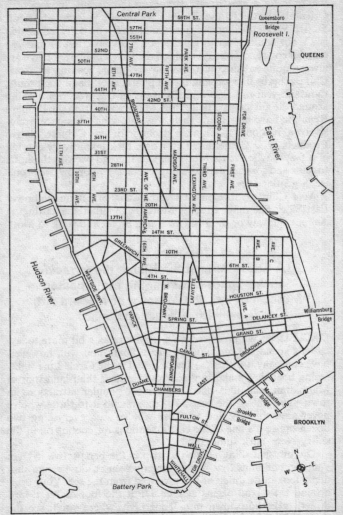

Upper Manhattan

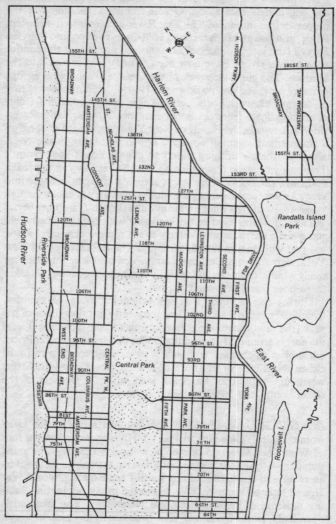

Brooklyn Navy Yard come into view. Up you go along the East River to view the splendor of the United Nations as seen from the sea, and farther along, Gracie Mansion, the home of the mayor, comes into view. The East River merges into the Harlem River, and you go north through Hell Gate, then on into Spuyten Duyvil (the last two, former navigational hazards at the confluence of two rivers, have now been tamed), and merge into the Hudson. The giant lacework of the George Washington Bridge emerges now, and you go down the Hudson, joining slews of tiny pleasure craft, work boats, perhaps even an oil tanker or freighter coming down from the upper Hudson. To your left is Riverside Park, where thousands of New Yorkers come to cool off on a summer's day; small boys are apt to be fishing in the river, although there's nothing much to catch. You'll spot Grant's Tomb as you come down along 122nd Street. As you approach midtown, the docks of the great shipping companies come into view. As your sightseeing yacht docks, you may be lucky enough to see a slew of tugs nudge a beauty like the *QE II* into her berth!

The sightseeing boat comes equipped with both a refreshment stand and a narrator who is likely to tell some very ancient jokes; but you will emerge rested, cool, and well-informed about New York. *Parent's note:* Children about 8 and over love this trip, but really young ones can get awfully wriggly; remember, it takes three hours, and you can't get off!

During the summer, trips are scheduled every 45 minutes, from 9:30 a.m. to 3:45 p.m., less frequently at other times of the year (the season runs from late March to mid-November), and the cost is around $10 for adults, $5 for children under 12. Prices are subject to change. To reach West 43rd Street, you can take either the 42nd Street (no. 106), 49th Street, or 34th Street westbound crosstown buses; all stop within a few feet of the ticket booth (tel. 563-3200).

INTREPID SEA-AIR-SPACE MUSEUM: Just a few blocks away from the Circle Line pier, at Pier 86, Hudson River and the foot of West 46th Street, is one of New York's newest—and most popular—attractions, the aircraft carrier *Intrepid,* a salty veteran of air and sea battles of the South Pacific during World War II, and later of Vietnam, now converted into a fascinating floating museum of naval history and technology. The museum is open daily, from 10 a.m. to 8 p.m. in summer, to 7 p.m. in winter (buy tickets at least two hours before closing). Admission is $6 for adults, $5 for seniors, $3 for children under 12 (tel. 245-2533).

Back on land now, try to find the time to visit the city's two major art museums: the Metropolitan Museum of Art and the Museum of Modern Art. You can have lunch in either one; then devote your afternoon to art.

METROPOLITAN MUSEUM OF ART: Whether you're interested in Egyptian artifacts or Roman armor or Chinese porcelain or Renaissance or impressionist painting, the Metropolitan is the place. You could spend weeks studying the collection of European and American paintings, a masterful group of Raphaels, Titians, El Grecos, Rembrandts, Picassos, Motherwells, Braques —enough to make the head swim. You'll surely want to visit the spectacular new Michael C. Rockefeller Wing, a stunning, $18-million showcase devoted to the primitive art of Africa, the Pacific Islands, pre-Columbian and Native America. You must not miss the new American wing, which has brought some of Central Park indoors in a glass-enclosed, 70-foot-tall garden that leads to three new floors of American paintings, furniture, sculpture, silver, glass, textiles, and decorative arts. Also high on your agenda should be the splendid André Meyer Galleries, showcasing the Metropolitan's extensive holdings in 19th-century European art, with particular emphasis on the impressionist and post-impressionist painters and a large collection of Rodin sculptures. The 32 dramatic Egyptian galleries, including the incredible Temple of Dendur in the Sackler Wing, are considered a triumph of art and scholarship, one of the most distinguished collections of its kind anywhere. The exhibit is absorbing for everyone, and the kids, especially, will love the mummies! The Metropolitan brings the world to New York, and, quite rightly, the world comes to its door (last year it counted 4,664,997 visitors. It is an SRO attraction, a major sightseeing target.

The Metropolitan is open Wednesday through Saturday from 10 a.m. to 4:45 p.m., on Tuesday until 8:45 p.m.; Sunday and holidays, from 11 a.m. to 4:45 p.m. Closed Monday and Monday holidays. There is a suggested admission charge of $4 for adults, $2 for students and senior citizens.

For recorded information, phone 535-7710; for news of concerts and lectures, 879-5512.

MUSEUM OF MODERN ART: Younger, brasher, and more daring than the Metropolitan, the Museum of Modern Art (MOMA), 11 West 53rd St., has been controversial ever since it opened in 1929. The Modern's early shows—of fur-lined teacups, Dada-esque landscapes of the mind, cubism, and abstractions—were considered shocking by the staid art establishment of the time; now there are painters and sculptors who actually picket the Modern, declaring it too old hat! Whichever side you're on, the Modern is a great, lively, wonderfully exciting museum which takes all of modern art and design as its province —and that includes photography, film, pottery, furniture, and architecture, as well as paintings and sculpture. As for the paintings, the "Old Masters"—the Picassos, Chagalls, Kandinskys, Mondrians, Tchelitchews—a visit to this collection is surely an essential part of a trip to New York. So is a look at the splendid outdoor Sculpture Garden with its Rodins and Calders and Nevelsons and Maillols; it is one of the most special places in the city. Devotes of old and new films practically make the theater of the museum a second home: it's the place to catch an early Garbo classic, a Flaherty masterpiece, your favorite Bogart flick, recent films you might have missed at the box office, as well as the work of new filmmakers.

Now that MOMA has completed its four-year, $55-million renovation, there is twice as much gallery space as ever before, and many new displays, one more dazzling than the next. Overlooking the Sculpture Court are two restaurants: the Garden Café, a cafeteria for the public, and the Members Dining Room. The musuem is open Monday, Tuesday, Friday, Saturday, and Sunday from 11 a.m. to 6 p.m., on Thursday until 9 p.m.; closed Wednesday. Admission is free for members, $4.50 for adults, $3 for students with valid ID, and $2 for children and senior citizens. Thursday from 6 to 9 p.m., it's "Pay What You Wish." Admission includes entrance to the movie. Because there is usually a heavy demand for tickets, it's advisable to get there as early as possible to commandeer a reservation. For information on current exhibitions, phone 708-9480; on films, 708-9490; for general information: 708-9500.

Schedule the next part of this odyssey for the late afternoon and/or early evening and plan to have dinner midjourney. For this is a visit to New York's most colorful area, Greenwich Village, and you'll want to have plenty of time to savor the sights and sounds.

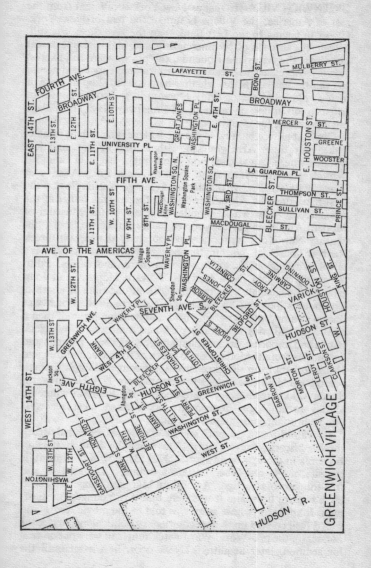

GREENWICH VILLAGE: Just as New York is different from the rest of America, the Village is unlike the rest of New York. Closer in feeling to the Left Bank than the East Side, it is still, despite the inroads of commercialism and high-rise apartment buildings, the American Bohemia, the place where self-expression is as necessary as bread. Its openness and ease are apparent to even the casual visitor, whether he comes to shop or stare or look at old buildings or drink espresso in the coffee houses or listen to folk music or catch an off-Broadway play. The Village has something for everyone.

Our best advice on how to see the Village is simply to ramble. Take your time. Arm yourself with a map or not, and just wander where fancy leads you. You might begin at Stanford White's graceful **Washington Square Arch,** Fifth Avenue at Waverly Place. Observe the statue of George Washington on the west flank done by Alexander Stirling Calder (the father of the Alexander Calder whose mobiles you saw at the Museum of Modern Art), then project yourself back into the world of 19th-century New York aristocracy as you study the elegant Greek Revival houses of Washington Square North. Henry James's novel *Washington Square* took place here, and James, Edith Wharton, William Dean Howells, Edward Hopper, and John Dos Passos have all lived on this block at one time or another. The houses look out on **Washington Square Park,** which was once a swamp, later a potter's field and hanging ground, then a public park. Today it is still a park and a mecca for Villagers, native and imported: ancient Sicilians playing chess, painters and composers from the lofts of Soho south of the park, children and their mothers from the expensive apartment buildings, hippies, beards, panhandlers, college professors from N.Y.U. On warm Sundays, kids from everywhere flock to the fountain where an all-day to late-night impromptu folk concert takes place. If you've brought your guitar, join in.

Or walk through the park and head down MacDougal Street; there's history at every turn. This was the headquarters of Bohemia in the tens and twenties. No. 137, now a restaurant, is the site of the old **Liberal Club,** a hotbed for anarchists and free-thinkers of all stripes. A youthful Margaret Sanger preached birth control here, and it was here that Art Young, Max Eastman, John Reed (whose story was told in the movie *Reds),* and Floyd Dell cooked up their revolutionary political magazine, the *Masses* (in the pre–World War I witchhunts, all were put on trial for sedition, later acquitted). Next door, in what is still the

Provincetown Playhouse, George Cram Cook and his wife Susan Glaspell, founded the Provincetown Players; in tow they had a promising young playwright named Eugene O'Neill and a young actress from Maine, Edna St. Vincent Millay. Today the atmosphere on MacDougal Street is still flamboyant, but it is not especially artistic: the street is a collection of shops, gimmicky coffeehouses, sidewalk stands selling pizza and shish kebab, all mobbed by throngs of gum-chewing teenagers who descend on the area weekend nights from everywhere (it's best to visit it during the week). Turn left on Bleecker and you'll see more restaurants, nightclubs, off-Broadway theaters, and coffeehouses where perhaps a young Joan Baez or Bob Dylan will be singing before an audience for the first time.

Or start your ramble on Seventh Avenue, at **Sheridan Square.** Nostalgia collectors who bemoan the tearing-down of old Village landmarks (on the site of the original Circle in the Square theater and the legendary Louie's Tavern now stands a modern apartment building, 3 Sheridan Square) will be rewarded by a walk down Seventh Avenue to Grove Street and **Marie's Crisis Café.** It was here that Tom Paine, a broken, defeated, old man, spent his last years; the brilliant spokesman for the American Revolution was unappreciated in his own lifetime. Continue down Seventh to Commerce Street, two blocks farther south, and walk past the lovely old homes to the **Cherry Lane Theatre,** founded by Edna St. Vincent Millay. "Vincent," one of the most authentic of the Village Bohemians, made her home at 75½ Bedford St., which is still known as the "narrowest house in the Village."

As you head back to Sheridan Square, note that this area is the center of New York City's gay population and nightlife, especially Christopher Street, west of the square. Now, amble down West 4th Street, an amusing shopping street with no less than two antique clothing stores, **Smitty's Antique Clothing** and **Tramps,** diagonally across the street from each other. Try on some glad rags, perhaps, and then have a drink or a burger with the large crowd that congregates at the very popular, very casual **Jimmy Day's,** at the corner of West 4th and Barrow. Or if your taste is running to coffee and wonderful tarts, truffles, eclairs or pralines, visit the authentic Pâtisserie Claude, a tiny charmer just across the street.

Perhaps one of the Village's best shopping streets is Greenwich Avenue, which you can reach by walking east on Christopher Street from Sheridan Square. This one block of Christopher Street alone has several charming boutiques: **Matt McGhee No.**

1 and **Matt McGhee 2,** the latter with almost everything made by hand—ceramic bowls, rugs, mohair throws; and across the street, two colorful shops featuring distinctive T-shirts, sweatshirts, and accessories for men, women, and children: the **Laughing Stork** at no. 19, **Design Point** at no. 15 (with the Oscar Wilde Bookshop upstairs). **Gingerbread House,** at no. 9, is a tiny treasure for little people, stocked with wonderful books and dolls and puppets, European toys and handmade rainbow clowns.

Bear left around Christopher, and you'll find yourself at a huge, busy center of the Village. Greenwich Avenue is lined with tempting shops. Note **Dorell Casuals,** no. 7, which has some of the nicest women's sportswear in the Village, and the **Pottery Barn,** nos. 49 and 51, where you can pick up inexpensive handblown glasses, hundreds of gourmet gadgets, and cookware items in tasteful, contemporary design. Don't miss a visit to Martin Proctor's **Unicorn City** at no. 55, where you can pet or purchase a mythological beastie—they come in posters, patches, pottery, pendants, and more, in a wide price range.

Cross the street now and walk Greenwich in the opposite direction. Stop in at the **Common Ground,** no. 50, to see a distinctive collection of American Indian jewelry, belts, rugs, and woodcarvings, mostly from Navajo and Zuni tribes. **Candy Kisses,** no. 58, does have candy kisses—and homemade fudge, fine chocolates, and all-chocolate novelty items, as well as rows of apothecary jars filled with oldtime penny candies—now gone up a few cents, alas. If you're hungry, stop in for a bite at the **Peacock,** at no. 24, an oldtime Village coffeehouse a few doors away. Have some torta verde di ricotta (spinach-and-cheese pie), a big plate of antipasto, or just some espresso or wine and pastry. If you're in the mood for pizza, **Famous Rays,** known for the best pizza in New York, is just a few blocks up Avenue of the Americas, at 11th Street. Across the street and one block farther north, at 12th Street, is the **Mad Monk,** where beautiful ceramic works are priced very modestly. Walk back south along Avenue of the Americas to 9th Street and have a look and a nibble at **Balducci's,** one of the city's most exciting and best stocked international food stores. Or just head for the big, busy corner of 8th Street and Sixth Avenue, and proceed to explore the intriguing shops as you walk along toward Fifth. And back you are at Washington Square Arch, the fountain, and the park. Sit down, relax, and contemplate the never-ending, always-absorbing Village scene.

Note: We've told you about the Village by day here: we'll explore the night scene in the Village in Chapter VIII.

AVE OF THE AMERICAS

SULLIVAN ST.

THOMPSON ST.

WEST BROADWAY

WOOSTER ST.

PRINCE ST.

GREENE ST.

MERCER ST.

SPRING ST.

BROADWAY

BROOME ST.

CROSBY ST.

LAFAYETTE ST.

HOUSTON ST.

CLEVELAND ST.

GRAND ST.

MULBERRY ST.

LITTLE ITALY

MOTT ST.

ELIZABETH ST.

BOWERY

THE SO HO AREA

W
S — N
E

SOHO: The last part of this excursion is not, admittedly, one of the "major sights" of New York, but for those who are particularly interested in art and artists and artistic shops, it might well be one of the most interesting. For New York's most vital art center is no longer Greenwich Village, or even Madison Avenue or 57th Street. About 2000 of the city's most serious artists—as well as crafts people and dancers and filmmakers and photographers and musicians and writers—live and work in a 50-block area of rundown cast-iron commercial buildings that stretches north from Canal to Houston Streets, west from Lafayette Street to West Broadway, just above Chinatown, just below the Village. This is Soho, and a Saturday afternoon here will give you a quick look at the latest movements in contemporary art, plus a chance to shop at some delightful boutiques and break bread with the Soho community in some neighborhood restaurants. Although the shops and galleries are open during the week as well, the area is noisily industrial during the week, and Saturday is *the* time.

If you're already in Greenwich Village, you can walk to Soho in about ten minutes; it's just south of Bleecker Street and Washington Square Village. Or, take the no. 5 Fifth Avenue bus marked West Houston Street and get off at the last stop—the corner of Houston and West Broadway. West Broadway is Soho's main thoroughfare, so start your leisurely promenade here, stopping in at galleries and shops as fancy leads you, admiring the distinguished 19th-century palazzo commercial architecture of the buildings (most are about 100 years old). Soho has a rich and varied street life: you might be able to pick up blankets or tops from Guatemala at low prices, buy paintings on the street, find news on a bulletin board of a lecture or happening (there are many of them going on here) that you might want to attend. A recent notice, for example, announced an evening of "Humming and Other Sensory Meditations—Sound Emerging for Trans-Perceptual Experience." The most important aspect of Soho, for us, is the feeling of aliveness and creativity in the area, the ambience created by serious and talented people exploring new ways of expressing their own reality.

Art in Soho tends to concentrate on works by younger artists and sculptors, and much of the work is massive (that's why the artist must work in lofts and why this small-industry neighborhood became an artists' colony). Styles vary from minimal to conceptual to pop to abstract expression to photo realism to you-name-it: about the only thing the artists have in common is that most of them are anti-establishment. 420 West Broadway is a good place to start your explorations: here's where **Leo Castelli, John Weber, Mary Boone,** and **Sonnabend Gallery** all maintain showcases. Take the elevator to the top floor and walk down: the crowd is on the steps, chatting and meeting and maybe celebrity-watching. Other galleries you might want to see include the pioneering **O.K. Harris, Nancy Hoffman, John Gibson, West Broadway,** and **Jordon Volpe.** Here too are the far-out interiors and sculptures of Rudi Stern's **Let There Be Neon.** If you can't afford a commission for your place back home, maybe you can afford one of the contemporary posters, which start at $10 unframed and unmounted, at **Poster Originals, Limited,** at 158 Spring St.

Roam the streets a little to find some of the other important galleries. **Paula Cooper,** an early Soho showplace, is at 155 Wooster St.; **Louis K. Meisel,** 141 Prince St., is one of the foremost galleries showing photo realism and abstract illusionism. Don't leave the area without at least a look at **Tropics Gallery,** 463 West Broadway, half-gallery, half-shop (see below), a stunner of a showplace for the fine arts and folk arts, the antiques, jewelry, textiles, and carvings of Bali and Java. Some of the museum-quality items here include extraordinary flying angels from Bali, antique Wayang Golek shadow puppets from Java, an extensive collection of Indonesian ikats (weavings), and opium beds priced upward of $10,000. If you're traveling heavy and can handle, say, a stained-glass window from an upstate New York church for $1500, make the acquaintance of **Urban Archeology,** 137 Spring St., a find for collectors of architectural ornaments. Traveling light? Then visit the **Spring Street Enamels Gallery,** 171 Spring St., to see some exquisite artworks in enameling: jewelry, sculpture, wall pieces. The gallery is one of the leaders in the current renaissance of this ancient and beautiful art.

For a new artistic experience, be sure to visit the **Museum of Holography** at 11 Mercer St., one block west of Broadway and north of Canal Street (tel. 925-0526). Holography, as most people do not know, is a new form of photography that uses laser beams instead of cameras to make three-dimensional images that seem to float before the eye. Admission is $2.75 for adults, $2 for students with current ID, $1.50 for children under 12 and senior citizens.

You can get the latest copy of *Art News* and browse through beautiful art books, many from Europe and Canada, at **Jaap Rietman Art Books,** upstairs at the corner of West Broadway and Spring Streets. For what the proprietors call "the largest collection of art postcards and notecards" in the world, visit **Untitled** (Harris Graphics), 159 Prince St. Cards are 35¢ and up.

In style, taste, and imagination, some of the Soho boutiques are an excursion unto themselves. . . . **Le Grand Hotel / Tales of Hoffman** at 471 West Broadway, looks like a 1920s movie set, with thick carpets, old-fashioned gilt mirrors, potted palms, and Billie Holiday on the stereo. There are men's and women's far-out shoes up front, Theda Bara-type dresses in the back. . . . The cavernous, mysterious interior of **Barone**, 414 West Broadway, purposely designed to "disorient the visitor" and remove the feeling of four walls and a ceiling, does just that. Exotic necessities like crystal mouches (beauty marks), and a far-out line of cosmetics and cosmetic accessories accentuate the surrealist atmosphere here. . . . **Pentimenti**, 126 Prince St., is the place for ruffles and laces and feather boas of half a century ago that look stunning on today's flappers. . . . Have a look at **This End Up Furniture Company**, 461 West Broadway, which shows rugged, hardwearing furniture handcrafted (by one person, from start to finish) of southern yellow pine. Inexpensive and handsome. (They have another shop at 1139 Second Ave.)

Balooms, 147 Sullivan St., is the place to treat yourself to an "air bouquet"—clear balloons filled with silk flowers. . . . We love the made-to-order dresses at **Tamala Design w/Bagel**, a cozy little store down a few steps at 153 Prince St. If you can't afford one of the hand-screened prints on cotton (from $125 to $150) or one of the hand-painted silks ($250 to $350), you can at least have a simple-yet-exotic snack like cream cheese and caviar on a bagel. . . . **Paracelso**, 432 West Broadway, is the place where well-heeled gypsies can stock up on colored silk dresses from Afghanistan and Japan (around $150 to $250), marvelous primitive jewelry, and heady perfumes from Arabia.

Food is raised to an art form at **Dean & De Luca**, 121 Prince St., where mounds of freshly baked breads and pastries, bins of coffee beans, stacks of dried nuts, perfect fresh fruits, compete for attention with delicious homemade pâtés, escabeche, chicken tarragon, coulibiac of salmon, and an exquisite selection of 300 varieties of imported cheeses. A visit here is reason enough to immediately plan a picnic.

Chapter VI

MORE SIGHTS AND SOUNDS OF NEW YORK

YOU'VE COMPLETED three days of sightseeing, and you're still thirsting for more. The possibilities are endless. While you certainly won't want to see *everything,* the following descriptions will give you an idea of what is available: pick and choose, according to your own time and interests. We've grouped them geographically—Midtown, Downtown, the Upper East Side, the Upper West Side, Points North, and Beyond Manhattan—so you can refer to this list when you happen to be in a certain area and have time to visit, for example, just one museum. **We've marked the exhibits that are of the most interest to the small fry with an asterisk.**

Note: We haven't attempted to cover everything in New York, since this is a guidebook and not an encyclopedia. Listed below are some major and minor sights of the city, chosen either for their importance or their special, if offbeat, charm.

Downtown

CITY HALL: City Hall Park at Broadway and Park Row. The mayor will be out to greet you if you're an astronaut, prime minister, or beauty queen, but you may not get to see him if you're just an ordinary mortal. You can, however, see the splendid building in which he works, a successful 19th-century blending of French Renaissance and Federal influences, considered to be one of New York's prime architectural treasures. Walk up the splendid marble staircase to the **Governor's Room.** It was once reserved for the use of the governor of the state when he was in New York, but now it's a museum with historic furniture (the desk George Washington used as president is here) and Trumbull portraits of George, Alexander Hamilton, and others. City Hall welcomes individual visitors Monday to Friday, 10 a.m. to 3 p.m. Groups of more than five may troop to City Hall only by appointment.

A lot of history was made at **City Hall Park** which, in the early days of New York, was a kind of village square: political riots, hangings, police wars, and one of the first readings, in 1776, of the Declaration of Independence to a group of New York revolutionaries, all took place here.

*FIRE DEPARTMENT MUSEUM: 104 Duane St., between Church St. and Broadway, three blocks north of City Hall (tel. 570-4230). We have yet to met the small boy who could readily be torn away from this one: three floors laden with antique fire-fighting equipment, including some splendid old engines dating back to 1820. Admission is free. Open Monday to Friday from 9 a.m. to 4 p.m.; closed weekends and holidays.

OLD MERCHANT'S HOUSE: 29 East 4th Street (tel. 777-1089). Miraculously saved from demolition, this splendid example of a 19th-century wealthy New York home is once again open for visitors. The Tredwell family lived in this house from 1835 to 1933, and its restoration has remained faithful to the original design. Household furnishings, glass, china are still as they were a century ago. Open only on Sunday, from 1 to 4 p.m. Admission is $2, $1 for senior citizens and students; those under 12 can enter free with an adult. The house is also open, by appointment, for groups of at least 20.

OLD ST. PATRICK'S CATHEDRAL: Corner of Mott and Prince Sts. Newly restored, this historic (1809) church is the predecessor of its grander sister on Fifth Avenue and 50th Street. In the cemetery outside the church is buried Pierre Toussaint, the former Haitian slave, who may one day be canonized by Rome.

WOOLWORTH BUILDING: 233 Broadway. Until the coming of the Empire State Building, this was the world's tallest—60 stories, pretty good for 1913. It's a lovely, lacy, Gothic frou-frou. Admire.

Midtown: East Side

*CENTRAL PARK: What Tivoli is to Copenhagen or Chapultepec to Mexico City, Central Park is to New York: the great public playground. A magnificent garden in the midst of the concrete canyons, it offers city-jaded New Yorkers a breath of the country, a chance to wander along bosky landscapes, climb rocks, listen to the song of birds, and stare at the sky. It also gives them the chance to stare at each other: Frederick Law Olmsted's 19th-century greensward is one of the most popular places in town. The park offers many recreational and cultural outlets. During the summer, there's the **New York Shakespeare Festival,** plus concerts by the Metropolitan Opera, the New York Philharmonic, and many others—most of them free. The Department of Recreation also sponsors many interesting events in the park, from free tennis lessons for kids to hula-hoop contests! So many things go on in the park, in fact, that daily reports are given via a recorded tape, on the telephone. Dial 755-4100, and if you need more information on any park facility or program, call 472-1003.

*The Park for Children

For kids worn out by too much sightseeing, an hour or so in the park is the perfect antidote. First, there is the **Central Park Zoo,** Fifth Ave. at 64th St., with an ample supply of lions, tigers, monkeys, and splashing seals in a pool, sure-fire kid pleasers. (The Zoo is currently undergoing a major reconstruction, to be completed early in 1985.) Kids also love the pony rides and the Delacorte Clock here; the carillon chimes and carved animals dance, every half hour. The zoo cafeteria, with its large outdoor terrace, is a good place to feed starving moppets. If you have really little ones, take them over to the adjoining **Children's Zoo,** where they can feed and pet animals, climb up Noah's Ark, and slide down Alice's rabbit hole. Then take them along to the **Carousel,** opposite 65th Street in the center of the park (a path leads here from the cafeteria). Or let them sail their model boats at Conservatory Pond near 72nd Street and Fifth, join the local youngsters flying kites, or work off some excess energy at one of the two inspired **Adventure Playgrounds;** there's one near 67th Street and Central Park West, another with an entrance on 60th Street and Seventh Avenue. Or they can listen to stories at the charming **Hans Christian Andersen** statue, near the model boat-house; the Public Library provides storytellers, usually on summer Saturdays, betwen 11 a.m. and 1 p.m. Most adult listeners seem as enthralled as the kids.

The Park for Adults: Boaters, Bikers, Riders, Skaters, Dreamers

One of the newer attractions in the park is the **Dairy**, a beautiful and historic restoration of one of Olmsted and Vaux's original park buildings, open Tuesday through Sunday from 10:30 a.m. to 4:30 p.m. Free concerts are held every Sunday at noon, followed by a walk/talk series; there are frequent exhibits; and walking tours led by the N.Y.C. Urban Park Rangers begin here every weekend. For more information, phone the Dairy at 397-3156.

With or without kids, don't miss taking a rowboat out on **Conservatory Lake** (72nd Street), an unexpectedly rural spot for New York. And when you've finished, join the throngs strolling around the beautiful Bethesda Fountain area, which is really the focal point of the park. The setting—with the fountain, the lake, the towers of New York in the background—is one of the most romantic in the city.

Other romantic ways to see Central Park: in a horse-drawn carriage (pick up a carriage at 59th Street and Central Park South, near the Plaza Hotel). The energetic among you can join the local jogging set, or rent a horse from the **Claremont Riding Academy**, 175 West 89th St. (tel. SC4-5100; about $18 an hour) and trot through miles of lovely bridle paths, or rent a bike from the bicycle concession near the boathouse at the 72nd Street Lake and join the throngs of New Yorkers—families, kids, boys looking for girls, girls looking for boys—who've discovered the joy of life on wheels. During the summer, the park is closed to traffic from 10 a.m. to 4 p.m. on weekdays, as well as all day on the weekends, so bikers, riders, and kids reign supreme. Tennis buffs can also find a home in Central Park; the courts at 93rd Street are insanely popular. Tennis permits cost $27.50, and they entitle you to unlimited play. There are also several bubbled courts that stay open during the winter. For information on permits and what courts are open, phone the Permit Office, 830 Fifth Ave. (tel. 360-8204). If roller skating is your thing, you can rent skates from **City Skates,** which has a concession in the middle of the park at the 97th Street North Meadows Playground (tel. 876-1118). Skating instruction is available. More sedentary types can enjoy browsing through the bookstalls (New

York's modest answer to the Left Bank *quais* of Paris) along the outer wall of the park, at Fifth Avenue and 60th Street. (There are also some great little kiosks serving all sorts of international snacks.) Eventually, many of the famed booksellers of Fourth Avenue's Book Row may relocate here.

Strawberry Fields

A living memorial to John Lennon grows in Central Park, in a hilly, 2½-acre area across the street from the Dakota Apartments, where Lennon was shot on December 9, 1980. Ground was broken for Strawberry Fields by his widow, Yoko Ono, who donated $1 million to the project, as this book was going to press. Some 25,000 strawberry plants will grow amid the trees, vines, shrubs, and perennials here, and gifts from foreign nations have been promised: a mosaic from Italy, flower bulbs from Holland, an oak tree from England, a fountain from France. For those who remember John Lennon, this is a very special bit of New York.

MUSEUMS, EXHIBITS, LANDMARKS: Asia Society Gallery, 725 Park Ave. (tel. 288-6400, ext. 229). Asia Society's splendid new building houses Mr. and Mrs. John D. Rockefeller III's collection of Asian art—sculpture, ceramics, and paintings from India, Southeast Asia, China, and Japan. In addition, an average of three loan exhibitions each year are shown in the C. V. Starr Gallery. Open Tuesday through Saturday from 11 a.m. to 6 p.m., Sunday from noon to 5 p.m.; closed Monday. Admission is $2.

Theodore Roosevelt Birthplace National Historic Site, 28 East 20th St. (tel. 260-1616). Teddy Roosevelt, the 26th president, was born on this site in 1858 and lived here until he was 15 years old. Five rooms of this reconstructed Victorian brownstone have been restored to look as they did during Teddy's boyhood. The house also contains a museum of Roosevelt memorabilia. Open 9 a.m. to 5 p.m. Wednesday through Sunday. Closed Federal holidays. Admission is 50¢; children under 16 and adults over 62, free.

Cooper-Hewitt Museum, the Smithsonian Institution's National Museum of Design, Fifth Ave. at 91st St. (tel. 860-6868). The only division of the Smithsonian to have its headquarters outside of Washington, D.C., Cooper-Hewitt is an exquisite gem of a museum, housed in the restored neo-Georgian Andrew

Carnegie mansion. The museum's holdings are acknowledged to be the world's finest collection of design and decorative arts, including everything from porcelain, embroideries, furniture, drawings, and prints, to birdcages, pressed flowers, and Valentines. Exhibitions, which change regularly, are always devoted to some aspect of design. Open 10 a.m. to 9 p.m. on Tuesday, to 5 p.m. Wednesday through Saturday, noon to 5 p.m. on Sunday. Closed Monday and major holidays. General admission is $1.50; senior citizens and students, $1. Free Tuesday after 5 p.m.

Frick Collection, 1 East 70th St. (tel. 288-0700). One of the most beautiful small museums in the world, this Fifth Avenue center, with its greenery and fountains, is an oasis. Concerts and lectures are held here, October through May. Phone 288-0700 for details. Open Tuesday through Saturday from 10 a.m. to 6 p.m., Sunday and minor holidays from 1 p.m. Closed Monday and major holidays. Children under 10 not admitted and those under 16 must be accompanied by an adult. Admission: Tuesday through Saturday, $1 (50¢ for students and senior citizens); Sunday, $2.

Guggenheim Museum, 1071 Fifth Ave., near 89th St. (tel. 360-3500). Frank Lloyd Wright's creation has both passionate defenders and detractors. It's a large, spiral ramp on which are displayed shows featuring works by established modern masters and artists currently involved in experimental approaches as well as Solomon Guggenheim's augmented collection of 20th-century art. The Justin K. Thannhauser Wing permanently displays such impressionist and post-impressionist masters as Picasso, Degas, and Cézanne. Open daily, except Monday, from 11 a.m. to 5 p.m., Tuesday until 8 p.m. Admission: $2.50; students with ID and visitors over 62, $1.50; children under 7, free. Tuesday evenings, from 5 until 8 p.m., admission is free. Restaurant offers lunch and snacks.

The International Center of Photography, 1130 Fifth Ave. at 94th St. (tel. 860-1777), is housed in a superb Georgian building, and is New York's only museum devoted to photography. It's a mecca for photography lovers and students of the art, who are attracted by a great variety of workshops and educational programs. Changing exhibits. Open Wednesday through Friday from noon to 5 p.m., on Saturday and Sunday from 11 a.m. to 6 p.m. Admission: $2 for adults, $1 for students, senior citizens free.

Japan House, 333 East 47th St. (tel. 832-1155). This stunning example of contemporary Japanese architecture, with its beauti-

Atriums, Unlimited

Not all the green space in New York is found in the city's parks. A new trend in the past few years has been for builders to include atriums and courtyards on the ground floors of new buildings, which are perfect places for sightseers, shoppers, and local officeworkers to have a rest, have a bite, and watch the passing parade. Here are some to look for:

The Market at Citicorp Center, 53rd and 54th Sts. between Third and Lexington Aves. One of the first of its type and one of the biggest, this seven-story, skylit atrium has hundreds of chairs and tables amid trees and shrubs, free concerts and entertainments every day, and dozens of shops and restaurants.

ChemCourt, 277 Park Ave. at 47th St. This three-story greenhouse atrium, with trees and flowers provided by the New York Botanical Garden, terraced pools, and a waterfall over a wall of white marble, is the largest indoor green space in New York.

IBM Atrium, 57th St. at Madison Ave. Stands of high bamboo shoots form a living canopy in this glass-enclosed, 68-foot-high atrium, bedecked with pretty marble tables and wire chairs. You can shop for gifts from the New York Botanical Garden shop here, or get a snack from the kiosk. The adjoining IBM Gallery of Science and Art has featured a fascinating array of exhibits. Admission is free.

Trump Tower, 56th St. and Fifth Ave. Manhattan's first vertical shopping mall is one of its most stunning spaces: floors and walls of rose-pink marble and gleaming bronze offset brilliant banks of flowers, potted palms, and an 80-foot waterfall plunging down from the skylight of glass and brass. The shops are among the priciest in town, and the restaurants are not inexpensive, but the piano and violin concerts at lunchtime are free. A must-see space.

Crystal Pavilion, 50th St. at Third Ave. Flashing lights, pink and white neon, and disco music set the tone for this very modern three-tiered atrium of gray granite and silver aluminum. Two walls of water, a gondola elevator, and plenty of greenery add dramatic accents. Restaurants, boutiques, chairs for sitting, and relaxing.

Olympic Towers Arcade, 51st St. and Fifth Ave., across from St. Patrick's Cathedral. Street benches and chairs surround a reflecting waterfall pool. Come to relax under the palms, catch a free concert, or try the nouvelle cuisine at La Cascade Restaurant.

Whitney Museum at Philip Morris, Park Ave. at 42nd St. An indoor garden setting of ficus trees and seasonal flowers serves as a green foil for a vast, high-ceilinged sculpture gallery, a satellite of the main Whitney Museum of American Art uptown. Gourmet desserts and snacks are available from the coffee bar.

ful gallery, library, and outdoor garden, is headquarters of the Japan Society. Concerts are held during the week, and there are regular series of contemporary and classic Japanese films on the weekends. Admission is $4. There are frequently special exhibits in the gallery. Even if nothing is going on, however, it's well worth having a look. The United Nations is just across the street. Open daily, 10 a.m. to 5 p.m.

*Jewish Museum, Fifth Ave. at 92nd St. Felix Warburg's splendid old town house is the setting for this distinguished collection—ceremonial objects, paintings, folk arts, silver, which trace the saga of the Jews through historical times, in their wanderings through many lands. A mosaic tile synagogue wall from 16th-century Persia and a 15th-century wooden ark from Italy are among the museum's unique treasures. The museum also presents major contemporary exhibitions of painting, photography, and sculpture.

Special events include films, concerts, lectures, and children's programs. The Jewish Museum is open Monday through Thursday from noon to 5 p.m., and Sunday from 11 a.m. to 6 p.m. Closed Friday and Saturday, major Jewish holidays, and certain legal holidays (call 860-1888 to check). Admission is $2.50 for adults, $1.50 for children under 16, students with ID cards, and senior citizens.

*Museum of Broadcasting, 1 East 53rd St. (tel. 752-7684). Want to catch up on the Ed Sullivan shows of the '50s, the Jack Benny broadcasts of the '30s? You can watch Uncle Milty cavort, hear FDR's campaign speches, and lots more at this enormously popular museum. Its collection includes just about everything that's ever gone out on the airwaves, and you're free to watch it or hear it at your own private console. Selected programs are also presented on large exhibit screens. A contribution of $3 for adults, $2 for students, and $1.50 for seniors and children under 13 is requested. Open Tuesday from noon to 8 p.m., and Wednesday through Saturday from noon to 5 p.m. Next door is vest-pocket Paley Park, a cooling place to sit and snack, watch the fountain and the people, if the museum is too crowded to get in.

*Museum of the City of New York, Fifth Ave. betwen 103rd and 104th Sts. For a capsule look at New York history, this is the place. You would do well to stop here, in fact, before beginning your historical tour of downtown Manhattan. Exhibits trace the city's history from the days of the Indians to the present, through costumes, old cars, photographs, prints, ship models, fire engines, maps, furnishings, theatrical memorabilia, toys. Don't miss the fascinating Dutch Galleries, with full-scale reconstructions of Nieuw Amsterdam, or the exciting "The Big Apple," a multimedia exhibition which tells the story of the city from 1524 to today. Children will dote on the "Please Touch" demonstrations which are given on Saturday from October through April, in a reconstruction of a 17th-century Dutch home; they'll also like the puppet shows, plays, and other programs in which they can participate, from October through April. And the gift shop, with many charming and inexpensive mementos of Old New York. Check the museum for its schedule of free Sunday afternoon concerts for adults (October through April).

A *special note:* During the warmer months, April through October, the museum offers a series of outstanding walking tours, under the direction of the distinguished historian Henry Hope Reed. The tours concentrate on architecture and social history, and are enormously popular; the cost is about $6. Phone LE 4-1672 for information.

The Museum of the City of New York is open Tuesday through Saturday from 10 a.m. to 5 p.m., on Sunday and holidays from 1 to 5 p.m. Free.

Whitney Museum of American Art, 945 Madison Ave., at 75th St. (tel. 570-3600). What many consider the very best collection of 20th-century American art is housed in Marcel Breuer's superb modernistic building, an inverted layer cake to which you gain entrance by crossing a bridge. Founded by Gertrude Vanderbilt Whitney, the museum opened in the Village in 1931, and is now in its third home. At least two major exhibitions are on view at all times, including selections from the permanent collection by such artists as Alexander Calder, Edward Hopper, Jasper Johns, Roy Lichtenstein, Reginald Marsh, Louise Nevelson, and Georgia O'Keeffe. The restaurant in a sunken sculpture court offers wines, light meals, and refreshments. Regular hours: Tuesday, 11 a.m. to 8 p.m.; Wednesday to Saturday, 11 a.m. to 6 p.m., Sunday, noon to 6 p.m. Closed Monday. Admission: $2.50; senior citizens, $1.25; children under 12 with an adult, and college students with valid ID, free; Tuesday evenings—6 to 8 p.m. free. Admission to programs in the New American Filmmaker Series is free with your ticket.

Note: The Whitney Museum has two branches in Manhattan. In midtown, there is the new sculpture court and garden, with an adjacent gallery for changing exhibitions, at the world headquarters of Philip Morris, Park Ave. and 42nd St., across from Grand Central Terminal (open Monday to Saturday from 11 a.m. to 6 p.m., Thursday to 7:30 p.m.). Admission is free (tel. 878-2550). Downtown, the Whitney at Federal Hall National Memorial, 26 Wall St. (at Broad St.), presents an active exhibition program and performing art series. Hours: 11 a.m. to 3 p.m. Monday through Friday, but often closed in summer. Call before going (tel. 431-1620). Free.

ART GALLERIES: There are probably as many art galleries on the East Side as there are grocery stores in some other cities: perhaps more. For art-happy New Yorkers, gallery-going is a favorite pastime, and the area of the East 70s and 80s is the new scene of the action, although many galleries still hold forth on the older gallery row, 57th Street. If your interest in art is more than casual, join the crowd.

Since there is no admission fee to galleries (unless there is a special charity benefit), you can come and go as you please. Where you go will be determined by what you're interested in: the moderns, the traditionalists, the old masters. The quickest way to find out who's showing where is to consult the art pages in the Entertainment Section of Sunday's *New York Times.* Some of the big names among the galleries showing the moderns: Betty Parsons, 24 West 57th St.; Leo Castelli, 4 East 77th St. (also in Soho at 420 West Broadway); Marlborough, 40 West 57th St.; Andre Emmerich, 41 East 57th St.; Fischbach, 29 West 57th St.; Tibor de Nagy, 29 West 57th St.; Saidenberg, 1018 Madison Ave.; Cordier & Ekstrom, 415 East 75th St.; Gimpel & Weitzenhoffer, 1040 Madison Ave.; Salander-O'Reilly, 22 East 80th St.; Terry Dintenfass, 50 West 57th St.; and Pace, 32 East 57th St..

Should your taste run more to the impressionists and French masters, relax at Hammer Galleries, 51 East 57th St., or Wally Findlay Galleries, 17 East 57th St. (which also shows contemporary Europeans and Americans). Findlay, in fact, is *the* art gallery for new cultural exchange: it has exclusive representation of many contemporary artists from the People's Republic of China; it also exhibits contemporary art from Senegal and tapestries from Africa, and shows the "British Primitive Fantastists" in association with the Portal Gallery in London. Visitors to the five-story town-house building are treated to guided tours by courteous and informed associates.

Hirschl & Adler, 21 East 70th St., specializes in American

paintings from the 18th century to the present, as well as French and European paintings from the early 19th to the early 20th century (during August, open by appointment only). Old masters? Get out your checkbook and head for the hallowed and haughty temples of Wildenstein, 19 East 64th St. (where you could also pick up an impressionist, post-impressionist, or 20th-century master), and M. Knoedler & Co., 19 East 70th St., which also handles old master paintings, 19th- and 20th-century and contemporary American and European paintings and sculpture.

AUCTION HOUSES: Scores of New Yorkers have become auction addicts. When they need to furnish an apartment, buy a painting, get a high chair for the baby, they wouldn't consider buying anything new or price tagged. For them, the game is in the bidding, the adventure in seeing who-gets-what. You can visit New York auction houses and bid for anything from sewing machines to silverware, from lamps to lorgnettes. Whether you're out for big game (or just spectator sport), the most exciting place is Sotheby's, 1334 York Ave. at 72nd St., where the cognoscenti vie for Rembrandts, pedigreed furniture, decorative arts, and precious jewelry. Many items, however, are not exorbitant, so don't be afraid to participate, especially at the "Arcade Auctions" held every other Tuesday, which feature sales of "affordable antiques." Illustrated catalog with estimated values are published for each auction. Sotheby's is really like a wonderful museum with an intimacy that museums can never achieve, in that prospective bidders are allowed to touch and handle the objects for sale in the preauction showings. Before a sale of antique books, scholars get to study; before a sale of rare violins, musicians may be allowed to try out the Stradivarius!

Christie's, 502 Park Ave., and Christie's East, 219 East 67th St., are prestigious British additions to the New York auction world. Old master paintings, furniture, fine art nouveau, art deco, foreign and ancient coins are some of the areas in which they deal. Important auctions in such fields as American paintings and sculpture and estate jewelry are among those at William Doyle Galleries, 157 East 87th St. Some very good bargains in art, Oriental rugs, silver, jewelry, furnishings, and bric-a-brac that you might want to take home with you can be found at Tepper Galleries, 110 East 25th St., one of the oldest American-owned auction galleries in New York; Manhattan Galleries, 1415 Third Ave. (at 80th St.); and Lubin Galleries, 30 West 26th

St. But be warned: once you start on the auction circuit, you may never get back to Macy's. And you may end up with a Louis XVI chair that you *really* don't need. That can happen.

For news of upcoming auctions each week, check the Antiques Pages of the Friday and Sunday *New York Times*.

West Side

TOURS: *Lincoln Center for the Performing Arts, 140 West 65th St. (tel. 877-1800, ext. 512). Whether or not you see any performances at Lincoln Center (more details in Chapter VII on evening entertainment), you should take a tour of this impressive complex of theaters and concert halls. Just to see the art and sculpture on the grounds is an experience in itself: Alexander Calder's *Le Guichet* in front of the Library and Museum of Performing Arts; Richard Lippold's *Orpheus and Apollo* in Avery Fisher Hall; Henry Moore's gigantic *Reclining Figure* in the reflecting pool in front of the Vivian Beaumont Theater; Marc Chagall's lilting paintings for the Metropolitan Opera House. The buildings themselves—the Metropolitan Opera House, the New York State Theater, the Vivian Beaumont Theater, Avery Fisher Hall, the Juilliard School—have been both criticized and praised: take a look and reach your own conclusions. You'll probably see all the buildings and may even get to watch rehearsals of some of the famed companies, like the New York City Ballet or the New York City Opera Company. But if you have your heart set on seeing the interiors of the theaters, do *not* come on a Saturday or Sunday afternoon; that's matinee time, and the doors are closed to tour takers. Tours are given between 10:30 a.m. and 5 p.m. daily, last an hour, and cost $5.25 for adults, $3 for children, $4.75 for senior citizens and for students (prices are subject to change).

LIBRARIES: *The Library and Museum of the Performing Arts, at Lincoln Center, 111 Amsterdam Ave. (entrance at 65th St.). A branch of the Public Library and of Lincoln Center, the Library and Museum of the Performing Arts is an entity unto itself, and one of the liveliest places in town. Everything is dedicated to the performing arts here and you can do a lot more than just borrow a book. You can sit down in a comfortable chair and listen to a recording of an opera or a musical (while studying the score at the same time), see excellent exhibits, catch concerts, plays, dance performances every night (more details in Chapter VII on entertainment), take the children to free story hours, puppet shows, concerts, dance presentations, films, in the Heckscher Oval. Best of all, it's all for free—a wonderful place. Hours: Monday and Thursday from 10 a.m. to 8 p.m., Tuesday to 6 p.m., Wednesday, Friday, and Saturday from noon to 6 p.m. Closed Sunday.

MUSEUMS: *The American Museum of Natural History, Central Park West at 79th St. (tel. 873-4225). One of the great scientific museums of the world, the American Museum brings the natural history of man and animals to vivid life for visitors of all ages. Added to such perennial crowd-pleasing (and kid-pleasing) exhibitions as the Hall of Minerals and Gems, the Hall of Man in Africa, the Hall of Reptiles and Amphibians, and the Hall of Ocean Life (with its 94-foot whale suspended from the ceiling), is the exciting Arthur Ross Hall of Meteorites, whose centerpiece is the largest meteorite ever retrieved. Another winner is the Hall of Asian Peoples, which explores the cultures that thrived on the Asian continent before the influence of the West. Some of the rare and splendid treasures seen here include two gold-leaf-covered buddhas from Japan and China and t'angkas from Tibet. You could spend days—no, weeks—here enjoying ethnological and anthropological collections, attending slide and gallery talks, seeing the animals in their natural habitats, and watching the dance, music, and crafts programs shown live at the People Center. And you won't want to miss seeing *To Fly*, the sensational movie on flight that also plays at the National Air and Space Museum in Washington; shown in the Naturemax Theater on a giant screen, it's a soaring (literally) experience. *To Fly* is shown every day, and on Friday and Saturday evenings it alternates with another giant-screen film, *Living Planet*. Admission charges are small (tel. 496-0200).

A big favorite with children 6 to 16 is the **Discovery Room**, in which 25 children at a time, each accompanied by an adult, play with learning games in a box—"Feel and Guess," "Reflections," "Skull and Mirror," and the like—for a variety of human and scientific experiences. Modeled after a similar room at the Smithsonian in Washington, the Discovery Room admits visitors on a first-come, first-served basis. Best to get tickets (free) at the Information Desk on the main floor when you enter. There's a lovely new restaurant (see Chapter IV) in the basement, plus a fast-food restaurant, and four wonderful gift shops, one just for children; take home an ancient Chinese puppet, beautiful Indian jewelry, or a colorful book of birds.

The American Museum of Natural History is open every day of the year except Christmas and Thanksgiving, from 10 a.m. to 5:45 p.m. Monday, Tuesday, Thursday, and Sunday; to 9 p.m. on Wednesday, Friday, and Saturday. There is a suggested admission fee of $3 for adults, $1.50 for children.

*The American Museum—Hayden Planetarium, 81st St. at Central Park West. This is one of the most exciting shows in town—for children, for adults, for anyone who ponders the mystery of man and the stars, of the great drama of outer space. Through the magic of the Zeiss star projector and hundreds of special effects, audiences can be shown the wonders of the night sky or taken to other worlds and beyond. Show topics range from black holes to the search for life in space to future travel to the stars. Sky shows are given every day except Thanksgiving and Christmas. Admission is $3.75 for those 13 and older, $2.75 for students and senior citizens, and $2 for children. For Sky Show information, call 873-8828. For Laser Show information, call 724-8700.

The New-York Historical Society, 170 Central Park West, at 77th St. (tel. 873-3400). The oldest museum in New York City has on permanent exhibit Audubon's original watercolors for *Birds of America*, an impressive collection of Tiffany lamps, outstanding landscapes of the Hudson River School, works by Thomas Cole, and early American portraits by John Trumbull, Gilbert Stuart, Charles Willson Peale, and Rembrandt Peale. In addition, the Society's museum presents a large number of special exhibitions. Open Tuesday through Friday from 11 a.m. to 5 p.m., on Saturday from 10 a.m. to 5 p.m., on Sunday from 1 to 5 p.m. Admission is $2 for adults, 75¢ for children; by donation on Tuesday.

Points North

THE CLOISTERS: In Fort Tryon Park (tel. 923-3700), this is one of the high points of New York, artistically and geographically. The Cloisters is a bit of medieval Europe transplanted to a cliff overlooking the Hudson. The Metropolitan Museum of Art, of which this is the medieval branch, has brought intact from Europe a 12th-century chapter house, parts of five cloisters from medieval monasteries, a Romanesque chapel, and a 12th-century

Spanish apse. Smaller treasures include rare tapestries like the 15th-century *Hunt of the Unicorn*, paintings, frescoes, stained glass, precious metals. All is set in tranquil gardens overlooking the Hudson; note the herb garden in the Bonnefont Cloister, planted with over 200 species used in Western Europe before 1520, and the garden in the Trie Cloister, planted with flora depicted in the Unicorn tapestries. Recorded concerts of medieval music are held at 12:30 and 2:30 p.m. every day. Since this extraordinary collection is one of the most popular in the city, especially in fine weather, try to schedule your visit during the week, rather than on a crowded Saturday or Sunday afternoon. The no. 4 bus which goes up Madison Avenue and is marked "Fort Tryon Park—The Cloisters" takes about an hour from midtown; quicker, but less scenic, is the Eighth Avenue IND A train to 190th Street (Overlook Terrace), which then connects with the no. 4 bus. Open Tuesday through Saturday from 10 a.m. to 4:45 p.m.; Sunday and holidays from 1 to 4:45 p.m. (Sunday from May through September, from noon to 4:45). Closed every Monday, Thanksgiving, Christmas, and New Year's Day. Pay-what-you-wish admission.

HISTORIC HOUSE: Morris-Jumel Mansion, in Roger Morris Park at West 160th St. and Jumel Terrace, just east of St. Nicholas Ave. (tel. WA 3-8008). Built in 1765 by Roger Morris, this Georgian mansion was headquarters for Gen. George Washington in 1776. Aaron Burr was married here in 1833. Open Tuesday through Sunday from 10 a.m. to 4 p.m.; $1 admission. Luncheon served to groups by appointment. To reach the Morris-Jumel Mansion, take the IND Eighth Avenue AA train to West 163rd Street. Sit in the last car of the train and you will get out at St. Nicholas Avenue, very near the mansion. You can also get there via bus no. 2, 3, 100, or 101.

Beyond Manhattan

BROOKLYN: *Brooklyn Museum, Eastern Parkway (tel. 638-5000). One of the best reasons for leaving Manhattan is to see the Brooklyn Museum, among the best museums in the country. It has superb collections of Egyptian, Oriental, American, and European art, as well as a fine primitive collection, 25 period rooms, and a Fashion Theater. There are new Japanese and Korean galleries. The Frieda Schiff Warburg Sculpture Garden is a repository for some of the architectural relics of the city: bits and pieces of the old Steeplechase Amusement Park in Coney Island and the Pennsylvania Station that was torn down to make way for the new Madison Square Garden, as well as the scene of changing exhibits. Don't miss a visit to the Gallery Shop, with its wonderful handicrafts from Mexico, Japan, South America, Scandinavia—all of it authentic, beautifully made, and well priced. The kids can stock up here on slews of inexpensive presents to bring their friends back home. The IRT Broadway–Seventh Avenue Express brings you to the museum's door at the Eastern Parkway–Brooklyn Museum Station. Open Wednesday through Saturday from 10 a.m. to 5 p.m., on Sunday from noon to 5 p.m.; holidays, 1 to 5 p.m. Suggested contribution: adults, $2; students, $1; free to members, seniors, and children under 12 accompanied by an adult.

Brooklyn Botanic Garden, 1000 Washington Ave. Next door to the Brooklyn Museum, and a major destination in its own right, the Brooklyn Botanic Garden is a glorious 50 acres' worth of flowers, trees, exotic plants. If you are in town in May, make a pilgrimage here to see the flowering of the cherry trees; they are even more beautiful than the ones in Washington, D.C. (Phone the garden at 622-4433 to check on blossoming time.) The Japanese mood also prevails in the traditional Japanese Garden. Other special treats include the Cranford Rose Garden, the Fragrance Garden for the Blind, and the Shakespeare Garden. You can browse through the greenhouses with their exotic tropical plants and be convinced you are light-years away from Brooklyn. The garden is open most of every day, but since hours change with the seasons, call 622-4433 for exact times. General admission is free, but on Saturday, Sunday, and holidays you'll pay 25¢ admission to the greenhouses and the Hill-and-Pond Japanese Garden. Closed Monday except holidays.

*Brooklyn Children's Museum, 145 Brooklyn Ave. (between Eastern Parkway and Atlantic Ave.). This is one museum that children will want to return to over and over; here they can do things with the museum's objects instead of just looking at them. BCM made "participation" its key principle at its beginning 84 years ago as the world's first children's museum. It recently replaced its two old Victorian mansions with a new $5-million building for children. The semi-underground structure is an architectural tour de force, a flexible five-level, learning-looking-growing environment, with its own windmill, greenhouse, steam engine, running water stream, workshops, and children's library.

Natural science, technology, cultural history, arts, and humanities are explored in unified exhibitions and programs. No one—from kids climbing through transparent plastic hexagons looming skyward to enthralled grownups—will want to leave. Admission is free. BCM is closed Tuesday, open from 1 to 5 p.m. on school days, and from 10 a.m. to 5 p.m. on Saturday, Sunday, and public school holidays. For subway and driving directions, phone 735-4400.

BRONX: ***Bronx Zoo,** Bronx Park (tel. 367-1010). For many years, the Bronx Zoo, one of the biggest (252 acres, 3500 animals) and the best zoos in the world, has been a prime visitor's magnet, and now it's better than ever. Traditional zoo cages are on their way out and, instead, natural habitats and moated exhibits like the African Plains and the Carter Giraffe Building are coming into the foreground. One of the newest of these features is Wild Asia, which offers a guided 25-minute safari, via monorail (the Bengali Express) through 46 densely forested acres where the elephants, tigers et al. roam free ($1.25 for adults, $1 for children 12 and under). Don't miss the architecturally exciting exhibits in the World of Birds, a $4-million, volcano-like exhibit building, complete with waterfalls, thunder, and other special effects in which visitors walk through rain forests and into jungles while birds swoop around their heads. A big one for the kids! Take the moppets to the newly reconstructed "Children's Zoo," where they can climb on a spider's web, try on a turtle's shell, and crawl through a prairie dog tunnel. They'll also love a ride in the **Skyfari,** a four-seater cable car ($1 for adults, 75¢ for children 12 and under). The zoo opens every day at 10 a.m. and closes anywhere between 4:30 and 5:30 p.m., depending on the time of year. Admission is free on Tuesday, Wednesday, and Thursday, but on other days you must pay $2.50 for adults, $1 for children under 12. Express bus service is available from midtown Manhattan to the zoo and the New York Botanical Garden (see ahead). The fare is $2.50 each way (exact amount required); phone 881-1000 for schedules. Or take the IRT Lexington Avenue subway, the no. 5 Dyre Avenue Express train to Fordham Road, change to the Bx 12 bus eastbound on Fordham Road; from the bus stop at Southern Boulevard, walk east on Fordham Road to the Rainey Gate entrance. On the West Side IRT, take the 241st Street–White Plains Road express train no. 2 to Pelham Parkway, and walk west to the Bronxdale entrance.

By car, take Exit 6 off the Bronx River Parkway. There's plenty of space to park, and the fee is $2.50.

New York Botanical Garden, Bronx Park (tel. 220-8700). Greenhouses, gardens, seasonal plantings, and an air of peace and quiet make this the place for a lovely respite from city tensions. See the Hemlock Forest, largely unchanged since the days of the Indians in Manhattan; the magnificent gardens of rhododendron, daffodils, azaleas, chrysanthemums. Newly restored to its turn-of-the-century elegance is the Crystal Palace, the 90-foot domed landmark Enid A. Haupt Conservatory (covering an acre of gardens under glass and similar to London's Kew Botanical Garden), with its coconut palms, jungle plantings, waterfall, desert areas, and seasonal floral displays. It's open six days a week from 10 a.m. to 5 p.m.; closed Monday. Conservatory admission is $2.50 for adults, $1.75 for senior citizens, children, and students. Stop in at the gift shop for unusual objets d'art and plants, have lunch at the romantic Snuff Mill Restaurant; it's on a terrace overlooking the Bronx River, which looks positively rural at this point. Admission to the grounds is free; they are open daily from dawn to dusk. Parking is $2.50 and includes one adult admission to the Enid A. Haupt Conservatory. By train: Take Metro North's Harlem line (20 minutes from Grand Central). By subway: Take the D, CC, or no. 4 train to Bedford Park Station; then walk eight blocks east. By car: The garden is on Southern Boulevard, south of Mosholu Parkway and north of Fordham Road and the Zoo.

SPECIAL TOURS: Dedicated theater-goers will love **Backstage on Broadway's** tours: they take you behind the scenes at a Broadway show, to meet the people—the stage managers, directors, lighting designers, etc.—who make the magic happen. Excellent for older children as well as grownups. Tours cost $5.50 for adults, $4.50 for students and senior citizens. Backstage on Broadway is at 228 West 47th St. (tel. 575-8065). . . . **Holidays in New York,** 152 West 58th St. (tel. 765-2515), arranges tours of unusual artistic and cultural merit: behind the scenes to the top wholesale fashion houses, tours of Jewish landmarks, and visits to artists' and dancers' studios. They also offer tours of Harlem and the Financial District, and general sightseeing. Sunday walking tours are held April to July and September through December. There are special tours for retired persons, students, and children, too. Special rates for groups. . . . Voluble **Lou**

Singer, a self-taught historian who must know more about Brooklyn than anybody, conducts absorbing tours focusing on Revolutionary and architectural Brooklyn, via bus or private car. You'll see the private parlors of restored Victorian brownstones, the masterful last landscape by Louis Comfort Tiffany, Stanford White's *Prison Ship Martyrs' Monument,* and much more. Unusual lunch stops are arranged. Singer, who teaches at Brooklyn College, will arrange special trips, to ethnic neighborhoods and elsewhere, for special interests. A Manhattan "Nosher's Tour" makes nibbling stops all over town, starting at the pickle barrels of the Lower East Side. Costs should run about $20 per person. A worthwhile and enjoyable excursion (tel. 875-9084). . . . For $10 each you can buy a 90-minute **Walking Tour Tape,** plug in your earphones, and take off to enjoy self-guided tours of Fifth Avenue; Wall Street and Olde New York; Greenwich Village; Chinatown, Little Italy, and Soho; or Millionaire's Mile (Upper Fifth Avenue). These entertaining and informative cassette tapes can be purchased at many bookstores (phone 757-1460 and they'll tell you where), or, in advance, by phoning that number collect and charging by credit card. . . . If you're in the city for an extended stay, it might be worth your while to pay the $35 annual membership fee and join **Adventure on a Shoestring,** a 22-year-old organization that takes its members on a variety of unusual excursions—a visit to a Broadway rehearsal or a Japanese Tea Ceremony, for example. Contact Howard Goldberg at 265-2663 or write to Shoestring, 300 West 53rd St., New York, NY 10019.

Chapter VII

THE BEST ENTERTAINMENT VALUES IN NEW YORK

BY NOW you've cased the town, you've dined and wined your way around the city, climbed to the top of the Statue of Liberty and explored the caverns underneath Rockefeller Center. But now it's time to put away the sightseeing maps, tuck whatever kiddies you may have into bed, and step out for an evening on the town. You didn't come all this way just to sit in your hotel room and watch your color television set. You want to see plays and movies, go to concerts and operas and nightclubs. But all that takes a bit of doing—and it's not just a matter of money. Too often, getting tickets to something in New York seems a matter of adding insult to injury. It's bad enough spending $60 to $90 or more for a pair of seats to a hit Broadway musical (especially when you want to see four of them) and even more for the Metropolitan Opera, but how to get the tickets in the first place? There is no need to despair. Provided you know the ropes, you *can* get tickets, you can see a lot more entertainment than you had even planned, and it may even cost less than you expect.

New York City is, of course, the entertainment capital of the nation, and it is here that you will catch not only Broadway theater and New York opera, but oustanding musical, dance, and theater groups from all over the world, everything from the Coldstream Guards to the Comédie Française. But that's just the beginning of the story. Since the city has literally thousands of young actors and musicians and dancers and other performers here studying or working their ways up the ladder, there are vast numbers of inexpensive entertainments to showcase these talents. Many are free; some charge modest admissions. In addition, there are innumerable lectures, poetry readings, offbeat entertainments that beckon the visitor. If you want to wander off the beaten track, you can have your horoscope forecast, do asanas with the yogis, or meditate with the Zen masters. All that is required is some pocket money and your own ardent interest in exploring the new and adventurous. First, though, some inside tips on one of the most subtle of the New York arts: Getting Theater Tickets.

THE RULES OF THE THEATER-TICKET GAME: The very name "Broadway" has become synonymous with the American theater, and whether you're a "tired business person" or ardent avant gardist, you will want to attend at least a few plays while you're in New York. But you will have two problems: first, getting seats; second, getting seats that you can afford. There are four general rules for dealing with this sticky wicket.

1. Do your homework. As soon as you know you are coming to New York—even if it's months ahead of the date—write to the theater box offices for the tickets you want. This is especially important for a hit musical, which is often sold out months in advance. (To find out what will be playing, consult the Entertainment Section of the Sunday *New York Times*, which is sold everywhere.) That way, you will be assured not only of a seat, but of a seat at box-office prices. If you wait until you get into town, you will probably have to resort to a ticket broker's services (they have branches in almost every hotel in the city), and then you must pay a commission on every seat. And you will have a hard time getting seats for the hits. *Note:* It usually works better to send your own mail-order requests from, say, Kalamazoo or San Diego than to have your cousin in New York go to the box office for you. Theater ticket sellers usually make a special effort to fulfill requests from out-of-town customers.

2. Avoid the weekend scene. Most New Yorkers work during the week, so they save their theater-going for weekends, and it's then that the prices are highest. Happily, you're here on vacation, and you can go during the week or to a Wednesday matinee when prices are lower. If you attend a musical on a Saturday night, for example, you'll have to pay from $25 to $45 or more for a seat. During the week, the range is usually from $20 to $30. On Wednesday matinees, perhaps $5 or more lower (prices vary from show to show). Prices for "straight" or nonmusical plays are slightly lower. *Motto:* Skip the music, head for a matinee, and see more shows for the money.

3. Pick the previews. Some years ago, it was *de rigueur* for Broadway shows to try out in either New Haven or Boston or Philadelphia before proceding to New York for the hoped-for opening-night triumph. All of that got too expensive and too complicated and so, in the last few years, the trend has been more and more to substitute New York "previews" for out-of-town tryouts. Philadelphia's loss is the New York theater-goer's gain, for you can often realize considerable savings on a preview ticket, even for musicals. There will be some changes before opening night, of course, when the shows are "set," and you are taking a chance since you have no reviews to guide you. But if, for example, it's a play that's been imported after a long and well-reviewed run in England, or has top stars, or is the work of an important playwright, you're not risking too much. So be your own critic. Preview dates are listed along with the regular ads in the *New York Times, New York* magazine, and the *New Yorker,* all good sources of detailed theater information.

4. If you don't mind waiting in line, the easiest way to get tickets for a show is to join the queue over at **TKTS (Times Square Theater Center),** at Broadway and 47th St. Half-price theater tickets are made available for the *day of performance only,* beginning at 3 p.m. for evening shows, at noon for matinees. Naturally, these are for shows that haven't sold out, so don't expect to get the "hottest" tickets this way. The center is open from 3 to 8 p.m. daily, from noon to 2 p.m. on Wednesday and Saturday (matinee days), and from noon on Sunday. There is a small service charge. There's a similar center downtown in the World Trade Center. Both centers, by the way, also sell tickets to Lincoln Center, opera, ballet, and concert attractions, as well as to Broadway and Off-Broadway.

5. Take the "twofers." When a show is not completely sold every night—perhaps it's at the end of its run or in previews—it often goes on "twofers." This means that, by presenting a slip at the box office, you are entitled to buy two seats for the price of one, on certain nights of the week. You're running little risk here, since any show lasting long enough to go on "twofers" has some merit: you will probably not, however, see the original cast. "Twofers" are available at many places: at most hotel desks, at restaurant cashier's booths, and, in large supply, at the offices of the Visitors and Convention Bureau, 2 Columbus Circle.

But let's suppose you just decided to come to New York last

week, nothing you want to see is available at TKTS, and you've just got to see the biggest hit in town. Your best strategy is to present yourself at the box office (or phone in advance) to see if standing room is available. Some 18 theaters on Broadway sell standing-room spaces (around $10) when their house is completely sold out. The view may be slightly obstructed in some areas, but usually it is excellent, and you can't beat the price. If, however, you are willing to pay full price and a little bit more, then go to one of the ticket brokers. The best seats in the house are usually commandeered by them, and they will certainly get you into something. You can often get a ticket for a nonmusical by just going to the box office a day or two before the performance.

Note: An easy way to get theater tickets is via *Ticketron,* a computer ticket service with convenient locations at major traffic areas. Service charge varies per ticket, but is nominal. You can find a Ticketron at Macy's (usually open until 6:45 p.m.) and at the Yankee ticket booth at Grand Central Terminal, on the mezzanine level, open to 5 p.m. (they also handle all major sporting events). For information on other Ticketron locations, phone 977-9020. To make phone reservations, phone **Teletron** at 212/947-5850.

MAKING THE OPERA SCENE: It used to be even harder to get tickets for the Metropolitan Opera House at Lincoln Center than it was for Broadway, but now that the novelty of the new house has worn off a bit, the situation has eased, and it is likely that you will be able to pick something up for most performances, even though most of the Metropolitan's seats are taken by subscribers. The best way to do it is via mail order, as far in advance as possible. To find out what and when, write to the Met for a schedule of performances, and enclose a stamped, self-addressed envelope. The address: Metropolitan Opera Mail Order Department, Lincoln Center, New York, NY 10023. An even neater trick is to persuade a friend who lives in the city to get to the box office on a Monday morning five weeks ahead of a scheduled performance to pick up a ticket (or phone 362-3000).

Failing all else, present yourself to a ticket broker or to the Metropolitan box office as soon as you arrive in town. Unless it's a *very* popular production, you will almost always be able to get a seat, although usually one in the orchestra at about $33 to $63 on weeknights, $35 to $65 on Friday, $38 to $70 on Saturday.

With a little more advance notice, you may be able to get a lower priced seat; they start at $13 in the Family Circle. The only way to really save money is to stand; standee's places are sold for $5 in the Family Circle, $7 in the orchestra; they go on sale the morning of the performance at 10 a.m. Usually, however, something will be found for you at the box office.

Happily, it's not quite as difficult to get seats for the **New York City Opera,** which also has a superb company, but slightly less cachet. Mail orders three or four weeks in advance will usually do the trick. Otherwise, try a ticket broker or the box office: it's also at Lincoln Center, at the New York State Theater. Prices go from $2.40 to $35. You can also buy tickets through **Chargit,** which will tell you if there are tickets in your price range (tel. 944-9300).

Bargains in Entertainment

Once you forsake the realms of the Broadway theater and the top musical companies, it becomes relatively simple to plan an evening out. Reservations can be taken care of by a simple phone call to the box office. Off-Broadway theaters are, unhappily, not as cheap as they used to be (when a show gets rave notices, some producers have a deplorable habit of raising the prices, sometimes to Broadway levels), but, typically, prices run from about $6 to $16. At most of the other events we describe here, admission will either be free, by contribution, or by paying a small admission charge, from $3 to $6. Best of all, you'll be catching some of the most exciting events in the city, where new ideas are being explored, new talents being perfected, new—and sometimes radical—innovations being made in the performing arts. To wit:

Theater

OFF-BROADWAY: New York theater-goers have been going "off-Broadway" for about 50 years now, ever since the Provincetown Playhouse set up shop on MacDougal Street to show the works of a young playwright named Eugene O'Neill. Off-Broadway went into high gear, however, in the '50s and '60s, the golden years of Circle in the Square, the Theater de Lys, and the Cherry Lane Theater. It was at places like this that Geraldine Page rose to stardom, that Edward Albee tried out his first works, and that names like Ionesco and Beckett and Bertolt

Brecht and Kurt Weill (his *Threepenny Opera* ran here for seven years) became household words. The longest running show, on Broadway or off, is Tom Jones's and Harvey Schmidt's *The Fantasticks*, now in its 25th year! It's at the Sullivan Street Playhouse.

The brightest news in the Off-Broadway scene in many a year has been the creation of **42nd Street Theater Row:** the transformation of the once-seedy block betwen Ninth and Tenth Avenues into a sparkling new theater neighborhood, complete with nine theaters—including the Harold Clurman Theater, Playwrights Horizons, INTAR (Hispanic-American Theater), Douglas Fairbanks, Jr., Theater, Lion Theater, Actors and Directors Theater, at least three cabarets, and half a dozen restaurants (our favorite is the charming Café Madeleine for light meals before or after the show). For news of productions on Theater Row, and to make phone reservations using major credit cards, phone **Ticket Central** at 279-4200, after 1 p.m.

Off-Broadway can still afford to be more daring than uptown theater, mainly because there is much less financial risk involved in mounting a production. The houses are much smaller than the Broadway ones (they are often converted factories, or church basements, or cellars); and the actors and technicians receive much less than a Broadway wage scale. This freedom sometimes leads to great artistic successes, to brilliant revivals of the classics, and sometimes to the merely inept and mediocre (there is, however, no shortage of the latter on Broadway, either).

Happily, it is much easier to get a ticket to an off-Broadway production than to a Broadway one. Check the listings in the *Times, New York,* or the *New Yorker,* phone the theater, and pick up your reservation about an hour before curtain time. The uptown Wednesday–Saturday matinee bit is usually waived in favor of a matinee Sunday at 3 p.m. and two performances on Saturday nights: at 7 and 10 p.m. Many off-Broadway playhouses will honor student ID cards.

OFF-OFF-BROADWAY: As off-Broadway aspires to become Broadway, so OOB hopes to make it to the "big time" of off-Broadway. Fledgling playwrights, directors, actors come together in small theaters, cafés, churches, school auditoriums, to do their thing; sometimes it's beautiful, sometimes unspeakable. The more professional—and at least more sane—productions will usually be put on by theater schools and repertory groups like the Manhattan Theater Club, La Mama E.T.C., and the Gene Frankel. Check the *Village Voice* for OOB listings and ads.

THE BARD—SUMMER AND WINTER: The New York Shakespeare Festival can be counted on all summer long for high-quality productions of the Bard and other entertainments in a delightful outdoor setting in Central Park. To get tickets for the free performances (every night except Monday from late June to early September), present yourself at the Delacorte Theater at 6:15 p.m. One ticket is given to each patron. Seats are reserved, and you can be seated between 7:15 and 7:45. So, take yourself off to dinner in a West Side restaurant nearby or, better yet, join the picnickers on the grass. The Delacorte can be approached from either 81st Street and Central Park West or 79th Street and Fifth Avenue.

During the winter, producer Joseph Papp and the other presiding lights of the Shakespeare Festival run the **Public Theater,** 425 Lafayette St., and let new playwrights have their fling. At this writing, there were some seven theaters under the Public Theater roof and the complex presents perhaps the most vital and compelling theatrical experiment in New York today. It was at the Public Theater that *A Chorus Line, That Championship Season,* and *For Colored Girls* got their start. At every performance, one-fourth of all seats (including those for the biggest hits) are saved for Quiktix, available at $7.50 and $9 instead of the usual $15 and $18. They go on sale two hours before showtime (tel. 598-7150).

REPERTORY COMPANIES: Repertory companies, long a fond dream for the American commercial theater, are finally becoming reality. In addition to the New York Shakespeare Festival, several other repertory companies can be counted on for quality new plays and significant revivals. Look for excellent productions at off-Broadway prices from any of the following: **American Place Theater, Manhattan Theater Club,** and the **Mirror Theater,** all uptown; **Circle Repertory Company** (on the Square). **Second Stage, WPA Theater,** the **13th St. Theater,** and **La Mama E.T.C.,** all downtown.

Equity Library Theater presents solid, highly professional (all the performers are members of the actor's union) revivals of classics like *Twelfth Night,* plays like *The Miracle Worker,* and musicals like *Follies.* The season runs from the middle of September through the end of May. Tickets can be reserved by calling MO 3-2028. A donation of $7 is requested. Performances are held at the Equity Library Theater, 103rd St. and Riverside Dr., Tuesday through Sunday evenings, with matinees on Saturday and Sunday.

The Library & Museum of the Performing Arts, 111 Amsterdam Ave. (65th St.), the New York Public Library at Lincoln Center. Since this unique and splendid institution believes in bringing the performing arts to life (as well as providing books, records, manuscripts, research materials about them), it runs a *free* winter series in its auditorium of concerts, dance programs, and plays. Recent theatrical events have included the Equity Informals (Equity Library Theater players trying out new ideas); the Comedia dell' Arte, and the Stage Directors and Choreographers Workshop. Performances are held at 4 p.m. weekdays and 2:30 p.m. on Saturday, from September through June. Tickets are on a first-come first-served basis, and the small auditorium fills up quickly, especially for dance events. Note, too, that there are frequent programs for children.

To find out what's going on, pick up a list of the New York Public Library's bulletin *Events,* published bimonthly, and available at any library branch (Central Circulation is at 42nd Street and Fifth Avenue). Or phone the Library & Museum of the Performing Arts at 930-0800.

Television

You say you've always wanted to be on television—even in the audience? Here's your chance. Tickets to many television shows filmed or taped in New York are free and are available at the offices of the Visitors and Convention Bureau, 2 Columbus Circle; pick them up as early in the morning as possible. They are also available at many hotel desks, restaurants, other places where tourists gather. For the most important shows, you should write in advance to the networks involved, or go directly to their studios on the day of the program, again, as early as possible. The addresses: Ticket Division, Columbia Broadcasting System, 524 West 57th St.; Ticket Division, National Broadcasting Company, 30 Rockefeller Plaza; ABC Guest Relations, 36 A West 66th St. You will also be well entertained and educated by taking NBC's 55-minute **Studio Tour** of its television and radio facilities. Tours leave from 30 Rockefeller Plaza between 10 a.m. and

4 p.m. Monday through Saturday; admission is $4.25. Children under 6 are not admitted. Phone 664-4000 for reservations.

Music

There is never a dearth of musical activity in New York. You can hear the lofty New York Philharmonic or a neighborhood symphony, the world's greatest soloists at Carnegie Hall or Avery Fisher Hall, or an aspiring young pianist at a local music school in dozens of musical events every week. While the very top music events are expensive, most are not, even at such prestigious halls as Town Hall and Judson Hall. And there are many, many concerts that charge $4 or $5, or are free. For week-by-week details on the inexpensive music scene, the *Village Voice* is your best source of information. The "Cue" section of *New York* magazine is also informative. They are available at newsstands throughout the city.

Be sure to pay a visit to the **Music & Dance Booth** at Bryant Park, just behind the New York Public Library on 42nd Street, between Fifth and Sixth Avenues. Half-price day-of-performance tickets for music and dance concerts are available; the box office is open from noon to 7 p.m. every day.

OPERA: There's more to the New York opera scene than the Met and the City Opera. A number of smaller companies present highly professional work with talented performers. This is also a good chance to catch aspiring singers on their way up. A New York standby for 36 years now, the **Amato Opera Theater** at 319 Bowery, corner of 2nd St., gives full productions, not workshops, of the classic repertory—Verdi, Puccini, Mozart, Rossini, and Donizetti—as well as rarely performed operas. Scores of its "graduates" have gone on to sing at the Metropolitan and the New York City Opera. Tickets are priced around $8 and can be reserved by calling CA 8-8200 up until a day before curtain time. Performances are usually given weekends over a ten-month season, and in July and August Amato is out singing in suburban parks.

The **Brooklyn Opera Society** is a major professional regional company which performs with national and international artists, orchestra, chorus, and corps de ballet. Performances are usually held at the Gershwin Theater of Brooklyn College, and in the summer, in the bandshell in Prospect Park. Tickets cost $5, $8, and $15 (tel. 643-7115).

AND SOME LIGHT OPERA: Should your taste run to Gilbert and Sullivan, don't miss the **Light Opera of Manhattan,** which performs at the Eastside Playhouse, 334 East 74th St. (tel. 861-2288). They are considered the finest of performers in the city of the Gilbert and Sullivan repertory, and of light opera by Victor Herbert, Rudolph Friml, Sigmund Romberg, and the like. Tickets range from $8 to $13.50, $7.50 for senior citizens; children, half price.

In search of more Gilbert and Sullivan, watch the papers for news of productions by the **New Empire Players** and the **Village Light Opera Group,** both at various playhouses around town in occasional productions.

CONCERTS AND RECITALS: To hear artists of the caliber of Andre Watts, Eugenia and Pinchas Zukerman, and Ruth Laredo, plus chamber groups like the Guarneri and Cleveland String Quartets playing in intimate surroundings, head for the **Kaufmann Concert Hall of the 92nd Street Y,** 92nd St. and Lexington Ave. (tel. 427-4410), one of New York's major recital halls. Concerts are given year round, and single admission is from $7 to $17.

The **Juilliard School,** one of the best performing arts schools in the world, schedules more than 300 performances from October through May to showcase the talents—and they are considerable—of their students. Major orchestra concerts take place Friday evenings at 8. Performances by the Juilliard American Opera Center, the Drama Division, and the Dance Division are scattered throughout the week in the school's four theaters and concert halls at Lincoln Center, Broadway at 66th Street. Almost all performances are free, except that contributions to scholarship funds are required for the opera, drama, and dance events. No tickets are required for the numerous student recitals, and available tickets for the Friday-night orchestra programs can be had three days in advance from the Juilliard Concert Office. Complete details about all Juilliard events can be had by phoning 799-5000, ext. 235. *Note:* Every Wednesday during the school year a free performance is given at 1 p.m. in Alice Tully Hall. These may range from orchestra and solo performances to choral, dance, and opera scenes. No tickets are necessary.

The **Library & Museum of the Performing Arts** at Lincoln Center is also very involved in the music scene. Showcases for young concert artists are held in the auditorium several times a week. Other branches of the **New York Public Library** hold frequent concerts, too. You might, for example, catch a classical guitar trio doing Paganini at the Hudson Park Branch Library in the Village, 10 Seventh Ave. South, or a violin-piano duo at the Donnell Library in midtown, 20 West 53rd St. (which also is the scene of many other events), or an ensemble group at the Countée Cullen Library in Harlem, 104 West 136th St. Check the *Events* calendar of the New York Public Library, free at all branches, or call the library's Telephone Reference Service, 790-6161.

The **Brooklyn Academy of Music,** 30 Lafayette St., Brooklyn, is home to the Brooklyn Philharmonia, various chamber and Next Wave music series, and guest artists. In addition to music, there's lots more going on in the four theaters of this oldest performing arts center in the United States: theater, dance, films, children's programs. The season runs from September to May. Ticket prices range from $6 to $25. For program information, call 636-4100.

Music in the Museums

What could be lovelier than hearing a major concert artist give a Sunday-afternoon recital, free, in the splendid setting of the **Frick Collection?** Phone them at BU 8-0700 for details on getting tickets. Or listening to live concerts or recorded music on certain Sundays in the medieval splendors of **The Cloisters** (part of the Metropolitan Museum of Art, but located uptown in Fort Tryon Park; tel. 923-3700 for ticket information)? These are only a few of the many fine musical offerings in New York's major museums. Check the papers for news of frequent concerts, too, at the **Metropolitan Museum of Art,** the **Museum of the City of New York,** the **New-York Historical Society,** the **Nicholas Roerich Museum,** and the **Brooklyn Museum.**

Music in the Churches

Some of the finest music in New York is heard in the city's churches—and it's all free. For example, during the fall and winter season, **St. Bartholomew's Episcopal Church,** Park Ave. at 51st St., noted for its mixed choir, presents a series of outstanding concerts most Sundays at 4 p.m. . . . At the **Riverside Church,** Riverside Dr. at 122nd St. (tel. 222-5900), a Service of Music is held occasionally on Sunday afternoons at 4 which includes organ recitals, orchestra, choral, and solo work by some of the world's top artists. Every Saturday throughout the year (and on Sunday at 2:30 p.m. as well), there is a carillon concert at noon. . . . Occasional concerts of great choral works are given Sunday at 8 p.m., in addition to organ recitals, at the **Church of the Ascension,** Fifth Ave. at 10th St. . . . **St. Peter's Lutheran Church,** in its stunning home at the Citicorp Center, 54th St. and Lexington Ave. (tel. 935-2200), offers a variety of musical programs, most of them free or at little cost. Its Jazz Vespers at 5 p.m. on Sunday are a vital part of the city's cultural fabric, and they are often followed at 7 p.m. by a jazz concert (admission charge). There's a 45-minute jazz concert at 12:30 on Wednesday too ($2 charge). Listings can be found in the *New York Times.*

Films

Most first-run movie houses in New York charge around $5 for admission; theaters showing revivals of top American and foreign films charge just a little bit less, mostly for afternoon showings. Note the **Thalia,** the **Regency,** and the **Carnegie Hall Cinema** uptown, and the **Bleecker Street Cinema** in the Village for especially imaginative programming. Film societies show documentaries and revivals for less, usually $3 to $4. Among these are the **Collective for Living Cinema,** 52 White St.; the **Millennium Film Workshop,** 66 East 4th St., and the **Film Forum,** 57 Watts St., all downtown. Films are included in the price of admission at the **Museum of Modern Art,** where you might catch up with Myrna Loy or Norma Shearer or the early Marx Brothers, and at the **Whitney Museum**'s "New American Filmmakers Series," featuring works by creative newcomers.

Want more? The **Public Theater,** 425 Lafayette St. (tel. 598-7150), in addition to live theater, also screens very special films most days of the week, with an admission charge of $4. The **International Center of Photography,** Fifth Ave. at 94th St. (tel. 860-1777), usually shows films of high artistic nature; admission is about $2. And you can often catch films by renowned Japanese filmmakers at **Japan Society,** 333 East 47th St. (tel. 752-3015). Admission is $4. Then there's **Theater 80 St. Marks,** 80 St. Mark's Pl., New York's original revival theater. Branches of the New York Public Library present free films. In the midtown area, **Donnell Library Center,** 20 West 53rd St., is the busiest, with everything from a Film Program for Preschool Children to a Film at Noon Program and evening programs, all free.

Dance

The top dance programs in New York will usually be held at Lincoln Center: at the New York State Theater, where the highly acclaimed **New York City Ballet** makes its home; at the Metropolitan Opera House, home base for the splendid **American Ballet Theater,** and host to many visiting foreign troupes; at the New York City Center, home to the exciting **Joffrey Ballet** and also to the **Alvin Ailey Dance Company,** as well as to numerous visiting groups. Both the Lincoln Center halls, City Center, and the Broadway theaters frequently play host to visiting modern-dance and folk-dance groups from overseas for short seasons: you may be lucky enough to catch the **Royal Ballet** of London or our own **Martha Graham** company if you're here during the winter; the **National Ballet of Canada** often performs during the summer. Carnegie Hall and Felt Forum often get into the dance scene, too, hosting the likes of the National Dance Company of Senegal or the Soviet Georgian Dancers. The Kaufmann Auditorium of the 92nd Street Y has been a prestigious haven for modern dance for many years, and is now the official home of the **José Limon Dance Company.** And the Brooklyn Academy of Music has lately presented such top names as **Merce Cunningham** and **Paul Taylor.** New York's dance offerings are among the greatest in the world. Prices are about the same for these events as for Broadway plays. There is also plenty of free and low-cost dance of high quality. For a start, you might try the following:

Cooper Union, 7th St. and Third Ave. (tel. AL 4-6300). From October to May in the Great Hall of Cooper Union, programs in the performing arts are given most weekday nights at 8. Dance performances may include anything from Olatunji and his African dancers to a Flamenco Fiesta. Admission is free (unless otherwise indicated), no reservations necessary. Just come early: the 900 seats get filled up quickly. Doors open at 7:30 p.m. To get a schedule of programs, write to Cooper Union Forum, Cooper Square, New York, NY 10012.

New York Offbeat
Entertainment for When the Spirit Moves You

Now here's some news for the esoteric set. If your idea of fun is casting horoscopes, chanting mantras, listening to talk on psychic phenomena, or learning to meditate with the yogis and the Zen masters, you've come to the right place. Spiritual, semi-spiritual, and occult groups have lately ben flourishing in our town to such an extent that, if not for the lack of palm trees, you might think it was Southern California. Herewith, a brief sampling, for those moments when you want to explore the world within.

YOGA: One of New York's reigning gurus, the genuine article is Swami Satchidananda of the **Internal Yoga Institute,** an Indian teacher whom almost everybody describes as "beautiful." The swami occasionally lectures in New York (call 929-0586 for details), but even if he's not in town, there will be plenty going on at the institute's two centers (there is one uptown at 500 West End Ave. at 84th St.; and in Greenwich Village at 227 West 13th St.): weekly programs in chanting and meditation and daily classes in Hatha Yoga, those relaxing-yet-energizing exercises that make you feel so marvelous. Should you want to spend a morning or an evening brushing up on your asanas, you are welcome to come by for a class. Bring a leotard or shorts. Admission is by contribution, minimum $4. The downtown branch also runs the "Lotus Light Café," serving vegetarian lunches and dinners, and **Integral Yoga Natural Foods,** at 240 West 14th St., open daily, with excellent prices.

Another place where you can come for an open class, maybe learn the headstand or the lotus, is the **Sivananada Yoga Vedanta Center,** 243 West 24th St. (tel. 255-4560). Classes cost $3 to $4.50 Visiting yogis frequently lecture here. Should you happen to be spending the winter in New York and need some respite from the cold, check with them about charter flights to their sunny yoga retreat on Paradise Island, in Nassau, Bahamas (about $30 a day, all-inclusive). They also run a yoga ranch in the nearby Catskill Mountains (around $20 a day, all-inclusive).

Everyone is invited to join the devotees of Swami Muktananda in daily meditation and chanting at the very beautiful **Siddha Yoga Dham of New York,** 324 West 86th St. (tel. 873-8030). There are free morning and evening programs, conducted by Western swamis, and delicious vegetarian meals are served at modest cost.

Swami Rama, founder of the Himalayan Institute, is known for his research work with the Menninger Clinic on the relationship of physiology and psychological states. His center in New York is at **East West Books** at 78 Fifth Ave. (14th St.). Besides an outstanding collection of books on spiritual subjects, it offers frequent classes in Hatha Yoga, and often presents holistic health and other New Age seminars (tel. 243-5994 or 243-5995).

You can spend an enlightening weekend in the country, courtesy of the **Yoga Society of New York,** which runs Ananda Ashram in Monroe, N.Y. (an hour's bus ride from the city). Ananda is a beautiful, 60-acre country estate with its own lake, sauna and massage facilities, vegetarian food, and a wide-ranging program involving yoga and other self-awareness disciplines. Costs are moderate. Phone 914/783-1084 for details. The Yoga Society also runs a series of programs downtown in the Wall Street area at its Holistic Health & Natural Life Center, 94 Fulton St. (for information, tel. 233-3887).

BUDDHISM, TIBETAN AND ZEN: New York has a huge number of Buddhist meditators. In Manhattan, the place to learn about Zen is the **New York Zendo,** a magnificent and authentic temple at 223 East 67th St. (tel. UN 1-3333), which admits the public once a week, on Thursday nights for *zazen*—zen sitting. Instruction is given to newcomers, but be sure to get there between 6:15 and 6:45 since there is often a crowd, and once the doors are closed they will not be opened again. A small contribution is requested. The subway or an express bus can take you up to the lovely Riverdale section of the Bronx to the Greyston Seminary, at 690 West 247th St., on the banks of the Hudson, the home of the **Zen Community of New York.** Under the direction of Bernard Glassman Sensei, an ordained Soto Zen Buddhist priest, this inter-religious Zen practice center regularly schedules classes, meditations, retreats, workshops, and celebrations of various religious traditions. The public is welcome to take beginning meditation instruction free every Sunday morning at 9 a.m., and a program of joint work, a lecture, and lunch follows. Nearby, at 5720 Mosholu Avenue is the **Greyston Bakery and Café** (tel. 543-2400), which features a delicious array of cakes and breads, light meals, and also a photo gallery, a poetry series, and a free 7:30 p.m. Sunday night ethnic dance or musical performance. For information on Zen Community programs, phone 914/543-5530.

The **Buddhist Academy,** 332 Riverside Dr. at 105th St. (tel. 678-9214), affiliated with the Buddhist Church, has many special programs open to the general public: in the fall there is a bazaar in which demonstrations of ikebana (flower-arranging), the Japanese tea ceremony, and the self-defense arts are given and authentic Japanese food is served; in June, there is the annual recital of Japanese classical dances; and in July, the most exciting event of the year, the Bon Dances. These ancient and beautiful Japanese religious dances celebrate the arrival in paradise of one's ancestors. They are held on the Riverside Dancing Mall at 105th Street, and are performed by hundreds of men, women, and tiny children in colorful kimonos. Should you care to attend the Buddhist Church, services in English get underway every Sunday morning at 11:30. Check the local papers or phone for information.

A leading center for the study and practice of Tibetan Buddhism in New York is **Dharmadatu**, 49 East 21st St., a meditation center under the guidance of Vajracarya, the Venerable Chogyam Trungpa, Rinpoche. Meditation instruction is available free of charge Tuesday evenings at 6:30 p.m.; on Wednesday at 8 p.m. there is an open-house program which includes a talk, discussion, and light refreshments. Dharmadatu is open to the public for meditation practice every evening and all day Sunday. Phone 673-7340 for exact schedule information.

MISCELLANY: The **New York Open Center**, 83 Spring St., in Soho (tel. 219-2527), offers many classes, workshops, and performances, exploring the integration of body, mind, and spirit. Speakers of the caliber of Robert Muller, assistant secretary-general of the United Nations have been presented. . . . Consciousness can soar while you float effortlessly in a **relaxation tank.** An hour of weightlessness at Alma Daniel's penthouse establishment overlooking Central Park costs $35 (tel. 799-0837). . . . Local headquarters for the popular **Movement of Spiritual Inner Awareness** (MSIA) are at 365 Canal St. (tel. 966-2249). Monday-night meetings present recorded video tapes by MSIA founder John-Roger. . . . A free introductory class is given every Tuesday at 6 at the highly regarded **School of T'ai Chi Chuan**, 47 West 13th St. (at Sixth Ave.) in Greenwich Village. Instruction in this ancient Chinese exercise art are given daily, and special Arica programs are held here as well (tel. 929-1981). . . . The **Silva Mind Control Center**, 6 East 39th St., promises to teach you how to get in and out of alpha states and beyond, in a four-day intensive training course that graduates swear by (tel. 684-6477). Free introductory lectures are given every Wednesday at 8 p.m. . . . It's a drive of about two hours to Rhinebeck, N.Y., and the beautiful summer campus of **Omega**

Institute, where weekend seminars and five-day intensive courses in the areas of health, the arts, social transformation, and spiritual studies take place throughout the summer. Programs, of the highest caliber, include leaders like Allen Ginsberg, Paul Winter, Holly Near, Bernard Siegal, Jean Houston, and George Leonard. For information, *before May 15,* call 914/876-2058; *after May 15,* call 914/266-4301, or write Omega Institute, Lake Drive, RD 2, Box 377-P, Rhinebeck, NY 12572.

THE STARS ARE FAVORABLE: Hung up on astrology? So, it seems, are half the people in New York. The **New York Astrology Center,** 63 West 38th St., Room 505, runs frequent lectures and classes, and reports that it has the largest collection of astrology books in the world, as well as books on natural healing and Eastern medicine, palmistry, and yoga. Phone 719-2919 for news of current happenings. They also have a computer center for casting charts. Uptown, **Mason's Bookshop,** 789 Lexington Ave. (between 61st and 62nd Sts.), run by Zoltan Mason, astrologer and teacher, is small, but has everything one could possibly want in the occult sciences. (Call for consultation fees.)

Note: For news of weekly events in astrology, yoga, and other spiritual matters, check listings and ads in the *Village Voice* or in the *Whole Life Times* (available in health-food stores); and watch the notices at **Weiser's Book Store,** 740 Broadway (at Waverly Place), which has probably the most extensive collection of occult books in the country; you could easily spend several incarnations here, reading everything from *The Egyptian Book of the Dead* to *Transcendental Magic.* It's an utterly absorbing place, even if just to look and browse.

A quarterly publication called *Free Spirit* has the most complete listing of events and organizations in the healing, holistic health, personal growth, and spiritual areas. You can probably pick up a copy at Weiser's or at many health-food stores, or phone 543-5536.

Chapter VIII

NEW YORK AFTER DARK

THE NEW YORK NIGHT has never been more vibrant, more alive, more dedicated—sometimes frantically, sometimes gracefully—to the pursuit of pleasure. Perhaps not since the '30s has it enjoyed such a renaissance of late-night and all-night activity. The real excitement is in a mixed bag of entertainment —country music is big, so is jazz, rock, folk, and cabaret and comedy are on the rise again. The glamorous supper club is back; the disco craze is calming down. Singles bars are more popular than ever. And for those quiet moments—of relaxing, or hand-holding, or people-watching—there are friendly pubs and trendy bars all over town.

In general, you should know that, barring Miami Beach, New York is the "latest" town in the country. Bars and lounges are permitted to stay open and serve liquor until 4 a.m. every night except Saturday, when the early-morning curfew is 3 a.m. Informality is the mode of dress—come-as-you-will—allowed everywhere, except in the top rooms where coats and ties are *de rigueur* for the men. Nowadays, with Women's Lib in the ascendant, women solo or in tandem can count on being welcomed everywhere. Drinks average $3 to $5 in the fancier places, somewhat less elsewhere. Even in the neighborhood pubs, the days of the 50¢ glass of beer are no more: plan to spend $1.25 and up.

How much will it all cost? Here, the latitude is enormous, and the choice is yours. You could easily spend $100 or more (for a couple, including tips) as you dine, dance, and watch the big names in entertainment. Or you can go pub crawling with the natives and spend about $25 for two. *Tips:* Many places have lower prices or no covers or minimums during the week; weekend prices soar everywhere. Also, a drink or two at the bar, plus a cover charge, can often be your price of admission to some of the best entertainment in town. Note that we have given charges only where they seem to be fixed; in the changeable nightclub scene, however, most covers and admissions will vary with the performer, the time of year, and the state of business. Except in the neighborhood pubs and the singles bars, reservations are imperative: for the major clubs, it might be wise to phone a day in advance.

SEEMS LIKE OLD TIMES: Remember the famous supper clubs of the '40s—the Copa, the Latin Quarter—those palaces of glitz and glitter with the big production numbers, high-stepping chorus lines of statuesque beauties dressed in little but their headdresses? Well, the old spectacles are coming back, and there are two places in New York where you are likely to catch the kind of show that you thought had migrated to Las Vegas and left New York for good. The first is the **Rainbow Grill,** on on the 65th floor of the RCA Building at 30 Rockefeller Plaza. This is the entertainment arm of its older sister, the Rainbow Room (which specializes in dining and dancing; see Restaurants, Chapter IV), and its views of the city are just as spectacular. Indoors, the view is of leggy chorines in a smartly paced revue, and of all manner of spectacle. Two shows nightly at 9:15 and 11:30 (no show Sunday), with dancing in between, and after the last show. There's a $10 cover charge during the week, $12 on weekends. À la carte entrees range from about $14 to $22 and go up. Reservations: PL 7-8970. Note to the budget-minded: The views of the city are all yours for the price of a drink in the South Lounge, which opens at 5 p.m.

"Paris in New York" is what the fans are calling **Café Versailles,** at 151 East 50th St., and the Paris they refer to, of course, is the one of Les Folies Bergère. The newest of the lavish supper clubs, built on the site of the old Versailles where Piaf held forth in the '50s, Café Versailles features a $40 prix-fixe dinner and an hour's worth of snappy entertainment, a combination of Parisian sauce and Las Vegas pizzaz, complete with showgirls, singers, dancers, and specialty acts. Showtimes are 9 and 11:30 p.m. every night. For reservations, phone 753-3471.

COMEDIANS AND CABARETS: Stand-up nightclub comics, long considered a casualty of television and changing times, are back again in New York. One of the best places to find them is at **Dangerfield's,** 1118 First Ave., near 61st St. (tel. 593-1650). Although Rodney Dangerfield, the comic who "don't get no respect" no longer makes appearances here, other top comics like Dennis Blair do. There's usually a cover charge of $8 to $15, plus a $7 minimum; on Sunday Comedy Showcase nights, it's a $6 cover and a two-drink minimum.

The **Monkey Bar** in the Elysee Hotel, 60 East 54th St. (tel. PL 3-1066), is well into its fourth decade now. Heretofore it has always been considered quite naughty, but in the light of the new permissiveness that reputation may have paled somewhat. But more or less continuous hilarity is still the order of the night from 9:30 on, with two or three acts incessantly bouncing off one another. Monday to Thursday the minimum is $7.50; Friday and Saturday, $10.

Undiscovered comics—and other entertainers—are always on hand, waiting to be discovered at a quartet of very popular clubs. **The Improvisation,** 358 West 44th St. (tel. 765-8268), was the original comics' showcase, and in its 20-year-history, it has launched some mighty names, from Rodney Dangerfield to the late Andy Kaufman (of TV's "Taxi") to singer Bette Midler. Open daily. . . . **Catch a Rising Star,** 1487 First Ave., near 77th St. (tel. 794-1906), where you can always catch the near-greats working on their material, and sometimes a visit by one of the big names like Dangerfield, Robin Williams, David Brenner, Joe Piscopo, or Joan Rivers, who might drop when they are preparing for a TV special or a live appearance. . . . **Comic Strip,** where you might occasionally see Eddie Murphy of "Saturday Night Live," who was discovered here. . . . **Chilies,** 142 West 44th St. (tel. 840-1766), where there's no cover charge on Monday audition nights. Tuesday is showcase night. Covers and minimums are modest at these clubs, the atmosphere is casual and relaxed, and food is optional and extra. Phone for details.

The cabaret area of the **Ballroom,** 253 West 28th St. (tel. 244-3005), is home to the enchanting singer Blossom Dearie; you can find her there most Tuesdays through Saturdays from 6:30 to 8:30 p.m. The restaurant part of this operation is called Rojas Lombardi at the Ballroom, and is quite special; it features a one-of-a-kind Spanish tapas bar with some 50 traditional appetizers for the tasting. Continental cuisine and a classical guitarists too, from 4:30 p.m. to 2 a.m., Tuesday through Saturday. . . . **Rachel's,** a very popular watering spot in Tribeca at 25 Hudson St. (tel. 334-8155), shows cabaret acts at 10 p.m. in its Little Room, Wednesday through Saturday. There's a $5 cover and two-drink minimum. . . . Performers of the quality of singer Phyllis Newman can often be found at **Freddy's,** 308 East 49th St. (tel. 888-1633), a popular East Side club. . . . Leave it to the

Village Gate, at Bleecker and Thompson Sts. (tel. 475-5120), now in its 26th year as a Village favorite, always to have a top cabaret show in at least one part of its fascinating complex, most likely at Top of the Gate, home to such hits as "A My Name Is Alice." . . . For cabaret in Soho, the place is **Upstairs at Greene Street,** 103 Greene St. (tel. 925-2415); downstairs, it's pop and jazz.

Forbidden Broadway

The classiest, sassiest cabaret act you're likely to see in New York is called **Forbidden Broadway:** it's been playing at a supper club called **Palsson's,** 158 West 72nd St., for about four years now, and we, personally, think it should go on forever. Gerard Alessandrini's fast-paced 1½-hour musical revue pokes brilliant and savage fun at the big names of Broadway, as a quintet of performers parade on stage parodying the likes of Richard Burton ("I wonder what the king is drinking tonight"), Liza Minelli ("I'm Liza one-note"), David Merrick (he has robots—"no contracts, no hassles"—playing in *David Merrick Street*), Patti Lupone ("Don't cry for me, Barbra Streisand"), and best of all, in a takeoff on *Fiddler on the Roof,* a group of actors living in the little village of Manhattan, bound together by a common theme: "Ambition!" Tickets are between $12 and $15, and showtime is Sunday, Tuesday, and Thursday at 8:30 p.m., on Friday and Saturday at 8:30 and 11:30 p.m. Come early for a delicious continental dinner in the restaurant ($10 minimum at the tables). Reservations: 595-7400.

SPECIAL EFFECTS: If atmosphere's the thing, it's hard to imagine a more deliciously *dolce-vita* club than **Roma Di Notte,** 137 East 55th St. (tel. 832-1128), where you can dine in a private cave, then dance on the marble floor to the soft strains of continental music. The food is very good and there is no cover or minimum. Music from 7:30 p.m. to 1:30 a.m., except Sunday. . . . **3 Mitchell Place** at the top of the Beekman Tower, 49th St. and First Ave. (tel. 355-7300), has breathtaking views along with songs and music at the piano bar. No cover, no minimum. . . . The most romantic spot in town for drinks and music? That could well be the **City Lights Bar** and the adjoining **Hors d'Oeuvrerie** restaurant at Windows on the World, atop the World Trade Center. There's piano music from 4:30 to 7:30 p.m., then a three-piece combo from 7:30 p.m. until closing, either for dancing or listening ($2.95 cover), marvelous international hors d'oeuvres for nibbling, and a billion city lights for backdrop. (There's a no-jeans dress code.) On Sunday it's tea dancing from 4 p.m. on (tel. 938-1111). . . . Nostalgia reigns in **Peacock Alley**, posh watering spot in the Waldorf Astoria Hotel, Park Ave. at 50th St. (tel. 872-4895); Cole Porter's splendid Louis XVI–style Steinway piano is played Tuesday through Saturday, and at the fabulous Sunday brunch, by leading pop/jazz pianists. . . . One of New York's most charming old brownstones, the home of actor John Drew way back when, is the setting for the **37th Street Hideaway**, 32 West 37th St. (tel. 947-8490). You can dance on the small parquet floor, or just listen to music and watch a show. No cover or minimum.

THAT MIDDLE EAST MADNESS: The old days of the ethnic Greek and Middle Eastern nightclubs in the 20s on Eighth and Ninth Avenues are long gone, but there at least two glamorous Middle Eastern clubs in midtown. Upstairs of the Café Versailles at 151 East 50th St. is **Club Ibis** (tel. 753-3471), where the tummy-twirling is fast and furious, and it's traditional for the men in the audience to shower the dancers with money and do some fancy stepping themselves. Cover is about $10 on weeknights, $15 on weekends, with a two-drink minimum. . . . **Club Sirocco**, 29 East 29th St. (tel. 683-9409), is another Middle Eastern extravaganza, with singing and dancing in many languages and lots of creative participation from the enthusiastic patrons. There's usually a minimum of $10 or $15, plus almost nonstop performances from 10 p.m. until the wee hours. . . . A favorite Middle Eastern oasis in the Greenwich Village sands is **Café Feenjon**, 117 MacDougal St. (tel. 688-8501), where shows get under way around 8:30 nightly (closed only summer Mondays), with music and minimums ranging from $2.50 to $5. Good Middle Eastern and American menu. Adjoining the Feenjon is a sister restaurant, the **Olive Tree**; here the entertainment consists mostly of playing chess and watching Charlie Chaplin movies. Open daily until 4 a.m.

SAMBA FEVER: A club with an international reputation, **S.O.B. (Sounds of Brazil and Beyond)** lures huge crowds to its cavernous space at 204 Varick St. (tel. 243-4940) for the best in authentic Brazilian food and music. The throbbing jazz sambas of

Brazil alternate with African, Latin, Caribbean and "World Music"; this is the only New York club that showcases third world music on a regular basis. The crowd ranges from the blue jeans set to the black tie set—there's something for everybody here. Come for a splendid dinner, Bahia style (entrees $10.95 to $15.95), partake of some of the national drinks like Caipirinhas or Batidas, and enjoy one of the most unique evenings north of Rio. Reservations are taken only for dinner; otherwise, it's first-come, first-served, but nobody will be turned away. Cover is $7 Tuesday through Saturday ($5 for dinner guests), $10 and $6 Friday and Saturday.

DISCO AND DANCING: What with rock and roll making such a big comeback, the disco craze has eased up a bit in New York. But Saturday Night Fever still exists, and the city still has plenty of places whose patrons share a passion for ear-shattering noise, mind-boggling light shows, and sardine-tin crowds. You should know that nobody who is anybody arrives until very late (from 11 p.m. on), that discos do not admit all comers (it all depends on the whim of the management), and that the door fee can be very high (up to $25 per person); those who have memberships ($150 to $250) have a slightly better chance of getting in and save a few dollars at the door. While disco clubs come and go with alarming rapidity and many are too special (for gays, blacks), faddy, or ephemeral to bear listing here (best check the local papers and magazines when you arrive), the following, in all likelihood, will still be doing business. Reservations are recommended everywhere.

Primarily a disco, although it also features New Wave, big bands, rock, and punk, **Xenon,** 125 West 43rd St. (tel. 221-2690), is known for its $100,000 sound system; your chances of being allowed in go up with the bizarreness of your costume. From 10:30 p.m. on, every day but Sunday; admission is about $18. . . . Remember the **Copacabana,** New York's legendary glamor nightclub of the '40s? It's reopened at the same old stand, 10 East 60th St. (tel. 755-6010), and now it's disco Friday and Saturday nights from 10:30 p.m. to 4 a.m. that brings the crowds, rather than the Copa girls of old. Admission is $12. . . . New York's newest "hot" club is the **Red Parrot,** 617 West 57th St. at 12th Ave. (tel. 247-1530), a barn-like space that occupies an entire city block. The crowd ranges from chic to freak, the music from disco to rock to the big-band sound, the admission from about

$10 to $20. . . . Unless you're a member in good standing of the Beautiful People, you won't know a soul at **Régine's**, 502 Park Ave. at 59th St. (tel. 826-0990). This international nightspot with mirrors reflecting the subdued lighting is very dressy, very "in," and the food is expensive and not as good as it used to be. The cover charge of $15 weekdays, $20 weekends, is waived with dinner reservations, and disco begins late and goes on until 4 a.m. . . . Disco is on from 10 p.m. to 5 a.m. on Friday and Saturday at glittery, hi-tech **Les Mouches**, 260 Eleventh Ave. at 26th St. (tel. 695-5190). . . . The closest thing you'll get to dancing in the streets is an evening at **Wednesday's**, 210 East 86th St. (tel. 535-8500), an underground street festival. This subterranean spot re-creates the ambience of a lively European thoroughfare: sidewalk cafés, wine and cheese shops, bistros, gas lights, and even trees! A disc jockey presides over the stereo set, the atmosphere is casual, and the menu features everything from steak to hamburgers. There is no cover charge on Sunday; it varies from $5 to $7 the rest of the week. Closed Monday. . . . Even **Roseland**, 239 West 52nd St. (tel. 247-0200), that mecca for ballroom dancers (see below), has gotten into the disco act, with midnight disco on Saturday; admission is $8 to $11, subject to change.

TOUCH DANCING: For those hankering after a nice old-fashioned ballroom fling, there's half-century-old **Roseland**, 239 West 52nd St., with a dance floor approximately the size of the Gobi Desert and a huge restaurant as well. Live bands play on Tuesday, Thursday, Saturday, and Sunday from 2:30 p.m.; and there's midnight disco on Saturday. Admission varies from $8 to $11, subject to change.

THE JAZZ REVIVAL: Jazz went through some lean years in New York, but now it's back, bigger and better than ever. So big has the jazz revival become, in fact, that a **Jazzline** (tel. 463-0200 to find out who's playing where) has been established and is flourishing mightily. On the club scene, much of the action is downtown. The **Village Vanguard**, 178 Seventh Ave., at 11th St. (tel. 255-4037), has been around since the 1930s with some of the best jazz there is. Both the giants (like Dexter Gordon and Bill Evans) and newcomers are showcased nightly except Sunday, starting at 10 p.m. No food, low admission, friendly crowd. The jazz action at the **Village Gate**, prestigious entertainment address at Bleecker and Thompson Streets (tel. 475-5120), takes place on Monday nights, when there is listening and dancing to "Salsa Meets Jazz," with name Latin bands and jazz soloists like Dizzy Gillespie and Wynton Marsalis. The rest of the week, it's Cabaret Theater; at the time of this writing it was the original Second City from Chicago, the well-known topical and improvisational group. The Sidewalk Café-Terrace features top-name jazz pianists like Tommy Flanagan, Hank Jones, and Ray Bryant, nightly from 9:30 p.m. (except Monday) until the wee hours. Sandwiches, soup, and chili are available. Call for information on the cabaret shows at Top of the Gate. . . . **Seventh Avenue South,** 21 Seventh Ave. (tel. 242-4694), a hip hangout for musicians, offers a diverse selection of live music, predominantly jazz and fusion. . . . **Blue Note,** at 131 West 3rd St. (tel. 475-8592), is large, comfortable, and features such top-name performers as Al Cohn, Zoot Sims, and Ahmad Jamal. You can catch all the action from the large bar for a one-drink minimum and $5 cover. . . . A relative newcomer to the Village jazz scene, **Lush Life,** 184 Thompson St. (tel. 228-3788), is a jazz club both informal and friendly, and the talent is tops: performers like Anthony Davis, Sheila Jordan, and the Cecil Taylor Expanded Unit make the scene here. . . . Five flights up in a cast-iron industrial building in the East Village, **The Jazz Forum,** 648 Broadway, at Bleecker St. (tel. 477-2655), makes its home. It's a lively spot, good for visiting, perhaps, after an evening at the nearby Public Theater. . . . Soho's big jazz spot venue is called **Greene Street,** 101 Greene St., near Prince (tel. 925-2415), a truck-warehouse turned nightclub and very successful at that. Pop and jazz singers and instrumentalists appear in a stunning supper-club environment, and the nouvelle cuisine is excellent (entrees run about $16 to $24 à la carte). You can watch the show at the bar sans cover. There's also live entertainment at Sunday brunch, noon to 4 p.m. In the same complex is **Upstairs at Greene Street,** 103 Greene St., for cabaret theater and a light menu; and the **Soho Kitchen and Bar,** a cafeteria-style restaurant. . . . The crowds don't mind going way west to Tenth Avenue and 17th Street to **West Boondocks,** at 14 Tenth Ave. (tel. 929-9645), where the relaxed atmosphere and moderate prices for the boss soul food (among the best in New York) compete with the good and easy top jazz. No cover, no minimum.

Sweet Basil Jazz Restaurant, 88 Seventh Ave. South, at Bleecker St. (tel. 242-1785), is highly rated among the Village jazz clubs, strong on talent. It consistently features top names in traditional and contemporary jazz, as well as very good international cuisine. A special treat is the weekend jazz brunch, with the music of the Eddie Chamblee Quartet on Saturday from 2 to 6 p.m., and the legendary trumpeter Doc Cheatham's Quartet on Sunday from 3 to 7 p.m. No cover. . . . Piano plus bass is the usual combo at **Bradley's,** 70 University Pl. at 11th St. (tel. 228-6440). The newest member of the trio is the **Knickerbocker Saloon,** 33 University Pl. at 9th St. (tel. 228-8490), a cozy spot to catch some of the greats. All three are known for commendable, medium-priced kitchens. . . . **Fat Tuesdays,** the downstairs room at Tuesday's Restaurant, 190 Third Ave. at 17th St. (tel. 533-7902), was a winner from the day it opened. The plush mirrored rooms with intimate seating features the best of avant-garde and mainstream artists (Michel LeGrand, Stan Getz, Dizzy Gillespie, etc.), food from upstairs. . . . In the mood for terrific Dixieland bands, Bourbon Street blues? Mardi Gras over to **Cajun,** 129 Eighth Ave., at 16th St. (tel. 691-6174), any Wednesday through Saturday (8 to 11:30 p.m.) or for the Sunday champagne jazz brunch (for $5.95, it's one of the best treats in town). Dine on inexpensive Cajun-Créole food or have drinks at the bar. No cover, no minimum. . . . **Angry Squire,** 216 Seventh Ave., at 23rd St. (tel. 242-9066), is another worthy jazz address in Chelsea, this one with a nautical flavor.

A spot for the best of traditional jazz is **Eddie Condon's,** 144 West 54th St. (tel. 265-8277), which has the Eddie Condon All-Star Jazz Band Monday through Saturday and guest bands on Sunday. Steaks, ribs, and burgers are served all the way until 2 a.m. . . . You can mix with the Columbia University kids and other enthusiastic jazz buffs at the **West End Café,** Broadway at 113th St. (tel. 666-9160), a very informal place for a mini jazz festival with legendary names from the swing era. No cover charge, moderate prices. . . . Another popular Upper West Side hangout is **Mikell's,** 706 Columbus Ave., at 97th St. (tel. 864-8832), which mixes Latin accents and rhythm and blues with traditional jazz notes. . . . There's always plenty of action at **Gregory's,** First Ave. at 63rd St. (tel. 371-2220), where a bevy of jazz masters hold forth. There's cocktail hour entertainment until 10 p.m., then a jazz trio until 3 a.m. . . . **Red Blazer Too,** 1576 Third Ave. (88th to 89th Sts.; tel. 876-0440), is making news by offering a different jazz band every night, with good food; no cover but there is a drink minimum. . . . **Michael's Pub,** 211 East 55th St. (tel. 758-2272), an English pubby type of place that everybody seems to like, has an eclectic entertainment policy—everyone from Mort Sahl to balladeers. They're big on jazz too, with Woody Allen's New Orleans Funeral & Ragtime Band occasionally checking in when the comedian is in town.

Most jazz clubs charge minimums of $5 to $10 and/or a one- or two-drink minimum, but it all depends on the performer. And with the jazz renaissance in full swing, new clubs are opening all the time. Check the listings in the magazines (the *New Yorker* has the best), also in the *Village Voice,* or call Jazzline to see just what's happening while you're here. It's best to make reservations, and check the credit-card policy of the club.

FOLK AND ROCK—SOME MIXED BAGS: Out of the folk and acid rock of the late '60s seems to have come a new melding of musical styles and appreciation, and New York's musical show-cases reflect this trend. There are few all-rock or all-folk stages or even artists left. And folk and rock are no longer the province of the Village alone. They have made their way uptown to larger quarters and have even, on occasion, taken over such prestigious halls of high culture as Carnegie Hall, Avery Fisher Hall, and the Metropolitan Opera House. Madison Square Garden and its neighboring Felt Forum have been the scene of many a rock concert, and the new Radio City Music Hall Entertainment Center presents occasional rock performers.

Although it's considered the preeminent rock club in the city —some say in the country—the huge, always-packed **Bottom Line,** 15 West 4th St. (tel. 228-7880), does not limit its acts strictly to rock—you might catch folk singers, jazz artists (of the stature of Don Shirley), even classical performers. The crowd is young, the food ordinary. No minimum.

The in place to dance to rock music at this writing is **Lime-light,** 47 West 20th St. (tel. 807-7850), a nightclub created out of a mid-19th century city landmark church (it was deconsecrat-ed some years back). Dancing takes place in the main sanctuary, and you can look down upon the goings-on from the choir loft above. There are four bars, a library, and many cozy nooks for sitting and talking. Crowds line up to gain access to this cavern-ous place (it can hold 2500 people), but the lines move quickly. Admission is $15, possibly cheaper on the nights of theme parties (call for information). . . . On Sundays, tea dances are held primarily for the gay community.

If you like to listen to high energy, high volume rock music while you eat, then be sure to dine at the very popular **Hard**

Rock Cafe, 221 West 57th St. (tel. 489-6565). Jammed with rock memorabilia (Elvis Presley's suit, Jimmy Hendrix' guitar, etc.), the café serves a menu that ranges from $5.50 hamburgers to steaks that go up to about $16.50. There's a soda fountain, and good desserts, too. Open daily from 11:30 a.m. to 4 a.m. They do not take reservations, and the line to get in can be quite long.

Back in the days when it was known as the Bitter End, the **Other End,** 147 Bleecker St. (tel. 673-7030), launched such superstars as Peter, Paul, and Mary. Still going strong, this is a smaller room, where you might even catch the likes of Bob Dylan every now and then. There's film night on Monday, comedy night on Tuesday. Admission is usually between $2 and $5, except for special shows. . . . **Folk City,** 130 West 3rd St. (tel. 254-8449), is another Village oldtimer that started some of the greats on their way. The talent is still worth catching. The range goes from folk to New Age on Friday and Saturday nights, but other eves there's cabaret, theater, comedy. Admission and drinks are modestly priced. Call for schedules. . . . Despite its location near the Ninth Avenue wholesale meatpacking district, the **Eagle Tavern,** 355 West 14th St. (tel. 924-0275), draws folk-music lovers from all over town on Monday, Wednesday, Thursday, Saturday, and Sunday evenings. It's traditional Irish folk music on Monday and Wednesday, bluegrass on Thursday and Saturday, finger-picking guitar on Sunday. The atmosphere is blue-collar bar, the crowd casual, and the cover charge about $5. . . . Not only is the Friday and Saturday night Irish folk music good at **Irish Pavilion,** 130 East 57th St. (tel. 759-9040), but the Irish coffee is so good it must have been made by the little people themselves (call to check if entertainment is on). . . . **Speakeasy Folkmusic Cabaret,** at 107 MacDougal St. (tel. 598-9670), presents both new performers and stars of the '60s. The cover fluctuates between $3 and $5. . . . A delightful place to hear folksongs or rock music or poetry reading is the **Cornelia Street Café,** 29 Cornelia St., between West 4th and Bleecker Sts. (tel. 929-9869). A cross between a European café and a Greenwich Village coffeehouse, it serves reasonably priced food in a new pleasant dining room with a fireplace and a full bar. Music, writing, and art programs continue every week.

Want a big rock club with a big dance floor? Try the **Ritz,** 119 East 11th St. (tel. 254-2800), where there's plenty of room to dance and to listen to top names. . . . **Peppermint Lounge,** 100 Fifth Ave., at 15th St. (tel. 989-9505), is still going strong after all these years, and the dancing is as wild as ever (bring your chiropractor with you). . . . Once known as a punk hangout, the **Mudd Club,** 77 White St., two blocks south of Canal St., between Broadway and Lafayette (tel. 227-7777), has become much more eclectic these days. Everyone's performed here at one time or another, from Frank Zappa to Joni Mitchell. . . . **Kenny's Castaways,** 157 Bleecker St. (tel. 473-9870), is popular with the younger set. The music and the food are both good here. . . . **CBGB & OMFUG,** 315 Bowery at Bleecker St. (tel. 982-4052), reverts back to its original punk rock formula only on Thursday ("Hardcore Night"); other nights, new and original bands play mainstream rock and roll. . . . The hours at **Danceteria,** 30 West 21 St., are 9 to 5—but that's 9 *p.m.* to 5 *a.m.,* the hours when a young, "partially crazed-out audience" gathers at this huge establishment to dance, watch videos, or visit the fourth floor, a "weird space for extreme avant-garde art exhibits, performances, and happenings." Thus forewarned, you are free to arrive there any night of the week, appropriately dressed (no suits or ties, please), and at least enjoy inexpensive admission prices: $1 on Sunday, Monday, and Tuesday; $5 on Wednesday and Thursday; $6 before 11 p.m., $10 after that, on Friday and Saturday. . . . And uptown at 100 West 72nd St. is **Trax** (tel. 799-1478), with a variety of acts (rock, New Age, and fusion) by both newcomers and top names. There's also a rock DJ for dancing. Call for a schedule of shows.

FREEBIES: During the warm weather, you can often hear some of the top club performers in the city doing their thing for free. It all takes place at the atrium patio of the **Citicorp Center,** at Lexington Ave. between 53rd and 54th Sts. Bringing in snacks or not to munch on, you sit at tables and watch the show. Usually from 6 to 8 p.m.; check the papers for details.

THE SOUNDS OF COUNTRY: Strange as it may seem to out-of-towners, the newest "in" thing in urbane, sophisticated New York at the current moment is country music. When Charlie Rich and Merle Haggard played the Felt Forum a few years back, the reception was overwhelming. Country music clubs have come and gone, but one that seems destined to remain forever is the very popular **O'Lunney's,** 915 Second Ave., between 48th and 49th Sts. (tel. 751-5470). It's a warm, woodsy, very western place: on one wall is a mural of a country boy with a guitar walking to the city—a prophecy? You can dine on moderately priced, basic American fare while listening to all the greats. Monday is talent night, Sunday from 8 p.m. on is given over to bluegrass, and the rest of the week, from 9 p.m. on, it's sincere, soulful country western—the kind you'd expect to hear in Nashville rather than New York. There's a $3 food or drink minimum at the tables (none in the bar area), plus a $3 entertainment charge. Open every day except Christmas.

Another big country, and rhythm and blues, mecca, home to leading touring country artists, is the **Lone Star Café,** Fifth Ave. at 13th St. (tel. 242-1664), where they serve Lone Star Beer, celebrate Texas Independence Day, and have a full Texas-American menu (try the chili, Texas ribs, and BBQ!). Despite its plush trappings—a marble staircase, lots of mirrors, brass, and mahogany—and its size—it seats 400 people on two levels, has upstairs and downstairs bars and two bands—the Lone Star Café has an intimate, casual air. Up on the big stage, under the golden horseshoe, you might catch acts like Hank Williams, Jr., the Blues Brothers, or Willie Nelson, plus other big names of country and western music as well as blues and rock artists. The music charge varies between $6 and $10, plus a two-drink minimum during the show.

Another honky-tonk where you can park your Stetson and take a spin on the dance floor to the strains of country is **City Limits,** Seventh Ave. at 10th St. (tel. 243-2242).

PUB CRAWLING ALL AROUND TOWN: 'Tis pleasant in the cool of evening to drop into a warm and/or atmospheric public house and slake the thirst with a brew, a drop of the grape, or a belt of the grain. In New York no one need go thirsty. At most places, mixed drinks will average $3 to $5.

Almost all visitors to Fun City find themselves at a Broadway theater on at least one evening. Say you want just a nightcap afterward and would like to stay somewhere in the area. The most obvious suggestion is **Sardi's,** 234 West 44th St. (tel. 221-8440). A contingent of authentic Broadway personalities can be depended on to arrive around 11:30 p.m., and the supreme vantage point for checking all comings and goings is the bar, just inside the entrance. Fine for an after-theater supper, too (see Chapter IV, Restaurants). On Eighth Avenue between 44th and 45th Streets is **Downey's Steak House** (tel. 757-0186), often called "the poor man's Sardi's." But here, too, certifiable show-folk—usually the younger, on-the-way-up variety—put in an appearance. Or there's the **Blue Bar** in the Algonquin Hotel, 59 West 44th St. (tel. 840-6800), which may be the petitest, chummiest lounge in Manhattan and where you'll surely be privy to every conversation. Here, too, celebrities, often itinerant actors or authors from Britain, materialize.

In full view of the Lincoln Center complex are the **Ginger Man,** 51 West 64th St. (tel. 399-2358), a charming watering hole with period-piece fixtures; and its brother enterprise, **O'Neal's Baloon,** 48 West 63rd St. (tel. 399-2353), easily recognizable by the theater lights on the canopy. Both have sidewalk cafés and are popular after-concert places. **The Saloon,** 1920 Broadway at 64th St., has roller-skating waiters and a huge sidewalk café. And at the lovely **Maestro Caffè,** 58 West 65th St., the drinks are accompanied by some of the best hors d'oeuvres in town—free.

Bookish types touring the Village will want to knock back an "arf'n arf" at the **White Horse Tavern,** at the corner of Hudson and 11th Sts., where Dylan Thomas dwelt and drank himself to death, and where such American literary lights as Norman Mailer, Louis Auchincloss, and Calder Willingham used to be regulars in the back room. A large and comfortable outdoor café offering light foods is open during the warm weather, usually from May 1 through early fall. . . . The **Lion's Head,** at 59 Christopher St., just off Sheridan Square, attracts younger writers, newspaper people (columnist Pete Hamill's favorite pump), and folk singers (notably the Clancy Brothers). . . . One of New York's first wine bars, **The Wine Bar** in Soho, 422 West Broadway, offers a huge selection of wines by the glass, plus the more usual hard stuff. . . . More than just traditional English brews, food, and atmosphere prevail at the jolly **North Star Pub,** at the South Street Seaport. There's usually a zany celebration of some sort taking place: a recent one, for example, was a "British forgive George Washington" bash!

The Gramercy Park neighborhood has at least two attractive dispensaries: **Pete's Tavern,** the oldest original bar in New York City, at 18th St. and Irving Pl., a 115-year-old shrine, habituated by O. Henry (who lived across the street) and commemorated by him in one of his stories; and **Molly Malone's Pub,** Third Ave. near 22nd St., a white-plaster, shingle-roofed Irish pub which exudes all those endearing Irish charms and draws unto it congenial, youngish souls from the high-rises around the lovely park, serving excellent Irish coffee.

Fifteen blocks or so north on Third is **Kitty Hawk's,** near 37th

St., a mini-museum of aviation memorabilia appropriately situated close to the East Side Terminal. Patronage is about equally divided between airline personnel and young dwellers in the Murray Hill neighborhood. In the East 40s, **Harry's New York Bar** at the Harley Hotel, 212 East 42nd St., is a convivial spot for a drink, madly popular at cocktail time when they offer an unbelievable selection of free hors d'oeuvres—shrimp, snow crab claws, hot appetizers, and the like—all free with the drinks. . . . At 6 p.m., the **Gold Room** of the Helmsley Palace Hotel, 455 Madison Ave. at 50th St., becomes perhaps the most splendid cocktail lounge in New York. Designed by Stanford White, the two-story room with vaulted ceiling has decorative panels based on the 15th-century Luca della Robbia panels in the cathedral of Florence, and demi-lunette paintings and stained-glass windows by artist John La Farge. And the drinks aren't bad, either. . . . **Onde's,** 160 East 48th St., is a comfortable spot frequented by business types; it's one of the few places where women can feel comfortable having a solo drink. Another seven blocks due north on Third, at 55th St., you come to **Clarke's** (only the noncognoscenti persist in calling it—incorrectly—P. J. Clarke's). This is truly a landmark and one which began its life as a workingman's saloon—and still looks the part. Now *tout le monde* turns up there. (Jackie Onassis digs the hamburgers the most.) The time to go is late (well after midnight), in time to catch the celebrity flow that sweeps in many a famous face, looking a little worse perhaps for the wear. That old booze picture starring Ray Milland *(The Lost Weekend)* was filmed here, by the by. . . . Another place to catch the celebrity scene is **Jim McMullen's,** 1341 Third Ave. at 76th St. Jim, a former male fashion model, has a huge crowd of buddies who hang out at the enormous bar in this art deco restaurant. It's always a party.

In the East 60s and 70s, the big action is the singles bars (see "Eating and Meeting at the Singles Bars"). Arrive at East 86th Street and you're in the heart of Yorkville, where the German-Viennese flavor is still noticeable, despite the French restaurants, rock clubs, and other more recent forms of divertissement that have moved on to the street. . . . **Elaine's,** Second Ave. between 88th and 89th Sts., is indubitably the most "in" joint on the East Side, and the people at the next table could well be Leonard Bernstein, Woody Allen, or one of that crowd.

Eating and Meeting at the Singles Bars

The singles bars movement which hit New York in the mid-'60s is still going strong. On the East Side, it swings primarily along First Avenue—known to habitués as "The Strip"—all the way from 60th Street up through the 70s. There you'll find mingling, mixing, eyeing, spying, and just plain good ole fun. And even if you don't find the one of your dreams, you're sure to fill your stomach 'cause there's food aplenty and the price is right. **Friday's**, at 63rd Street, was perhaps the first of the bunch and is the granddaddy of several other nightspots around town (**Tuesday's**, Third Ave. near 17th St.; **Tuesday's West**, 72nd St. and Columbus Ave.; and **Wednesday's**, 210 East 86th St.). It's got low lighting, a crowded bar, booths, semi-outdoor seating, good drinks, and some of the solidest food around. The burgers are thick and done as you like. The spare ribs have a delicious sauce. Prices run from $2.95 to about $12.

Across the street is **Adam's Apple**, near 61st Street, now in its tenth year. Much larger than Friday's, it has two dining rooms, a bar area, and two suspended dance floors. It's been opulently revamped with lush, live foliage and tropical lighting. Food is à la carte, $3.50 to $23.50.

Who's On First, at 65th St., offers good food and fun, while **Carnaby St.**, near 64th St., has drinks, rock and roll music, and dancing, but no food.

Maxwell's Plum, at the 64th St. corner, is the finest and classiest of the lot and draws an older, well-heeled crowd. Glittery with Tiffany-style lamps and art deco frills, it has an enormous, diversified menu, with diversified prices—most of which are slightly higher than elsewhere on the Strip. Late-night dinner dancing, too.

In the last few years, the singles turf has expanded across town, across Central Park and over to Columbus Avenue. Here, in the blocks just above and below 72nd Street, is another outrageous fashion parade, another place to see and be seen. Center of the action, at the moment, is **Ruelles**, at 75th St., which draws some very chic celebrity types—designers, actors, even a mayor or two (see "Restaurants," Chapter IV).

Chapter IX

SECRETS OF THE NEW YORK SHOPPING WORLD

WE KNOW quite a lot of people—and not all of them women —who come to New York for only one reason: to go shopping. Not for them the excitement of Broadway, the dazzle of the nightclubs, the adventures into the exotic world off the beaten path. For them, the greatest show in town begins right on Fifth Avenue. One woman we know flies in regularly from Detroit, checks into her hotel, grabs a cab, and heads immediately for Saks. "Then," she says, "I know I'm in New York."

What our friend senses, of course, is the fact that New York is one of the great fashion capitals of the world, a city where *Women's Wear Daily* sits on the best coffee tables, where the fashion business provides a living, a *raison d'être* or, at the very least, a subject of conversation for thousands of people. As a result of this high-keyed fashion consciousness, the New York woman, regardless of her income, is one of the best, most individually dressed women in the world. Close at hand she has the great department and specialty stores like B. Altman, Lord & Taylor, Saks Fifth Avenue, Bergdorf Goodman, Bloomingdale's, Macy's, and Gimbels. She also has hundreds and hundreds of small boutiques and shops where she can buy anything from a Paris evening gown whose price tag runs into four figures to a Mickey Mouse T-shirt for $6. She can suit her flights of fancy with a pair of fine Italian boots, a silken sari from India, a peasant dress from Morocco, or a poncho from Mexico. She can rummage through old capes and costumes in the Village, or pick the cream of the Puccis at SFA. It's a wide-open, exciting scene, and one that any woman (or man, for that matter, since men's boutiques are proliferating almost as widely as women's) with an ounce of fashion curiosity will find absorbing.

The Department and Specialty Stores

If you've been following our sightseeing suggestions, you've probably already been to **Macy's,** 34th St. and Herald Square, which, as the world's largest department store, has it all, from elegant boutiques like the Little Shop to the Cellar, a street of gourmet shops in the basement. Selections in every department are vast and always of good quality. Across the street is **Gimbels,** another friendly giant (check its basement for occasional close-outs from its more elegant sister store, Saks Fifth Avenue), and both could keep you busy for weeks. As if that's not temptation enough, in between them is **Herald Center,** the $60-million, seven-acre, 200-retail-store shopping complex (still a-building at press time), themed to capture the varied neighborhoods and styles of Manhattan. A skylit food court and atrium with views of the city will offer an array of foods from New York's best known restaurants. Walk east along 34th Street now until you get to **Ohrbach's,** one of New York's great bargain stores (about which more later). At 34th and Fifth is prestigious **B. Altman & Co.,** an oldie with a young contemporary as well as classic reputation, emphasizing top designers in women's, men's and children's fashion, unique gifts and china, Oriental objects, gourmet delicacies, rare books and autographs, and the refreshing Charleston Garden for breakfast, lunch, tea, and Thursday dinner. Proceed up to 38th Street and Fifth, and there's 150-year-old **Lord & Taylor,** with its shimmering street floor, the swinging Young New Yorker shop, beautiful antique furniture, many lovely, lovely things for every member of the family. Its Bird Cage is a busy lunch- and tea-time aviary. The next big stop is at 50th Street and Fifth and that, of course, is **Saks Fifth Avenue** —a name long synonymous with fashion elegance. Here's where you can indulge yourself in a Revillon fur, revel in a whole shop of Louis Vuitton luggage and accessories, and shop the top French and American designers' collections in their own boutiques. Twice a year, in January and June, Saks runs storewide clearances, and everyone in town shows up for the bargains. **Bergdorf Goodman,** at 57th and Fifth, and **Henri Bendel,** just west of Fifth, present the ultimate in fine clothing and accessories. Both are filled with charming little boutiques and all sorts of nooks and corners for precious goodies. Cross the avenue to inspect the luxuries of the stunning new **Trump Tower** and the adjoining **Bonwit Teller.**

Head east to Lexington Avenue and 59th Street now (and if you have children with you, you'll undoubtedly have to make a stop at the corner of Fifth and 58th at **F.A.O. Schwarz,** America's most famous toy store), to **Bloomingdale's.** Bloomie's, as it is affectionately known to the chic sophisticates who practically make it a second home, has the latest in everything from forward fashions for juniors on the second floor to designer clothing on the third, to the trendiest houseware on the sixth. On the main floor is the energized world of cosmetics, skin care, and accessories, plus a marvelous bakery-gourmet department. Uptown, at 86th Street and Lexington Avenue (a short subway ride from Bloomingdale's), is the area's newest and northernmost department store, and that's **Gimbels East,** more sophisticated than its downtown sister, with good values in every category, and, again, a very good bakery/gourmet section.

Jewelry and Gifts

New York is the diamond center of the country, and if you're convinced that diamonds (or even pearls) are a girl's best friend, you should have a look at some of the town's outstanding jewelry shops. Start at the top with the splendor of **Tiffany's** (which surprises with inexpensive gift items in addition to the likes of emerald brooches and diamond necklaces) and **Cartier,** Fifth at 52nd Street (also at Trump Tower), where you can find old Cartier designs of the '20s and '30s as well as today's classic jewelry, plus Paris-designed watches, jewelry, and small leather goods at "young prices" in the Les Must de Cartier boutique. A stroll along 47th Street, between Fifth and Sixth Avenues, where diamonds are being traded on street corners, polished in workrooms, and sold in a number of small jewelry stores, puts you right in the heart of the jewelry world. To catch the Village jewelry scene, walk on West 4th Street between Sixth and Seventh Avenues; here and elsewhere in the Village you'll find any number of small shops selling avant-garde rings, pins, brooches, that are both beautiful and/or way out.

The Best of the Bargains

But we promised to let you in on some special secrets of the New York shopping world, on the essential information that will tell you where to pick up an $85 dress for $35, a mink coat for $1000, or a great pair of pants for $15—or where to get designer's originals for one-third the price in the salons. So let's begin at **Ohrbach's,** 5 West 34th St., where the biggest selection of high-fashion, bargain-priced women's clothing is to be found.

The only trouble is that those millions of other shoppers are pushing and shoving and poring over the counters in a mad scramble for the same dresses, handbags, gloves, sweaters, lingerie, etc., that you are. There are also good men's and young men's departments, and lovely children's clothing at below-usual prices. *Tip:* Come early in the morning before the crowds get thick, and try to avoid the lunch hours, noon to 2 p.m.

On you go, to **Alexander's**, Lexington Ave. at 58th St., where the values are good in every department, but especially outstanding in knitwear and sweaters. We once coveted, but did not buy, a $44 Paris-imported sweater set in an uptown boutique: the next week, there it was in Alexander's, priced at $24! Furs and cashmeres are other good buys here, and so are children's toys and games. The first-floor handbag department often has amazing values.

If French designer's clothing is what you covet, *allez vite* to **Azriel Altman**, Fifth Ave. near 25th St. (tel. 889-0782). Altman has taken over the premises of a former bank, and now its assets include cachet names like Ted Lapidus, Pierre Balmain, and Bernard Danae of Paris, as well as a few American designers. Prices are not inexpensive, but the finest suits, coats, raincoats, leather coats, precious silks, are all 25% to 30% less here than elsewhere. Imported shirts and sportswear for men, too. There's another A. Altman at 182 Orchard St. on the Lower East Side.

Current, top-brand fashion at about one-third off department store prices—that's what you'll find at **Bolton's**, uptown at 1180 Madison Ave. (near 86th St.); also on the East Side at 225 East 57th St., 4 East 34th St. (near the Empire State Building); and on the West Side at 53 West 23rd St., 27 West 57th St., and 2251 Broadway (near 81st St.). Bolton's is also located in the Village at 43 East 8th St., and at 59 Liberty St. (near Wall St.). Fresh selections arrive twice a week and include a fashionable mix of famous-label dresses, suits, coats, contemporary casuals, and accessories. Dresses range from about $40 to over $100.

Top names like Nipon, Liz Claiborne, and Cathy Hardwick are among those found at **Designer Liquidators**, 2045 Broadway, near 71st St. (tel. 787-3954), all at prices of 20% to 70% off list. It's all current, first-quality merchandise, and new shipments arrive all the time. Open every day.

Call **S. & W. Famous Designers Apparel** "off Seventh Avenue," if you will. It features name brands from the Seventh Avenue houses, at excellent prices. There are actually four stores in the complex, all located on the corner of Seventh Avenue and

26th Street. At 165 West 26th St., the upper level shows top-designer suits, dresses, and sportswear: the lower level is the "After Five" department and the lingerie section. Around the corner at 283 Seventh Ave., you'll find shoes, handbags, and accessories; 287 Seventh Ave. has designer coats in suedes, wools, and leather; 291 Seventh Ave. is the place for medium-priced designer sportswear. Closed Saturday, but open Sunday through Friday (tel. 924-6656).

Close by, and with the same pipe-rack ambience, but with similarly extraordinary values, is the **New Store**, 289 Seventh Ave. (tel. 741-1077), which stays open every day of the week. Prices run a good 40% and more off on top-name designer clothes: skirts, pants, blouses, jeans, blazers, and much more. Beautiful designer shoes, too. A few doors away, **Harris's**, at 275 Seventh Ave. (tel. 989-9765), also has fine women's designer fashions at savings that are usually 33% to 50% off regular prices. This store is a bit larger than the others and there is more personalized service. Open every day.

It's worth a trip downtown to the financial district to pay a visit to **Century 21**, 12 Cortlandt St. (tel. 227-9092), near the World Trade Center, which may be New York's most spectacular discount department store, with everything from toys to TVs and designer wear for women, men, and children at prices that are often 30% to 50% off the regular tabs. We've seen Jones New York pants, Christian Dior beachwear, Jack Mulqueen silk dresses, Vittorio Ricci shoes. The biggest bargains are in women's lingerie and shoes, but everything is well priced here, including electronic games, small appliances, and men's sport shoes. Century 21 is open weekdays only, from 7:45 a.m. to 6:15 p.m.

While you're downtown, take a look, too, at the women's department of **Syms**, 45 Park Pl. (tel. 791-1199), "where an educated consumer is our best customer," to quote their ads. Syms *does* offer the consumer good value: designer clothes sold for about one-third off regular prices, with a progressive mark-down policy (*if* you wait long enough, and *if* nobody else gets it first, you could conceivably get a $100 garment for about $25). Selection is top-notch, decor is minimal, and the lunchtime crowds are horrendous. Well worth a try, however, early in the morning or later in the day when the crowds have thinned out. Open Monday through Wednesday from 9 a.m. to 7 p.m., Thursday until 8 p.m., on Saturday from 9 a.m. to 6 p.m.

CLOSEOUTS: Where, under one roof, might you find $250 watches for $55, $30 sneakers for $7.95, a $90 set of cookware for $30, a $20 name-brand perfume for $2.95, or a $2 lip gloss for 29¢? These are the kinds of bargains New Yorkers are crazy about, and you will be too, once you discover the stores of either **Odd-Job Trading Company** or **The Pushcart, Job Lot Trading Company.** Both of these companies do an amazing business in brand-name goods acquired at auctions and closeouts or as overruns. Stock changes constantly, but it's always worthwhile to see what they have in camping and sporting goods, hardware, pet supplies, kitchenware and china, toys, linens, stationery, party goods—to name just a few categories. Odd-Job has huge stores: one at 3 East 40th St., another at 66 West 48th St. The Pushcart has its original store, downtown at 140 Church St. in the City Hall area, in an atmosphere re-creating the oldtime pushcarts of the Lower East Side, and a newer store, uptown at 412 Fifth Ave. at 37th St. At all of these stores, the crowds are apt to be fierce, especially during lunch hours, so arrive earlier or later. For the downtown Pushcart, take the IND or IRT subways to Chambers Street.

THE LOWER EAST SIDE: You could spend a week shopping the Lower East Side and we could write a book just telling you about the bargains here, in these narrow, tenemented streets where New York's immigrant Jewish colony once flourished. Many of the shopkeepers live uptown or in the wealthy suburbs now, and so do most of the customers. But they still keep coming down here for marvelous bargains in just about everything, and now, with inflation rampant, business is brisker than ever. We'll simply point you in the direction of a few of our favorites and let you take it from there. Remember to bring plenty of cash, wear good walking shoes, be prepared for inconvenient or nonexistent fitting rooms, and a strict no-return policy. Try to come during the week, since most places are closed late Friday and Saturday, and Sunday is total insanity. Take the F train (Queens line) on the IND subway or the QB, M, or J trains of the BMT to Delancey and Essex Streets, or the D train (Sixth Avenue line) on the IND subway to Grand Street; you should be there in about 20 minutes from midtown Manhattan.

Let's start with women's clothing: our favorite places are **Fishkin's,** at 314 Grand St. and also at 63 Orchard St. (which also carries shoes and handbags); **Breakaway Designer Fashions and**

Furs, 88 Rivington St. and 125 Orchard St.; **Forman's,** 82 Orchard; **M. Friedlich,** 196 Orchard; and **A. Altman,** 182 Orchard (see above). All have top-name designer and imported dresses, suits, tops, pants, coats, etc., at remarkable prices. Men can be well outfitted at **G & G Projections,** 53 Orchard St.; **Haar & Knobel,** 49 Orchard St.; and at **Charlie's Place,** 61 Orchard (which has a huge selection of London Fog raincoats for women, too). They can pick up designer's shirts at, of all places, **Ezra Cohen,** 307 Grand St., who is best known for buys in designer linens, towels, bedspreads, etc., as is **Harris Levy,** 278 Grand, which has been selling to New York's finest families for many a long year. (Harris Levy is also a direct importer of fine bed and table linens and features a complete bath shop.) You'll be dazzled by the array of beautiful handbags at **Fine & Klein,** 119 Orchard St. Pick up your couturier underwear at **Mendel Weiss,** 91 Orchard, and see the nice people at **D & A Merchandise Company,** 22 Orchard, for all kinds of lingerie and underwear for everybody in the family (catalogs will be sent on request). **Goldman & Cohen,** 54 Orchard St., discounts at least 20% to 25% on fine-quality women's lingerie and loungewear; you'll want to stock up when you see the prices!

All leather gloves, mostly imported from Italy, are a bargain at **Bernard Krieger,** 316 Grand St., and so are ski gloves, wools and suedes, and some attractive women's hats. You can buy the kids their new wardrobes at **Rice and Breskin,** 323 Grand St., and shoe-shop at **New Grand Street Bootery,** 65 Orchard St., or the front part of **Fishkin's,** 314 Grand St. (for women). Pick up some knitting or crocheting supplies—and get some free instruction if you want it—at booming **Bell Yarn Company,** 75 Essex St., and some fine fabrics from **Samuel Beckenstein,** at 130 Orchard.

There's nothing like shopping to whet the appetite—and tire the feet—so have a rest and enjoy either a dairy meal at **Ratner's,** 138 Delancey St., where the pastries are mind-boggling, or a meat one at **Katz's Delicatessen,** 205 East Houston St., where the corned beef and hot pastrami are legendary. (Ratner's, a New York tradition since 1905, serves from breakfast to after-theater.) It would be unthinkable to come home from the Lower East Side without "a little something for later"—perhaps a knish or a kugel from **Yonah Schimmel's Knishery,** 137 East Houston St. (The same family has owned the knishery for over 90 years, bakes 12 varieties of knishes daily in a 100-year-old brick oven, and has a yogurt culture that has been ongoing for over 80 years!)

Or pick up some lox or caviar or pistachio nuts from **Russ & Daughters,** 179 East Houston St., which happens to be one of the city's most prestigious appetizing stores. Taste, shop, enjoy!

SOMETHING FOR THE MEN: With the price of men's suits rising astronomically, many of the better heeled men in town have left their usual haberdashers and are now shopping the outlet stores. There are many such stores advertised, but not all deliver first quality: some simply buy last year's or unpopular styles. The ones that we mention here (husband-tested) carry fine clothing and prices of about 30% to 40% lower than elsewhere. Most levy a slight charge for alterations. The decor is pipe rack, but service is usually good—and you can't beat the prices. Our favorites include **Syms,** 45 Park Pl., in the financial district (tel. 791-1199), which also boasts an excellent women's designer discount department; **Gorsart,** at 122 Duane St. (tel. 962-0024), also downtown; **Mernsmart,** Madison Ave. at 54th St. (tel. 371-9175), and also at 75 Church St. (tel. 227-5471); and **Burton Ltd.,** 475 Fifth Ave. at 41st St. (tel. 685-3760). **Harry Rothman,** 111 Fifth Ave. at 18th St. (tel. 777-7400), has a customer roster that reads like Brooks Brothers; more than half a century old, it is the granddaddy of the discount stores. **Saint Laurie, Ltd.,** 895 Broadway (20th St.), has been manufacturing classic men's clothing since 1913, and it is sold at some of the finest stores in the country. Prices at the factory outlet store are about one-third less (women's classic business suits, too). **NBO,** in a handsome new store one block from Lincoln Center, on Broadway near 67th St. (tel. 595-1550), offers a top-flight selection of designer menswear at very good prices. Open every day, including Sunday.

In Search of Serendipity

Those three ancient kings who went in search of serendipity—looking for something rare, undiscovered, exceptional—would have had a splendid time shopping in New York. The unusual shop, the one-of-a-kind discovery, abounds here. Below, we'll tell you about some of our personal favorites off the beaten path, uptown and downtown, where you might pick up the perfect gift for your friends back home—or for yourself.

APPETIZING: Not an adjective but a New York noun (or state of mind) that means salty smoked fish and pickled herring and

Almost Wholesale on Seventh Avenue

Gaining access to New York's famed wholesale houses, unless you have a connection, is not so easy. But we've discovered something that we like even better: shopping at the showrooms of the jobbers and exporters who are the middlemen of Seventh Avenue. Besides carrying a vast array of merchandise from many manufacturers, they welcome retail customers, provide fitting rooms (nonexistent in wholesale houses), courteous service (you are usually not allowed to browse), and exceptional merchandise at prices that may range from as little as 20% to as much as 50% or 60% of what you would have to pay retail. Usually, it's cash only, and no returns.

Start your Seventh Avenue expedition at **Abe J. Geller,** on the fifth floor of 491 Seventh Ave. (37th St.). You'll be dazzled by racks and racks of stunning clothes, all with the top designer's labels still in them! Mr. Geller claims that prices are 40% to 60% lower than they are in the fancy stores. Open weekdays from 10 a.m. to 5 p.m., on Saturday until 3 p.m. (tel. 736-8077).

You may have to wait a little while to be waited on at **Ms., Miss Or Mrs.,** on the eighth floor of 462 Seventh Ave. (35th St.), but we can assure you that it will be worth every minute. MMM represents close to 350 of the top-name manufacturers on Seventh Avenue. Their merchandise is first quality, and runs from name-brand sportswear to all-wool coats, fake furs and fur-lined coats, raincoats, goose-down-filled quilts and jackets, and imported tweeds to an extensive selection of designer dresses priced from $45 up to $500. Their markup is very low, your savings are phenomenal (40% to 50%—and more at the time of seasonal closeouts). They ask that you phone them at 736-0557 first, and tell them you read about them in this book. Open weekdays from 9 a.m. to 6 p.m., on Thursday to 8 p.m., on Saturday to 4 p.m. Closed Saturday in July and August. Diagonally opposite Macy's.

Despite its name, **National Ladies Specialty Corporation,** on the second floor of 470 Seventh Ave. (35th St.), is not just for the ladies. Sure, they have scads of dresses and suits, including designer names ($35.75 to $199.75); plenty of skirts ($59.75 to $75); synthetic fur coats, coats, and raincoats ($199.75 to $250) for women, but they also have a complete men's haberdashery. Designer handbags and accessories and brand-name lingerie, too. Free alterations on womens' clothes over $35.75 add even more to the 20% to 40% savings on all merchandise. Open weekdays from 9 a.m. to 6 p.m., on Saturday until 4:30 p.m. (tel. 695-1350). All major credit cards.

lusty breads and fragrant coffee beans and heady pâtés and delicate cheeses—and much more. New York has at least four appetizing emporiums to which the faithful make pilgrimages from near and very far. Each is gigantic, mind-boggling in its variety of offerings, and purveys food (including gourmet takeout) of superb quality. Make tracks to, on the West Side, **Zabar's,** 2245 Broadway at 80th St. (tel. 787-2000), which also has a mezzanine full of housewares and gourmet kitchen gadgets at the best prices in town; on the East Side, to **Fay and Allen's Foodworks,** 1241 Third Ave. at 71st St. (tel. 794-1101); in the Village, **Balducci's,** 426 Avenue of the Americas at 9th St. (tel. 673-2600); in Soho, **Dean & De Luca,** 121 Prince St. (tel. 254-7774). All are open seven days a week and provide some of the most entertaining shopping and people-watching in New York.

ANTIQUES: Hung up on patchwork quilts? **America Hurrah Antiques,** 766 Madison Ave., at 76th St. (tel. 535-1930), has the world's largest collection of antique American quilts, most made between 1830 and 1930 in New York and Pennsylvania (many Amish quilts) at prices averaging $300 to $1200. They are familiar with European bed sizes and can advise Europeans precisely which quilts will be suitable. Also beautiful: folk art and Americana like hooked rugs, paintings, pottery, handmade antique weathervanes, baskets, and country accessories.

A campy, funky collection of '40s, '50s, and '60s *objets* is the stock in trade at **Carol Alderman Antiques,** 353 Third Ave. at 26th St. (tel. LE 2-7242). You might find anything from antique clothes and furs to antique cooking equipment, mirrors, chandeliers, candlesticks, and a vast collection of jewelry: necklaces, bracelets, and especially earrings—many one-of-a-kinds, made from old findings. Ms. Alderman also boasts the largest collection of stained-glass panels in New York. Everything is eminently affordable. Many models and photographers make this a regular stopping place. It's a great fun stop for incurable collectors, with many good bargains.

Antiques and potpourri are the specialties of **Cherchez,** 864 Lexington Ave., at 65th St. (tel. 737-8215). Prices range from $6 for a French herbal moth bag ("an antique recipe to deter moths") up to the hundreds for antique paisleys, chemises, table linens, lace collars, Chinese robes. Scented notepapers and envelopes, dried flower wreaths, herbs and spices for potpourri would make charming small gifts.

Want to do all your antique hunting under one roof? The **Manhattan Arts & Antique Center,** 1050 Second Ave. at 56th St. (tel. 355-4400), is a handsome, enclosed mall where some 85 collectors have gathered their wares. The range goes from country furniture and art nouveau to rare Chinese porcelains, from African masks to temple hangings from Tibet. Collect a print or a Persian carpet, a music box or an old master, depending on what the budget will bear. Open daily from 10:30 a.m. to 6:30 p.m.; and Sunday from noon to 6 p.m. Convenient parking.

BALLOONS: New York's only all-balloon store nestles in Soho at 147 Sullivan St. Ray and Marlyne, the creators of **Balooms,** can provide you with the kind of presents to send home that your friends will never forget: imagine mylar balloons popping out of boxes with your message inscribed on them, or a customized "Observation Balloon"—a hot-air balloon in a wicker basket. Or send flowers—i.e., an air bouquet of clear balloons stuffed with feathers or confetti or silk flowers. Prices start around $25. Balloons can float to any address. If you can't get to Soho, you can order by phone at 673-4007.

BOOKS: Curious about Oriental philosophy or acupuncture or herbal remedies or flying saucers or parapsychology? Get on your magic carpet and fly down to **Samuel Weiser,** 740 Broadway, near 8th St. (tel. 777-6363), which is the largest, most internationally respected occult, philosophical, and metaphysical bookshop in the country, possibly in the world. Its carefully selected stock of a quarter of a million volumes (including secondhand and rare tomes, some dating back as far as the 17th century), attracts countless scholars, collectors, scientists, philosophers, and just plain interested people. Or steer the carpet toward **East West Books** 78 Fifth Ave. at 14th St. (tel. 243-5994), which boasts a similarly absorbing eclectic collection.

Barnes & Noble, at the corner of 18th St. and Fifth Ave., has what is perhaps the largest collection of books in the country, displayed in a highly browsable fashion. If you can't find what you want here, chances are it's just not findable. Directly across the street is its Sales Annex, a veritable supermarket of books. Since prices seem cheaper here than they are at regular supermarkets, you'll probably come home with bagfuls of books—everything from bestsellers to children's books to publisher's overstock—for anywhere from 10% to 70% off. Sunday afternoon at the Sales Annex is a great New York pastime. The uptown Barnes & Noble Sales Annex, at 48th St. and Fifth Ave., is another must for bargain-hunting bibliophiles. And there are more Barnes & Nobles scattered around town.

CAMERAS AND ELECTRONICS: **47th St. Photo,** 67 West 47th St. and 115 West 45th St. (tel. 260-4410), consistently has top discount prices on cameras, computers, audio and video equipment, telephone answering machines, and all manner of electronic wonders. Check their double-page ads which appear almost daily in the *New York Times* for an idea. You'll find the 45th Street store bigger and less hectic than the 47th Street one, but service is knowledgeable and helpful at both. Open Sunday through Friday (closes at 2 p.m. on Friday); closed Saturday.

CERAMICS: Those who love hand-thrown and hand-built ceramics—at very reasonable prices—should make tracks to the Village and the **Mad Monk,** at 500 Avenue of the Americas and 12th St. (tel. 242-6678). The genial Carl Monk, who presides over the store, shows the work of over 75 upstate and New England potters; their handsome teapots, casseroles, ornamental mirrors, jars, pitchers, planters, and the like, range mostly from $6 to $75, although very special pieces may go much higher. Also sold at reasonable prices (discounts of 20%) is a fine collection of books on East-West philosophy.

CHOCOLATES: Chocaholics rejoice! The perfect chocolates—or at least those as close to perfection as we've found—are alive and well and living in a bandbox little store called **Chocolates by M** at 61 West 62nd St. (between Columbus Ave. and Broadway), just across the street from the New York State Theater at Lincoln Center. The reason they're so good is that Mamie Lee makes them fresh, in the back of the store, in small quantities every day; no artificial binders or stiffening agents need be used. Mamie's rum balls and perfect, fresh strawberries coated with bittersweet chocolate are our favorites, but the Kahlúa truffles, caramels, stem cherries in Grand Marnier, and fudge are all wonderful, too. If you want to give somebody a very special present, buy them two theater tickets, and have Mamie put them inside a giant chocolate fortune cookie ($14). Prices range from $12.95 per pound for the fudge, up to about $24 for the chocolate-covered fruits. Try the chocolate cookies, too. Open six days from 10:30 a.m. until 7:30 p.m., and often on Sunday (tel. 307-0777).

COLUMBUS AVENUE—HEARTS AND FLOWERS, HAND-CRAFTS, AND WINDUP TOYS: Columbus Avenue, in the four or five blocks above and below 72nd Street, has turned into a wonderful shopping/eating/people-watching scene—a kind of Greenwich Village in miniature. All the shops here are serendipitous, but we have a few special favorites. **Only Hearts,** 281 Columbus Ave. at 73rd St. (tel. 724-5608), is a little shop where everything has to do with hearts. Whether you fancy a heart safety pin for $2 or a hand-painted wooden heart mobile for $70, there is something here you'll have to have: perhaps heart-shaped earrings, oversize-heart-bedecked T-shirts, lingerie, or even a waffle iron that makes hearts! . . . **The Last Woundup,** 290 Columbus, between 73rd and 74th Sts. (tel. 787-3388), has an incredible collection of wind-up toys and music boxes. Amid a scene of happy Victorian clutter, modern and antique toys range from fire-spitting apes for about $2.50 to a camel that moves in steady gait across the desert for $18. Wonderful operatic music boxes are about $40. We especially like the T-shirts here: one reads "Don't Postpone Joy"; and another, "Youth Has Nothing To Do With Age." This shop is irrestible for kids of all ages. . . . **Handmaiden,** 104 West 73rd St., just of Columbus (tel. 787-2664), is a real find for anyone who loves handcrafts. Barbara Mundy and Georgia Hearn, two talented ladies, have put together a collection of soft sculpture, folk art, hand-knit children's clothing, pottery, porcelain wood chimes, and much more, all of it handmade, in excellent taste and very well priced. Especially joyful are the hanging topiaries by Phil, made in the shape of ducks or mushrooms, frogs, puppies, hearts—or our personal favorite, a dolphin jumping through a hoop. The ivies implanted in these moss-and-wire topiaries (priced from $14 to about $30) will grow in about a month and do not need direct light. Note, too, the wooden trolls from the Smoky Mountains ($25), and the patchwork quilts for babies (from $40 to $60). Closed only on Monday. . . . At **Southflower Market,** Columbus Ave. and 68th St. (tel. 496-7400), exotic blossoms are picked by you right from the floor and sold at prices below those at other stores, since these people are direct importers from Holland and South America, and bypass the wholesale flower market. Pick yourself a perfect tulip, perhaps, for under $1. The exciting shopping on Columbus continues uptown and downtown for several blocks. Not far from Lincoln Center, this area is well worth a special trip.

HERBS, SPICES, AND SOAPS: Kiehl's Pharmacy, 109 Third Ave. (13th St.), has been known since 1851 for one of the largest selections of herbs (and their own herbal products) in the country—for herbs to ward off a spell or ward off a cold, for exotic potions, homeopathic remedies, their own perfumes, bath and facial preparations. Alas, they no longer carry leeches (the demand for blood-letting has died down), but they stock every modern as well as time-tested remedy available. When you can find frankincense and myrrh, ginseng and pennyroyal and raspberry leaves (helpful in childbirth), and penicillin and vitamins under one roof, you have to be at Kiehl's.

The oldest chemists and perfumers in the United States, Caswell-Massey, Lexington Ave. and 48th St. (also at the South Street Seaport), in business for 230 years, still carries the same colognes that were favorites with George and Martha Washington and the Marquis de Lafayette! Sarah Bernhardt used their cucumber cold cream (and so can you), and you can also pick and choose from the largest collection of imported soaps in the world. There's imported shaving equipment, pomanders, potpourri, cough drops and lozenges from England and France. A wondrous nostalgic place full of things you can't get elsewhere. For their fanciful catalog ($1), write to: Catalog Department, Caswell-Massey Co., Ltd., 111 Eighth Ave., New York, NY 10011.

Cambridge Chemists, 21 East 65th St. (tel. 838-1884), is the kind of place that makes visiting Europeans feel they're right at home. Here's where one can buy pure and natural products by Cyclax of London (they are the only U.S. agents for these beauty products used by Queen Elizabeth), Floris and G. F. Trumper of London, and a variety of other toiletries, cosmetics, and treatment preparations from England, France, Switzerland, and Germany. Although a listing of their clients might read like a page out of the *Social Register,* everyone is treated with old-fashioned courtesy. A wooden shaving bowl, a natural clove pomander in a bed of potpourri, a perfume vaporizer, or a crystal atomizer are a few unique gift possibilities here.

Should you wish to have your own individual fragrance custom-blended and then put into hand lotion or bubble bath, perfume or shampoo—make an appointment with the nice people at **Scentsitivity**, 870½ Lexington Ave., at 65th St. (tel. 988-2822), a small charmer of a shop that creates "signature scents" for many of New York's leading celebrities. The consultation is free, the prices fair (hand lotion, for example, is $10 to $17.50), and nobody but you can get the formula. The shop also has fragrant potpourri, many imported skin care and cosmetic lines from Europe (Taylor of London, Norfolk Lavendar, etc.), and their fragrant house blends ("Rain" is our favorite) of "Positively Essential Oils" ($15 for a quarter ounce, $25 for a half ounce); use them as perfume or put a few drops on a lightbulb to make your home smell wonderful.

INTERNATIONAL GIFTS: Noto, 245 West 72nd St., west of Broadway (tel. 877-7562), is a friendly little boutique, jam-packed with treasures from around the world, all well priced. Note, for example, the very special Balinese jewelry—hand-worked sterling-silver rings and earrings with semiprecious stones, from $15 to $35. Victorian brass reproductions, Peruvian boxes and mirrors done in reverse painting on glass, and a wonderful selection of baskets from China and the Philippines—many with a French Country look—suggest the intriguing international mix. And be sure to see the shop's own hand-cast reproductions of antique artifacts—Notre-Dame gargoyles, art nouveau and Mediterranean mirrors, European carved heads, from under $10 to $35. The price range here goes up to $200, but there are many tasteful and inexpensive small items. Open every day.

MUPPETS: Believe it or not, there is a store specializing in nothing but **Muppet Stuff;** it's at 833 Lexington Ave. at 63rd St. (tel. 980-8340), and it's sheer heaven for anyone with a fondness for the likes of the Cookie Monster, Miss Piggy, Ernie, Kermit the Frog, and more friendly folk. The shop abounds with all the licensed Jim Hensen Associates products—toys, clothing, books, dolls (the Muppet Babies are especially wonderful), gifts, home videos—and it's popular with everybody from kids, who throng the store on Saturday (and can usually be found around the TV set in back watching videos of Fraggle Rock or Sesame Street or the Muppet Show), all the way up to corporate types who love the Kermit the Frog tie, $15, and exclusive here. Most items are in the $5 to $10 range. Open Monday to Saturday from 10 a.m. to 6 p.m.

PATCHWORK: Domino Patchworks, in a cheery loft on the 14th floor of 100 Avenue of the Americas, near Grand Street, turns out enchanting appliqué baby quilts, beautiful enough to hang on a wall, quilt accessories, and wonderful sleeping bags shaped like clowns or robots or Humpty Dumpty, and sells them to the public at about 25% less than the prices they command at specialty stores around the country. Quilts average $70 to $86; sleeping bags, $112. Call first for a weekday appointment: 226-3195.

RECORDS: New York has many record stores, but there's never been anything before quite like **Tower Records,** 692 Broadway, at East 4th St. in the East Village (tel. 505-1500). Tower is a scene, a happening, a place where people go to be seen as much as to buy records; as many at 6000 people are said to pack the aisles on Saturday and Sunday. Called "the world's largest record store," Tower stocks half a million records and tapes in every conceivable category, sells many of them at discount prices, and also shows all-rock cable television on 17 video screens. It's also in the midst of a trendy new shopping neighborhood that includes other such fascinations as the Unique Clothing Warehouse, 712 Broadway, with huge selections of hip, chic, and cheap military surplus; the Antique Boutique, next door, for antique clothes; and Star Magic at 743 Broadway, with a large collection of crystals, of both the leaded and gemstone varieties.

UNICORNS: "Now I believe there are unicorns," said William Shakespeare in *The Tempest,* and you will agree with him when you walk into **Unicorn City** at 55 Greenwich Ave. (tel. 243-2017). Here, assembled under one roof, are all the crafty unicorns in captivity, captured in silver and gold pendants, pillows and T-shirts, wallets, picnic bags, posters, and more. Pick up a lovable baby unicorn doll for the kids to play with ($20), a sterling-silver unicorn pendant as a good-luck symbol (Bette Davis swears by hers), for $25. Costumed Commedia del 'Arte Pierrot dolls ($20 to $75) are also great finds here.

BEST BUYS: It often happens: you shop New York and you become addicted. If you'd like to continue to shop the city after you get back home, you may want to subscribe to *Smart Living* Magazine. Dedicated to finding top value for the consumer dollar, *Smart Living* comparison-shops the city each month and reports on the lowest prices in brand-name merchandise in many fields, from clothing to computers to major appliances. Almost everything can be ordered via mail or phone. A year's subscription is $20. Write to *Smart Living*, 747 Third Ave., New York, NY 10017, or phone 212/675-4777.

NOW, SAVE MONEY ON ALL YOUR TRAVELS!
Join Arthur Frommer's $25-A-Day Travel Club

Saving money while traveling is never a simple matter, which is why, over 22 years ago, the **$25-A-Day Travel Club** was formed. Actually, the idea came from readers of the Arthur Frommer Publications who felt that such an organization could bring financial benefits, continuing travel information, and a sense of community to economy-minded travelers all over the world.

In keeping with the money-saving concept, the annual membership fee is low—$15 (U.S. residents) or $18 (Canadian, Mexican, and foreign residents)—and is immediately exceeded by the value of your benefits which include:

(1) The latest edition of any TWO of the books listed on the following page.

(2) An annual subscription to an 8-page quarterly newspaper *The Wonderful World of Budget Travel* which keeps you up-to-date on fastbreaking developments in low-cost travel in all parts of the world—bringing you the kind of information you'd have to pay over $25 a year to obtain elsewhere. This consumer-conscious publication also includes the following columns:

Travelers' Directory—members all over the world who are willing to provide hospitality to other members as they pass through their home cities.

Share-a-Trip—requests from members for travel companions who can share costs and help avoid the burdensome single supplement.

Readers Ask . . . Readers Reply—travel questions from members to which other members reply with authentic firsthand information.

(3) A copy of *Arthur Frommer's Guide to New York*.

(4) Your personal membership card which entitles you to purchase through the Club all Arthur Frommer Publications for a third to a half off their regular retail prices during the term of your membership.

So why not join this hardy band of international budgeteers NOW and participate in its exchange of information and hospitality? Simply send $15 (U.S. residents) or $18 U.S. (Canadian, Mexican, and other foreign residents) along with your name and address to: $25-A-Day Travel Club, Inc., 1230 Avenue of the Americas, New York, NY 10020. Remember to specify which *two* of the books in section (1) above you wish to receive in your initial package of members' benefits. Or tear out this page, check off any two books on the opposite side and send it to us with your membership fee.

FROMMER/PASMANTIER PUBLISHERS Date_____
1230 AVE. OF THE AMERICAS, NEW YORK, NY 10020

Friends, please send me the books checked below:

$-A-DAY GUIDES
(In-depth guides to low-cost tourist accommodations and facilities.)

☐ Europe on $25 a Day	$10.95
☐ Australia on $25 a Day	$9.95
☐ England and Scotland on $25 a Day	$9.95
☐ Greece on $25 a Day	$9.95
☐ Hawaii on $35 a Day	$9.95
☐ India on $15 & $25 a Day	$9.95
☐ Ireland on $25 a Day	$9.95
☐ Israel on $30 & $35 a Day	$9.95
☐ Mexico on $20 a Day	$9.95
☐ New Zealand on $20 & $25 a Day	$9.95
☐ New York on $35 a Day	$8.95
☐ Scandinavia on $25 a Day	$9.95
☐ South America on $25 a Day	$8.95
☐ Spain and Morocco (plus the Canary Is.) on $25 a Day	$9.95
☐ Washington, D.C. on $35 a Day	$8.95

DOLLARWISE GUIDES
(Guides to accommodations and facilities from budget to deluxe, with emphasis on the medium-priced.)

☐ Austria & Hungary	$10.95	☐ Cruises (incl. Alaska, Carib, Mex, Hawaii, Panama, Canada, & US)	$10.95
☐ Egypt	$9.95	☐ California & Las Vegas	$9.95
☐ England & Scotland	$10.95	☐ Florida	$9.95
☐ France	$10.95	☐ New England	$9.95
☐ Germany	$9.95	☐ Northwest	$10.95
☐ Italy	$10.95	☐ Southeast & New Orleans	$9.95
☐ Portugal (incl. Madeira & the Azores)	$9.95	☐ Southwest	$10.95
☐ Switzerland & Liechtenstein	$9.95		
☐ Canada	$10.95		
☐ Caribbean (incl. Bermuda & the Bahamas)	$10.95		

THE ARTHUR FROMMER GUIDES
(Pocket-size guides to tourist accommodations and facilities in all price ranges.)

☐ Amsterdam/Holland	$4.95	☐ Mexico City/Acapulco	$4.95
☐ Athens	$4.95	☐ Montreal/Quebec City	$4.95
☐ Atlantic City/Cape May	$4.95	☐ New Orleans	$4.95
☐ Boston	$4.95	☐ New York	$4.95
☐ Dublin/Ireland	$4.95	☐ Orlando/Disney World/EPCOT	$4.95
☐ Hawaii	$4.95	☐ Paris	$4.95
☐ Las Vegas	$4.95	☐ Philadelphia	$4.95
☐ Lisbon/Madrid/Costa del Sol	$4.95	☐ Rome	$4.95
☐ London	$4.95	☐ San Francisco	$4.95
☐ Los Angeles	$4.95	☐ Washington, D.C.	$4.95

SPECIAL EDITIONS

☐ How to Beat the High Cost of Travel	$4.95	☐ Marilyn Wood's Wonderful Weekends (NY, Conn, Mass, RI, Vt, NJ, Pa)	$9.95
☐ New York Urban Athlete (NYC sports guide for jocks & novices)	$9.95	☐ Museums in New York	$8.95
☐ Where to Stay USA (Accommodations from $3 to $25 a night)	$8.95	☐ Guide for the Disabled Traveler	$10.95
☐ Fast 'n' Easy Phrase Book (Fr/Sp/Ger/Ital. in *one* vol.)	$6.95	☐ Bed & Breakfast-No. America	$7.95

In U.S. include $1 post. & hdlg. for 1st book; 25¢ ea. add'l. book. Outside U.S. $2 and 50¢ respectively.

Enclosed is my check or money order for $_____

NAME_____

ADDRESS_____

CITY_____ STATE_____ ZIP_____